IN DEFENCE OF

JESUS

THE CHRIST

CHALLENGING THE BOOK CHRIST OR DEVIL?

G. C. EZEIGWE

authorHOUSE

AuthorHouse™ UK
1663 Liberty Drive
Bloomington, IN 47403 USA
www.authorhouse.co.uk
Phone: UK TFN: 0800 0148641 (Toll Free inside the UK)
        UK Local: 02036 956322 (+44 20 3695 6322 from outside the UK)

Scripture quotations marked NKJV are taken from the New King James Version.
Copyright © 1982 by Thomas Nelson, Inc. Used by permission. All rights reserved.

Published by AuthorHouse 09/03/2021

ISBN: 978-1-6655-8995-6 (sc)
ISBN: 978-1-6655-8996-3 (hc)
ISBN: 978-1-6655-9253-6 (e)

Contents

Acknowledgements ix
Introduction xi

Chapter 1   Preface to Christ or Devil? 1
Chapter 2   Acknowledgements of Christ or Devil? 25
Chapter 3   Introduction to Christ or Devil? 31
Chapter 4   What Is Religion? 40
Chapter 5   Origin of Christianity 67
Chapter 6   Christ 73
Chapter 7   Christ's Teachings 121
Chapter 8   Christians 136
Chapter 9   Spread of Christianity 165
Chapter 10 Challenges to Christianity 171
Chapter 11 Corruption in the Vatican 174
Chapter 12 The Modern World and Its Church 183
Chapter 13 Christian Religion and Education 209
Chapter 14 Christian Religion and Morality 220
Chapter 15 Traditional African Religion—Prospect 224
Chapter 16 Conclusion 248

This book is humbly dedicated to the late *Ichie* James Nwafor Ezeigwe (my father); the late Mrs Ukachukwu Victoria Ezeigwe, alias 'All-Weather' (my mother); and last, but in no way least, the late elder and chief Bassey Ekanem (my father-in-law).

My parents, as my role models, led exemplary, simple, godly, honourable lives with ease. Today I am struggling with the difficult prospect of doing the same.

God, may their souls rest in your perfect peace, in your kingdom.

Acknowledgements

Goodness demands that I acknowledge with pleasure the support I received from some magnanimous people while I was writing this book.

I cannot fully express my thanks to the potential Ichie, engineer S. Chianumba (ex-lecturer in engineering), and his family, for their hospitality and tolerance. I bored them with my habit of using their flat, every so often, as a place for diversion during my writing.

To Mr James Okereke (an unsung public relations / marketing officer) and his dear, noble wife, Augustina, both of whom showed interest in the aim of my book and, like midwives, watched and looked forward to its birth, I say, thank you very much.

My appreciation goes posthumously to the late, honourable Mrs Winifred Moneke, alias 'Magi', the epitome of a sociable personality, who tirelessly made sure my 'wisdom box' (tobacco snuffbox) suffered no starvation; I am addicted to snuffing at intervals while I read or write.

I am solemnly saddened that she did not live to witness the publishing of my book or enjoy with me the sweet smell of success. What a very sad reflection for me to bear! May her soul rest in God's peace.

Sometimes pessimism fathers optimism. My worthy wife, a brilliant, learned friend (legal practitioner), voiced the opinion that I would not be able to sufficiently gather myself together to work successfully to the end and see my manuscript published. To prove her wrong, I strengthened my determination and redoubled my efforts to see my dream come to fruition.

I would, therefore, be remiss if I were to fail to give her a huge loving hug for the boost that her pessimism obliquely gave me, increasing my optimism. I am obliged to her.

There are many others who have earned my thanks. Chief among them is Ichie Ephraim Anyaegbunam, an architect. Others can identify themselves. To all go my sincere thanks.

Although the aforementioned persons each gave me a helping hand in one way or another, not all, I need emphasise, share all the opinions I express in my book. The responsibility for all points made in the book falls squarely upon my shoulders.

At this stage, I wish to add that my manuscript for the book gathered dust for a long time while waiting for a typist. Like a bolt from the blue came one, Ms Emelda Kajoina, who took it up and, with her nimble fingers, gave it a professional touch. She earns my praise for her great job of reading my awkward handwriting and typing the manuscript.

My proofreader also deserves my appreciation. My manuscript was a jigsaw puzzle to him. He took pains in reshaping it, correcting my grammar, spelling, and punctuation.

I hope that any criticisms of my book be made public so that any third party interested may enjoy the privilege of hearing from all sides before airing his or her views on any issues raised. Let the principle of *audi alteram partem* (hear the other side) apply.

To all who contributed in any positive form to the production of this book, *In Defence of Jesus the Christ*, I make a simple request: join me in riding triumphantly the crest of the wave of my success.

Introduction

This book challenges the book *Christ or Devil?*, which denies and rejects the existence of the deity (or gods). It criticises and condemns Jesus the Christ and Christianity.

Anene Obianyido is the author of the book, and Tai Solarin is the author of the preface to the book.

Challenging the above-named book, *In Defence of Jesus the Christ* concentrates more on matters concerning atheism and Christianity and pays less attention to other religions.

At first sight of the book *Christ or Devil?* I found the title inviting and seducing. Politely, I requested one Mrs Nwazota (Matthew), who at the time was reading a copy, to pass hers on to me when she was done with it so I could share my opinions about it with her. She exclaimed 'Um' and paused. After hesitating for a while, she replied, 'So far as I have gone, I do not like it one bit.' She stared at me thoughtfully for a while, then said firmly, 'If you like, you can have it and keep it from this minute. I have no more use for the rubbish.' I grabbed it from her like a starving wolf, with a flash of thought in my mind—*One man's meat is another's poison*—hoping to find it interesting even though she did not.

My great anxiety to read it derived from the riddle posed by the title *Christ or Devil?* The English word *or* is a conjunction usually used to link or introduce alternatives. *Or*, therefore, means 'if not this, then the other'.

The two alternatives in the title of the book are *Christ* and *Devil*. Therefore, if the person to whom the title refers is not Christ, then he or she is the Devil. *Who then is this person described by the title of the book?* I wondered.

With my foreknowledge of scriptures (the Bible), I preconceived that although Jesus was not expressly or overtly mentioned in the title, he was most likely the one being silently or obliquely referred to as being either the Christ or the Devil. Which of the two alternatives, then, does the author of the book consider Jesus to be? I desperately wanted to find out.

My strong desire to find out forced me to leap frantically to turn the pages of the book curiously, like an archaeologist excavating for a special find. I read inquisitively for which of the two alternatives the author considered Jesus to be, in fact.

The first few pages of the preface to *Christ or Devil?* transmitted early signs of what I was likely to find. Soon I began to realise that Obianyido saw Jesus as a devil. I shuddered! I felt a sharp sting in my heart since I am a staunch believer in Christianity. I became huffy! My feeling added strength to my desire to write a book to challenge *Christ or Devil?* The result is *In Defence of Jesus the Christ*.

Although my book is decked out with the title *In Defence of Jesus the Christ*, I confess that the surface meaning of the title somehow differs from what my book in fact represents. The Christ is not in danger and never will be. The title is therefore extraordinary in form. I know this, and yet I stuck with the title, feeling that I must find a way to challenge *Christ or Devil?* My book's title, therefore, suits my aim.

As I mentioned earlier, the Christ is not in danger. Christhood is impeccable and impregnable. The divine status with a spiritual aura surrounding it provides a sort of self-defence mechanism that readily lays waste to any attacks or criticisms against it. Christianity, therefore, needs no one to defend it. And anyway, who am I to defend the Christ?

I suggest that the title of my book be looked at as a form of decoration for a particular purpose.

That conclusion prompts the questions 'What is the purpose?' and 'What is *In Defence of Jesus the Christ* about?' The purpose of my book is to certify that the book *Christ or Devil?* which attacks and criticises the Christ, is superficial and of no consequence. The reason I chose the title *In Defence of Jesus the Christ* for my book is that I believe it will have, by its nature, a magnetic effect to entice readers, drawing them to the book and keeping captive the attention of those who are inquisitive about the Christ as they scour the book.

The first thing the readers of my book will find is that the author of the preface to *Christ or Devil?* effusively praises Obianyido, the author of *Christ or Devil?*, for his atheism and his faith, and supports Obianyido's criticisms of Jesus Christ, Christianity, and God.

Necessarily, I ask if Obianyido's book has anything substantial or spectacular to attract such a degree of praise as Tai Solarin has for it. This is a vital question, to which my readers are to find the suitable answer after they have scoured my book. As for me, I readily grade the praise as irrelevant exaggeration.

Anyway, propelled by the strong current of my desire to discover all the book had in store for its readers concerning God, Jesus the Christ, and Christianity, I calmed my emotions, pressed on, and followed the faffing of the book to its unmeritorious end.

I found, after all, that the book contains nothing but allegations, speculations, lies, and groundless attacks, all knitted together as a campaign of singular viciousness against Jesus the Christ, Christianity, and God.

In the preface, Tai Solarin confesses atheism as his faith. From that perspective, I was able to see the affinity between the body of the book *Christ or Devil?* and the preface. That revealed to me that Tai Solarin, who wrote the preface, and Obianyido, the author of *Christ or Devil?*, worked in concert to produce the book in question.

After I had carefully gone through the book, it became clear to me that their joint mission was to destroy Christianity in Africa and replace it with atheism, starting with their country, Nigeria. Tai Solarin, a resolute atheist, harried Obianyido into adopting that ambition, I believe.

To say the truth, I am very unhappy about their character, not because of their criticisms and attacks against Jesus the Christ, Christianity, and God, but because of the words and expressions they chose to use for the attacks. They savour of uncivilisation and barbarism, and for the most part, they are sacrilegious. Every matter in the Bible and elsewhere that smells of Jesus the Christ, Christianity, or God is senselessly, rudely abused.

I have heard of, and read, books criticising Jesus the Christ and/or Christianity, but never before had I come across anything close to what is contained in the book *Christ or Devil?* in terms of vulgarity, incivility, and prejudice. It is easy to see the book as raw and worthless.

When a book seems worthless, it sometimes pays to see it as such and consider the ideas in the book as pedantic, and the book's criticisms of the subject matter (in our case, the criticisms of the Holy Bible and its contents) trivial and of no consequence. For our present purposes, although the book *Christ or Devil?* seems trivial on the surface, it is, in fact, dangerous beneath the surface because of what it harbours there. If left unchallenged, the campaign in the book is likely to cause social disruption. Societies will lose the teachings of Christianity that help to keep people in good moral shape so they may conduct themselves well. To prevent this from happening, the campaign of atheism against Christianity must be tackled head-on and defeated.

The campaign against Christianity by the loony partners Tai Solarin and Anene Obianyido spans a variety of issues. I have made those issues the battleground between the book *Christ or Devil?* and my book *In Defence of Jesus the Christ.*

Of necessity, some of the issues are mentioned as follows so as to allow my readers a bird's-eye view of what to expect:

(a) *Christ or Devil?* does not promote belief in God. That is, it does not accept that God exists or that the universe and the things therein are God's creations.

(b) It doubts that the man Jesus of Nazareth ever existed on this planet. It conceives that Jesus Christ was an imaginary figure conjured up by Christians, or that he was a mythological personage.

(c) It contends that if God exists, Jesus Christ was not, and is not, the Son of God.

(d) It asserts that if Jesus Christ did perform miracles, whatever he performed was done by the power of Devil—that he acted by witchcraft.

(e) It doubts that the teachings in the New Testament ascribed to Jesus Christ are indeed Jesus's.

(f) Relying on a book, *The Holy Blood and the Holy Grail*, it alleges that Jesus Christ, if he ever existed on this planet, escaped crucifixion and eloped with Mary Magdalene to a foreign land, where they got married and had a child, and that someone else was crucified in the place of Jesus Christ.

(g) It alleges that Jesus Christ broke away from Judaism to form his own religion, taking advantage of the Jews' turbulent social condition with their neighbours and the Roman authorities.

(h) It asserts that if Jesus Christ did live on earth and taught, his teachings are of no benefit to our modern world.

(i) It asserts that if Jesus Christ ever lived, he was crucified as a slave for his criminal acts.

(j) It asserts that Jesus Christ went about with political thugs.

(k) It alleges that Jesus Christ, his disciples, and their religion (Christianity) were most hated and despised by the people in the time of Jesus Christ.

(l) The author, Anene Obianyido, alleges that once a TV debate took place in Nigeria between an atheist friend of his and a Christian on whether or not God exists. He concluded that his atheist friend proved that God does not exist and won the debate.

(m) The book states that the Christianity of Jesus Christ is responsible for the backwardness and nondevelopment of African countries.

(n) It alleges that Jesus Christ was aggressive and abusive towards those he addressed during his mission.

(o) It queries the popular Christian concept of the Virgin Birth, i.e. that Mary did not conceive Jesus by the power of the Holy Ghost without Joseph (Jesus's earthly father).

(p) It treats the concept of the Holy Trinity with contempt and disdain, and totally disregards it.

(q) It ridicules the statement Jesus the Christ made to Peter concerning the handing of the key of heaven to Peter.

(r) It suggests that Judas Iscariot and those Jews who conspired to bring about the death of Jesus be praised by Christians since Christians believe that the death of Jesus washed away their sins.

(s) It doubts the authenticity of the gospels of the New Testament, referring to them as worthless hearsay evidence.

In *Christ or Devil?* there are more issues that combine with those mentioned above to make up the criticisms the author has against Jesus the Christ, Christianity, and God. Those are not named at this stage, though they are given attention in *In Defence of Jesus the Christ* as they crop up.

When addressing the issues, I bore in mind the revolting, rude, uncivil words and expressions employed by the author in criticising and attacking God, Jesus the Christ, and Christianity. For that I employed similar expressions and words (strong enough) so as, at least, to get even with the author of that book in the use of foul language.

I hope to be forgiven by my readers for this.

Some of my readers, I guess, might like to ask, 'Are Tai Solarin and Obianyido not entitled to freedom of expression in our civilised society?' My immediate reply to such a question would be, 'Of course they are.' My attitude is that one's freedom of expression is to be exercised within the province of civilisation. Where one strays outside that, one automatically forfeits the protection guaranteed by civilisation and exposes himself or herself to all possible attacks. The writer of the book *Christ or Devil?* did just that—overstepped the boundary of civility and exercised uncultured principles by their manner of criticism and attack against Jesus the Christ, Christianity, and God, ignoring all sense of propriety. That amounts to abuse of civility. Therefore, the author at once lost the protection offered by civilisation to be dealt with in a civilised way.

'He who seeks equity must come with clean hands,' say those white wigs in law court. The crude manner of the writer provoked my use of strong language in challenging them. I had to fight them within and without the arena of civilisation with words and expressions similar to theirs in rudeness, being mindful of the Roman saying *Similia similibus currantur* (Fight fire with fire).

I have made no secret of my preference for Christianity over atheism. Atheism is an enemy of humans, I conceive it has nothing to stand on, and nothing to offer humanity. Christianity is built on God, the uncreated Creator of all things and beings, and offers love, peace, and happiness in our present life, and happiness in our life to come (eternal life).

Do not misconceive my interest in Christianity: it begins with and stops at the principles taught by Jesus the Christ. Most present-day Christian churches with buildings labelled 'church', 'temple', or 'cathedral', and with ceremonies, festivals, rituals, and so forth, have no place in my concept of Christianity. Personally, I conceive that God (i.e. the Christian God) has his temple within humankind, wherein lives the Christ, the aspect of God (the special Son of God) (Colossians 2:8). I completely accept the saying in the New Testament that God does not live in a house built by hands. It is my belief, therefore, that to look for God in buildings (churches, temples, cathedrals, mosques, synagogues, shrines) is to move farther away from God.

Important Remarks about My Book

Firstly, some of the points made herein are likely to be found strange and hard to grasp. This is due to the nonuniversality of the facts imparted by the points made herein, coupled with the unique words and expressions used to support them. Most of them are the knowledge revealed to my inspired mind.

I strove to make every expression as simple as the nature of the subjects they related to would allow. For tackling any such problem, I give the tip to my readers that the matters be approached with slow, sober strides and keen interest, and from a spiritual perspective. A literal approach alone is likely to mislead in many cases. So follow a systematic approach: gnaw at the problems conscientiously with the teeth of the inner spiritual mind until the shells, containing the facts, the truth of the matter, are broken through and the spiritual nectar within the subjects is gained. Pearls are scarcely found on the surface.

Secondly, Anene Obianyido's book *Christ of Devil?* repeats many of its subjects which I challenge. It reconstructs some of the already discussed subjects and adds to them trivial points that are irrelevant. That style bored me beyond description as I followed his argument.

I could resolve to ignore such trivial additions to matters previously treated and avoided chasing Obianyido round and round in his recycling fashion. I did not. I feared that any passivity on such issues could give the wrong impression, such as that I was lacking in reply to, or shied away from, those trivial matters as if they were difficult to address.

I, therefore, in detail followed Obianyido's repetitions and replied to his irrelevant add-ons, not allowing them to suffer neglect. I make this fact known in the hope that my readers consider it and do not accuse me of unnecessary repetition and triviality.

Thirdly, though I am responsible for writing *In Defence of Jesus the Christ*, I must confess that some of the ideas it carries are not originally mine. I incorporated such ideas into my book after I had come to consider them as thoroughly acceptable.

Many other facts or ideas are originally mine (I later rejoiced to find that they agree with those of spiritual and scriptural luminaries). These facts (ideas) came to me I know not how! I should say through spiritual inspiration. In any case, I found them at home in the truth they impart.

My readers, I trust, will find the entire book informative, revealing, thrilling, and scripturally nourishing. If the book is followed thoroughly with an open mind unmarred by bigotry, it will be seen to answer many of the long-standing scriptural and spiritual conundrums, the mind-boggling matters that have been bothering Christians and non-Christians for ages.

I therefore suggest that my readers, before beginning to read this book, first of all shelve, as much as possible, those notions they have long held relating to the subjects they come across in this book. In this way, with somewhat of a virgin mind, they may go through the entire book undisturbed by their previous knowledge of the issues before them. Thereafter, they may decide whether or not to go back for their shelved knowledge or abandon it for good and rely on their new findings in my book.

Remember to search the scriptures, as did the people of Berea (Acts 17:11). By so doing, you may evaluate my references to the Bible.

Finally, I make a modest claim: my book is an exciting challenge to the book *Christ or Devil?* by Anene Obianyido. I am convinced that atheism, which the book *Christ or Devil?* preaches, is will-o'-the-wisp.

My book is determined to see that the seed of atheism which *Christ or Devil?* attempts to sow in Africa, beginning in Nigeria, will find no fertile soil anywhere in Africa.

I have made no claim to be a religious or scriptural luminary, but I feel proud to say that I am sufficiently knowledgeable in scriptural and spiritual matters to be able to successfully combat atheism to the point of demolition.

I have written not to directly sway my readers, but to challenge the points in Obianyido's book, most of which have been long-standing moot issues, and then allow my readers to be swayed to any side by their findings.

I do not envisage that my book will be immune to attacks. No doubt it will incur some criticisms and questions, in some cases stir up debates, and in others provoke anger about the points given. In any such circumstances, where possible any questions about unclear claims in my book should be directed to me, the author.

I predict that those who will find problems with my book are those who will fail to sweep away the soot of wrong teachings, long deposited in their heads before they embarked on their journey through my book.

Better it is, then, that my book be studied in a fresh, sober atmosphere with patience, but devoid of previous knowledge or concepts about the subjects herein, i.e. with an open mindset.

To my zealous readers: may you be guided by divine light (as I was while writing) as you undertake the task of studying this book. May the atheists among you, at the end, find sufficient reasons to be convinced to exhale atheism and inhale deity, through the Christ in them, in the manner reminiscent of that of Saul of Tarsus, who later, after his change of faith (he was an ardent persecutor of the Christ), became baptised as Paul and passionately followed the teachings of Jesus the Christ (Acts 9:1–22).

Though I worked laboriously while writing, I enjoyed every bit of the time spent on the work and took pleasure in seeing it completed. It was to me akin to a woman in travail who, after the successful birth of child, rejoices.

As a staunch Christian, I am fighting atheism to defend my civic rights. It is hoped my readers will enjoy their journey through my book and, in the end, derive a good measure of scriptural knowledge, and spiritual uplifting and satisfaction, from reading it.

I wish every one of the readers a rewarding journey through my book.

PREFACE TO *CHRIST OR DEVIL?*

The major aim of the preface to the book *Christ or Devil?*[1] is to criticise and condemn Jesus the Christ, Christianity, and God so as to find grounds for promoting atheism. Based on that, the author of the preface, Tai Solarin extols Anene Obianyido, the author of the book *Christ or Devil?*, for his efforts in contributing immensely to this aim.

The main issues in the preface are herein introduced under the subheading 'Tai Solarin', and under the subheading 'Reply', my responses and challenges to his claims and assertions follow.

Since it is not convenient to present in full the book *Christ or Devil?* I consider this format sufficient enough to give my readers the simplification and clarity they expect when I am speaking about the preface. The format is a device like that used in question-and-answer or for catechism.

I trust my readers will be delighted with the style since it is to make the book thrilling and informative.

Here we go.

---

[1] Throughout, I refer to the work by Anene Obianyido entitled *Christ or Devil? The Corrupt Face of Christianity in Africa* (Delta of Nigeria, 1988).

TAI SOLARIN: By faith I am an atheist.

REPLY: Who is an atheist by the way? By a common definition, an atheist is one who believes that God does not exist.

This is a simple and popular definition. Personally, I would define an atheist as one who ignorantly does not apprehend what God is, or is unable to understand that God exists or how God exists.

At the end of this chapter, I expatiate on my personal definition of an atheist under the caption 'The Possible Roots of Atheism'. For now, allow me to discuss some of the views of preeminent (knowledgeable) figures concerning the existence or nonexistence of God:

Francis Bacon

'A little philosophy inclineth man's mind to atheism, but depth in philosophy bringeth man's mind about to religion.'

This simply means that reasoning deeply and wisely turns a person's mind from atheism to Godism.

Lord Kelvin

Lord Kelvin was among those scientists who gained early knowledge in electricity. His view on atheism: 'I believe the more thoroughly science is studied, the further does it take us from anything compared to atheism.'

Albert Einstein

Einstein was a scientist, though an atheist. He went on to confess, 'It is enough for me to reflect upon the marvellous structure of the universe, which we dimly perceive, and to try humbly to comprehend even an infinitesimal part of the intelligence manifest in nature.'

Here one can easily see that in Einstein's equivocation, the scale weighs in favour of his belief in the existence of God.

Dante Gabriel (1828–1882)

Gabriel's view is 'The worst moment for the atheist is when he [or she] is really thankful and has nobody to thank.'

Luis Bunch (1628–1688)

'I am still an atheist, thank God.'
Is he not unblinkingly idiotic?

H. B. Stove (1811–1896)

In a writing by Stove, a child was asked, 'Do you know who made you?' After struggling preposterously for an answer, the child said, 'Nobody, as I know,' with a short laugh. The child went on, 'I 'spect I grow'd.'

Atheists are by analogy like that child. They are mentally fogbound and cannot see beyond their existence to the fact that their existence has a Source, the Source that is the Source of itself as well as the Source of all that exists, and that Source is called God.

Ivy Northage Chan

In Chan's book *Spiritual Realisation*, she writes, 'A philosopher once said, "No man could look upon rose and remain an atheist because in their beauty they have done more to promote the reality of God than humans—our teachers—and philosophers of the past."'

Professor Walter C. Kaiser Jr.

'The Bible is guilty by virtue of its divine claims, miracles and talks about God.'

Whatever that means! I take it that he doubts the existence of God, or else he blames the Bible for not making its teachings on God clearer.

C. S. Lewis

'I surrendered to the unrelenting approach of Him [God] whom I so earnestly desired not to meet, I prayed, I suddenly met him. I admitted God was real, I was no longer an atheist.'

A. C. Grayling

'Some scientists, amazingly, are religious, and they are apt to argue that the best argument they can give for having religious beliefs is the so-called "argument to the best explanation", which in this case says that given the inconclusiveness of our state of knowledge, the best account we can give of the world is that there is a God.'[2]

King Solomon

'Let us hear the conclusion of matter: Fear, and keep His [God's] commandments: for this is the whole duty of man' (Ecclesiastes 12:13).

---

[2] A. C. Grayling, *Meditations for the Humanist: Ethics for a Secular Age* (Oxford: Oxford University Press, 2003).

Boethius

In his book *The Consolation of Philosophy*, book one, Boethius quotes the Pythagorean maxim as 'Follow God.'

Now I suppose that the quotations so far given are enough for my purpose. So I stop here and suggest that my readers ponder over the much that has been offered.

In addition, my readers are to consider the fact of symmetry seen in the natural elements of the universe—the sun, the moon, the stars, the animals, the insects, the plants, and so on. Too, let them consider the purpose or function of those natural elements, their interrelationship (interdependence), and the various roles being played by each creature and creation (the inanimate things) within the natural set-up of the universe. My readers are not to be unmindful of the fact that each of these natural elements strictly adheres to its own peculiar laws while interacting with other elements in order to bring the right fruitage and harmony to the entire world's natural system. The aggregate of these scenarios points to the fact of a superlative Intelligence behind the whole arrangement.

It is therefore my contention that the concept of atheism is a philosophical absurdity for failing to observe the display of the superlative Intelligence in the structure of the natural elements and the orderly and harmonious functions immanent in the system of the universe and to perceive that all emanate from an all-embracing Intelligence, omniscient, omnipotent, and omnipresent, that is necessarily the Source of itself and exists independently of any other thing. Here I am talking of the Alpha and Omega in the universe, the Being we wisely call God.

NB: Throughout, I have given enough illustrations in support of the fact that God exists and that he is the Creator of the universe and all therein.

For further information on the subject, refer to the January 2015 issue of the Jehovah's Witnesses magazine *Awake*, pages 3–7, where you will find the article entitled 'How Did Life Begin?'

I need to reiterate this: All the facts mentioned above, and more that I've left out, point compellingly to a system of teamwork in nature designed by a most superior Intelligent Being, not visible to our physical eyes. That Being is what is universally known as God or whatever other befitting name anyone else chooses.

TAI SOLARIN: The author of the book *Christ or Devil?* earns my praise for expressing very strong and unreserved opposition against Jesus Christ and Christianity.

I believe that there are many others who share his view but, being terrestrially bound, are unable to come into the open.

REPLY: *Terrestrially,* the word used by Tai Solarin, refers to Planet Earth (the world). It is in contrast to the word *celestially,* which means 'heavenly; the spiritual realm of God'. The idea of terrestrial, therefore, presupposes the recognition of the existence of the celestial, that is the realm of God. In short, *celestial* is opposite of *terrestrial.*

Tai Solarin does not believe in the existence of God, yet he recognises the existence of the terrestrial. By deduction, he therefore recognises the celestial. The state of being terrestrial coexists with the state of being celestial.

Where things go in pairs, the recognition of the existence of one accords automatic recognition to the other—the opposite in this case.

According to Paul the apostle, 'There are celestial bodies, and bodies terrestrial' (1 Corinthians 15:40). In vain, therefore, does Tai Solarin deny the existence of God. He is deceiving himself, being merely ignorant and confused in his claim to, or proposition of, atheism.

In connection, I call attention to the view of Bertrand Russell, a philosopher, who rightly said, 'No satisfaction based upon self-deception is solid, and however unpleasant the truth may be, it is better to face it, and proceed and build your life in accordance with it.' Tai Solarin is deceiving himself for not accepting the fact.

The truth is that from whichever perspective we approach the enquiry of whether or not God exists, without being unnecessarily dogmatic, we must arrive, at the end, where the fact of the existence of God stands firmly, staring unblinkingly at us.

TAI SOLARIN: I know at least two Igbo priests [in Nigeria] who share the view of the author's [Obianyido's] criticism of Jesus Christ and Christianity but who lack the courage to declare their stand. I admire courage and detest bravado.

My Mayflower school was unfounded on faith in God, in 1956, and is today making tremendous progress.

REPLY: Immediately after Tai Solarin made his statement of 'I admire courage and detest bravado,' he acted in contradiction to that: 'My Mayflower school was unfounded on faith in God, in 1956, and is today making tremendous progress.' What bravado by one who claims to detest bravado! He has only shown courage in doing what he self-admittedly detests.

He made the foregoing statement not caring that in any enterprise it is the end that counts, not the beginning, not the progress (the middle stage).

According to him, he admires courage. Why then has he failed to name the two Igbo priests? Why keep their identities under wraps? Veiling the identities of the priests does not show courage.

There are many instances of Solarin's bravado in *Christ or Devil?*: 'If there were twenty different schools looking for a job, the Mayflower school graduates would get, if not the first place, certainly the second'; 'The graduates from Mayflower school are miles ahead of their contemporaries.' These are dowry claims, among others not mentioned, which he makes. They are nothing short of vain bravado. How can he then shamelessly claim that he detests bravado in the face of his braggadociousness and ostentatiousness? Of what concern, after all, are the bits and pieces of those instances of blowing his own trumpet in the preface to *Christ or Devil?*

Solarin was expected to write about the author (Obianyido) and his book, not about the Mayflower school and atheism. His praises of the school and atheism are obvious misfits in the preface. Hypocritical is his vaunted claim that he admires courage and detests bravado.

TAI SOLARIN: The commonplace saying among some Nigerian Christians that 'education without religion is like a cup of tea without sugar' is a cheap aphorism palatable only to people who do not know that the Chinese, who gave tea to the world, never drink tea with sugar.

REPLY: The line of reasoning followed by Tai Solarin in his attempt to refute the said Nigerian Christian aphorism is fussy, sheer fiddle-faddle. His argument is stunted and deformed in that he takes no account of many relevant facts inherent to the aphorism he criticises. Words, phrases, sentences, and expressions, including aphorisms, derive their true meanings from the circumstances (the context) amid which they appear. China might have given tea to the world, but Chinese tea in the context of Solarin's comment refers to the original raw tea which the Chinese used as a medicinal herb. The tea Solarin talks about was not originally used as a beverage or as part of a meal, as is the case today.

Based on that fact, his view is archaic. The idea of having tea without sugar is an anachronism, belonging to the culture of ancient China. Today, Chinese people have their tea with sugar. Solarin, with his weak reasoning, attempts to put new wine in an old bottle (Matthew 9:17). He lives in the past!

Today, people of the world (including, of course, Chinese people), Nigerians in particular, invariably have their tea with sugar. The purpose of the saying (the aphorism) that 'education without religion is like a cup of tea without sugar' is to explain that education requires religion (in the form of moral knowledge) to be meaningful, useful, and tasteful, just as a cup of tea needs sugar to make it tasty, or palatable, to the majority of Nigerians.

We are talking about Nigerians, not about the Chinese, in the matter of the aphorism. Nigerians see tea without sugar as no good. Analogously, they see education stripped of religion (moral education) as useless, as tasteless, as something that is to be rejected. Why?

The reason is that religion is expected to inculcate people with good morals and excellent behaviour, whereas education, lacking moral teaching or knowledge, simply educates the head and fails to humanise the people being educated, instead turning them into a type of machine or leaving them in a natural, beastly state.

If the Chinese take tea, processed or not, without sugar, that is entirely their concern, no matter who introduced tea to the world.

In the matter described above, Tai Solarin's interpretation of the aphorism is far removed from reality and truth. As a result of his disconnection from reality, Solarin misapplies the aphorism. His argument accordingly collapses, giving the chance for the Nigerian Christian's point of view to prevail.

TAI SOLARIN: The popular saying among Nigerian Christians that 'if the Lord does not build the house, then the builders work in vain' is arrant nonsense. My Mayflower school adventure, founded in 1956, was set up without the hand of God.

REPLY: Tai Solarin is childish in making his claim. This claim is the offspring of his immature character. I see it as crass propaganda, vainglorious self-praise blended with impiety and blasphemy born of self-intoxication. Tai Solarin is very vain, very full of himself, very egocentric, and very puffed up, and passes himself off as an important member of the intelligentsia or a polymath. Imagine the magnitude of his claim; imagine how unnecessarily he preens himself in making his empty assertion!

Solarin deeply hates Christianity and the idea of belief in God. Given this, one expects him to keep far away from anything that has any connection with Christianity. The word *Mayflower* is the name of the ship of a Christian religious group, the English Pilgrim Fathers. In that ship, the group of Christians, in order to find a safe haven and a better life elsewhere (this was during the Great Schism of the Christian church, between the Roman Catholics and the Protestants, concerning Pope Clement VIII of Rome and the English monarch Henry VIII, which trouble was tearing apart the Pilgrim Fathers' home in England), set out for North America around 1642.

An Igbo tribe (in Nigeria) has a saying, 'Onye mu na ya nadighi namma, ahu onyuru anaghi: esim isi.' The English translation is 'I do not have anything whatever to do objectively to connect me in any way with my mortal enemy. Even where the enemy's fart stinks like hell, in no way do I openly or objectively react.' On that note, what beats me is why Tai Solarin, an inveterate enemy of Christianity, chose to baptise his school with the name Mayflower, a name historically tied to a band of Christians. Could he not have steered away completely from that, which has to do with Christians? I wonder!

In any case, let me investigate the Christian maxim which Tai Solarin quarrels against. He criticises the maxim because he is starkly ignorant about God. God is omnipresent, omnipotent, and omniscient. God is the Creator of the universe and of all within it. In having created the universe, he set the laws to govern it and the things within it, including the events that take place in it. Whatever comes into existence or does not go according to the physical laws does not stand.

In his bald ignorance of the laws, Tai Solarin misunderstands the quotation and, as a result, misinterprets the maxim. Anything done that is against the laws of God is like a house built upon sand, which the wind or a flood, at the right time, sweeps away (Matthew 7:26–27). One can build without the sanction of God, but the building either stands or falls later according to whether the setting up of the building agrees with God's laws.

Tai Solarin expected God to have come 'in the likeness of man' and to have been seen founding his school or stopping him from founding it. It is easy to determine a child's age from the child's utterance, just as it is easy to guess Tai Solarin's downright lack of knowledge of God's ways, as well as his very poor spiritual station and the level of immaturity in his reasoning, shown in his claim to have founded his school without help from God.

All he wants to say is that God does not exist; otherwise God would have stopped him from founding his atheist school, or immediately punished him for setting up the school. God does not do such things just to demonstrate his absolute supreme authority over his creatures and creations; everything in the world is under God's divine laws, which function accordingly at the right time, in the right situation, and in the right measure. The working of God's laws follows God's divine agenda.

Let us not forget the freedom of choice of action—*free will*—given to human beings to choose between good and bad actions, good and bad behaviours.

If this were not so, then every person would be a sort of machine or robot designed for either good conduct or bad conduct. The world would not have had the two opposing types of conduct—good conduct and bad conduct. There would have been simply conduct! Consequently, there would have been no expectation of punishment or reward.

As we have it, from the time of Adam and Eve, today there is good conduct and bad conduct. The choice between the two is always the individual person's.

'After all, God makes his sun to rise upon the good as well as upon the bad; his rain is for the righteous and for the unrighteous' (Matthew 5:45). 'For my thoughts are not your thoughts, neither are your ways my ways; says the Lord' (Isaiah 55:8).

God is impartial in his grace; his grace is universal and nondiscriminatory. By that I mean that a person enjoys the aggregate of God's blessings, be the person righteous or unrighteous. Also, God distributes his punishments impartially, nondiscriminatorily, and universally. But then everyone has deductions from their said aggregate of blessings when they suffer punishment, one way or the other, for their sinful conduct. So a human being lives on the balance of the credits and debits predicated upon his or her moral conduct. That is what determines a person's fate. The fate takes effect at the time it matures, following God's law, which is not necessarily immediate.

Therefore, Tai Solarin's assumption that he set up his school without the hand of God and that the school is 'making tremendous progress' is nothing short of petitio principii (begging the question).

TAI SOLARIN: By criticising Jesus Christ, the author [Obianyido] has written galore and emerged as Africa's Thomas Paine, or Charles Bradlaugh, or Robert Ingersoll.

Any Nigerian, nay, any African who reads this book *Christ or Devil?* by the author is bound to succeed in life, for he will have learnt, for once, that his success lies absolutely in his own hands, that he is the master of his fate, the captain of his soul.

REPLY: Tai Solarin talks crap! How dare he laud Obianyido and liken him to Thomas Paine, Charles Bradlaugh, or Robert Ingersoll? How dare he compare the writing of Obianyido to that of the Europeans named earlier? Why has he presented Obianyido as a fit African to match those European intelligentsias of the classical era? What greater affront than that to Africans? Africans have so many intelligent writers far better than Obianyido whose writings can be fairly compared to those of the named Europeans. Obianyido has not earned the heights given him by Solarin. He is by no means close to the Europeans in intelligence, even though some of those Europeans could be confused, screwy philosophers.

A search with a fine-toothed comb is likely to yield that Obianyido picked up some crumbs of the misconceived philosophical ejaculations of some among the intelligentsia to write his book. In that case, there seems little trace of freethinking or original ideas in his work.

The quality of his book, in terms of knowledge, reasoning, and expression, is worse than the quality of the writing of the worst European writers. I venture to opine that he even pillaged from those Europeans.

The Europeans were open-minded in their discourse. They made philosophical enquires into the things they proposed, and searched for facts. They questioned what they considered to be unclear or to be gaps in the subjects before them, investigated these things, and waited for answers. In Obianyido's case, he made blanket, sweeping negative conclusions about the subjects before him without any prior investigation.

The book *Medieval Thought*, by Gordon Leff, has this: 'By doubting we come to enquiry, by enquiry we perceive the truth.' That prudent path to follow when in doubt was not followed by Obianyido in his writing. Instead, he indulged in a hasty, illogical process with predetermined conclusions that often resulted in his blind criticisms and prejudices.

On this matter, if the Europeans' writings lead to knowledge, then Obianyido's writing is bound to lead to ignorance. That means Tai Solarin, unfortunately, passed over excellence for a state below mediocrity and, in so doing, attempted to slaughter intelligence before Obianyido's ignorance.

In Africa, particularly in Nigeria, the country from which Tai Solarin and his 'Siamese twin' fighter against Christianity hail, society is wallowing in an ocean of monstrous social failures, namely, corruption, kidnapping, lack of jobs, lack of electricity, and lack of adequate medical service, among other festering social ills of many shades. The ills are daily eating into and corroding the sinews of the country's social system. Everywhere there are signs of retrogression and decadence. All Tai Solarin offers as a panacea to those multiple and proliferating complex social disharmonies is the book entitled *Christ or Devil?* written by Anene Obianyido. Shit! Sorry!

If the book indeed had the 'magic wand' ascribed to it by Solarin, then Africa, Nigeria in particular, would not today be sprawling, making no material progress, and going down a slippery slope towards a deplorable, despicable political, social, economic, and moral abyss, as had been the case since the book went into circulation in 1988. Waving the book as a 'magic wand' cure for lack of progress in Nigeria sounds like the adverts one comes across frequently in Nigeria when quacks struggle to sell their dysfunctional wares and inefficacious medicines in open places and on buses. I am afraid that the prescription of reading the book *Christ or Devil?*, if followed, is bound to constipate Nigeria and make its matters worse. In Virgil's phrase, it will result in *aegrescit medendo* (the disease worsening with the treatment).

The prescription by Tai Solarin is therefore nothing less than a recipe for disaster!

It is also Solarin's view that reading *Christ or Devil?* will make the reader the master of his or her fate, the captain of his or her soul. This is an expression Solarin cribbed off a poet, W. E. Henley (1849–1903). Anyway, let us not be too mindful of the fact of the cribbing.

The important questions that will hang over people who read the book—those who swallow Solarin's prescription—are: Who was the master of your fate when you were formed in your mother's womb? After that, who captained your soul's entrance into this world; and who is to captain its exit from this world?

Any attempt to answer those questions is bound to take Tai Solarin to God. He is so allergic to the word *God*! So, he would remain mute, not daring to attempt an answer.

Now let me attempt a precise explanation of that adage that talks about one becoming the master of one's fate and the captain of one's soul. Fate and the soul are of the invisible spiritual realm. As a result, they are beyond human control. *The Collins Cobuild English Language Dictionary* describes fate as 'a power that is believed to control and decide everything that happens in a way that people cannot prevent, or change'. It describes the soul as the part of a person that is believed to continue existing after the body is dead.

The dictionary has made it clear that no one has power or control over any of the two elements in life. Reason: these elements are spiritual and are therefore beyond human power or control. In this circumstance, the real meaning of the adage is found far below the surface. The adage is couched in cryptic language with spiritual connotation buried in poetic expression. The words *fate* and *soul*, indicating things of a spiritual nature, are governed by spiritual laws that are under God's grace.

In order to earn that grace, the favour from those laws, human beings must keep the laws that govern their lives by controlling their conduct.

Jesus Christ knew of the connection one's moral conduct has with one's fate and one's soul. Speaking of this matter, he said to Peter, 'Put up again the sword in its place, for all they that take the sword shall perish with the sword' (Matthew 26:52). With the parable of the rich man and the poor man (Lazarus), Jesus Christ illustrated how the unrighteous personal conduct of the rich man captained his soul to hell (bad fate), while the poor but righteous man captained his soul to Paradise (good fate) (Luke 16:19–31). Paul, Christ's apostle, too, knew how one was to be the master of his or her own fate, the captain of his or her own soul, when he said that one receives according to his or her moral conduct (Ephesians 6:1–9). In Galatians, Paul also said, among other things, 'Be not deceived; God is not mocked: for whatever a man soweth, that shall the one reap' (Galatians 6:1–10). This is also about personal conduct as a means of being the master of one's fate or the captain of one's soul.

In conclusion, it is a person's moral conduct in his or her present or past life (or the life before the present one—I believe in reincarnation) that determines a person's fate and what happens to his or her soul.

Therefore, Tai Solarin's recommendation that one read the book *Christ or Devil?* as a means of becoming the master of one's fate and the captain of one's soul is utter rubbish. Shamefully, he failed to understand the saying (with hidden meaning) he adopted from Henley. As a result, he misapplied it. Whatever one does in order to be the master of his or her fate or the captain of his or her soul, one must take on board his or her own moral conduct. 'You reap what you sow.'

Tai Solarin has the habit of taking the surface meanings (the literal interpretations) of sayings, i.e. the maxims, aphorisms, proverbs, witticisms, and adages, and using them raw as they are given. He fails to dive deep for the meanings. We have observed this shallow practice when he was misinterpreting the sayings 'Education without religion is like a cup of tea with sugar' and 'If the Lord does not build, the house builders work in vain,' to mention a few. In such cases, he should have dived beneath the surface meanings to get at the real meanings, the aims of the sayings. Pearls are scarcely found on the surface.

If Tai Solarin had reflected on the adage in question, he would have realised that God's law has the final say in whatever one thinks or does. Mastery of one's fate and captainship of one's soul must always yield, at last, to the overpowering, ever-present law of God, no matter how long that takes to happen.

That a Christian church found its way to Solarin's atheist school, and that Solarin passed away prematurely (almost at the prime of his life) are striking testimonies that Solarin (a human being) was not after all, despite his boastings, the master of his fate or the captain of his soul. There is an Authority, a Source of all things, beyond the control of human beings. That Source, the ultimate, is God!

What is made clear with the preface written by Tai Solarin is that the book *Christ or Devil?* is a point where Tai Solarin and Anene Obianyido meet. At that point, an alliance was forged between them as they were intent on criticising and attacking Jesus the Christ, Christianity, and God.

If Obianyido is truly for indigenous African religion as he claims throughout his book, a religion that is, no doubt, about a deity (God or gods), then his alliance with Solarin is an unholy and inharmonious one. I expect that it makes for a very uncomfortable bed to accommodate them as odd fellows, one believing in no God, the other believing in God. Tai Solarin, who, no doubt, is in the driver's seat of the alliance, has mercilessly thrown dust into Obianyido's eyes with the contents of the preface and has kicked him right in the teeth with malicious joy. Thus, Obianyido got more than he bargained for when he allowed Solarin to write the preface to his book.

Solarin made a bad job of the preface, which says little or nothing about the subjects and scope of the book. Instead, he enjoyed the opportunity to use the book as a launching pad against theism (deity) and, at the same time, as a vehicle for campaigning for and promoting atheism and the Mayflower school that Tai Solarin, the writer of the preface, founded. In fact, he took Obianyido for a rough ride!

So far in this work, I have dealt with the preface written by Tai Solarin, a confused and treacherous atheist. Now I intend to round up this chapter, which is largely about atheism, under the subheading 'Possible Roots of Atheism'.

Possible Roots of Atheism

A human being is a reasoning machine. Except in an involuntary, reflexive, accidental, or unconscious situation, a human being steps into action or belief after necessarily weighing the pros and cons of his or her intended step. Everyone's normal action or belief is preceded by reasoning.

Because of the role reasoning plays in decision, one's belief (faith) in deity (theism) or atheism is the outcome of one's reasoning. That means everyone's faith has reasons or roots in support. Theism has reasons (roots) leading to it. So has atheism.

Right now, I am considering atheism: what are the possible reasons for believing in it, or what are the possible roots that lead to it?

There are many. From among them, I have economically chosen those that appear to be the cardinal ones. They are three: the invisibility of God; scientific advancement; and anthropomorphism. I intend to analyse them, one after the other, below.

Argument of Invisibility

Does an atheist reasonably deny the existence of God? My simple and direct answer is, I do not think so. What the atheist tends to deny is the manner in which God is presented or represented.

Some Christians, even though they believe God is invisible, portray him as if he has a visible form. For that, the atheist, who by character wants empirical evidence about things, questions the reason God cannot be seen or touched physically. Since God has been presented as having a form, if he cannot be seen or touched, then his existence is in doubt, reasons the atheist.

But there is this point: the atheist believes there is an invisible source of life (energy or force), the effect of which we all experience and observe in ourselves and in other elements in nature around us. I personally contend that that Source is God. According to Joel S. Goldsmith, 'The multiplication of coconuts on a coconut tree is dependent, not on the tree, but on the invisible Source that operates in the tree, through it, upon it, and ultimately as the tree. The world [of course the atheist included] calls it a force of Nature without ever knowing what a force of

Nature is. Actually, it is a name given to the Unknown Invisible activity that produces fruit where there was none before.'[3]

Although that force is invisible (cannot be seen with mortal eyes), its existence is never in doubt. It is supported by the power of reason, which is drawn upon experience, which experience has physical expressions. The Source of that experience exists, and it is God, though he is not visible. 'Absence of evidence is not evidence of absence': the maxim from the known to the unknown applies.

To further illustrate the point, I pose this question: does anyone see the wind? Of course no one does. What one sees or observes are the effects of the wind. Yet everyone believes the wind exists. Our knowledge of the existence of the wind is certainly predicated upon our knowledge of the visible or tangible effects of the invisible wind. Analogously, since we accept that the wind, though invisible, exists, because we can observe and see the effects of it, we have no reason not to accept that God, whose effects we observe and experience in many ways, exists even though he is invisible.

There must necessarily be a Being that is the beginning of itself and is independent of every other being, with said Being being the Source of itself and the beginning of all other things that exist. Gordon Leff shares this wisdom when he quotes Aristotle as saying, 'No being in potentiality can pass into act except by influence of another being already in act.' He goes on to conclude, 'The dictum makes necessary Being alone actual and caused, the cause of possible being. Necessary Being in contrast to possible must be by virtue of its own nature; it cannot not be. Thus, since possible beings could not exist on their own, and since they do in fact exist, they must have a cause—necessary Being. This is God, who is first Being, and whose essence is identical with His existence.'[4]

---

[3] Joel S. Goldsmith, *Beyond Words and Thoughts* (New York, Citadel–Kensington, 1976).

[4] Gordon Leff, *Medieval Thought* (1970), 50.

The foregoing analysis reveals that without knowing or intending it, the atheist believes in the existence of God.

Argument of Scientific Advancement

Scientists (including technologists) are today steadily encroaching upon areas of knowledge previously considered to be the exclusive areas of God. A few examples are cloning, grafting, artificial insemination, the transplanting of parts of the human body from one body to another, the space shuttle, and landing on the moon. 'Playing God' is the popular description for such feats. Daily the frontiers of such feats are being pushed forward. As a result, the atheist concludes that since humankind can do such things previously thought to be incredible and exclusive to God, the idea of God is fanciful, or God is redundant.

My view is that reasoning along these lines is blind. Scientists depend upon theories, observations, and trial and error to arrive at their achievements. Before setting out in search of whatever they want to achieve, scientists preconceive the possible existence of their quest. They may or may not find their object (quest) in the end. Yet the crucial question is, whatever the object of the search, who or what is responsible for its existence? Why is it invisible, and where is it at the material time it is being searched for?

Paul the apostle knows where. He says, 'Whatever is without is from within'—i.e. within the spirit of humankind, the abode of God. So, the scientist has to go within the abode of God by means of trial and error for the relevant natural laws to apply in order to make manifest his or her object that is within and visible.

This means that which the scientist looks for, if it is, must already be in existence in the invisible world at the material time it is being looked for. All the scientist searches for is the relevant law or laws that can be applied for the quest to become manifest (visible).

In that light, the scientist does not create anything, nor does he or she set up the law or laws that make anything happen. He or she simply looks for the laws already in existence in the invisible realm and applies the relevant one when found so as to make things happen. In other words, scientists rely on the natural laws (God's laws) already in existence to perform or achieve their feats. To put it in a simple form: scientists move from the known to the unknown.

Since the atheist depends upon the possibility of science to perform extraordinary feats that seem close to supernatural to deny the existence of God, the atheist wallows in shameful ignorance for not realising that the science upon which he or she relies in turn relies upon the law(s) of the invisible force/energy (that is God), which of necessity is the source of any other things.

In such a case, the atheist, without realising it, believes in the existence of God since he or she believes in science.

Argument of Anthropomorphism

The atheist considers another viewpoint, namely the attributes that Christians ascribe to God, and concludes that God does not exist.

Below, I intend to discuss that issue in two phases to make my opinion easy to understand.

The first phase: Some Christians rely on the section of Genesis where God is reported to have said, 'Let us make man in our image, after our likeness' (Genesis 1:26–27), to say that God resembles a human being in appearance, feelings, or behaviour, and vice versa—a concept that equates with anthropomorphism. In such a case, God has been presented by Christians as having human physical form and character. Some Christians even go further to conceive that God sits in the sky as his Paradise, from where he oversees his universe.

The atheist challenges that concept and poses the view that if God is like a human being with human form and characteristics and cannot be seen or touched, then he does not exist. That, to me, is a reasonable challenge. The interpretation that many Christians have of the section of Genesis in question is wrong. The section refers not to the physical form of humankind, but to the quality of a person as having a soul (spirit), having free will, and having intelligence that enables him or her to be a creator of events and circumstances in his or her world.

God is Spirit (invisible) and cannot be seen or touched; he has no human form and no human characteristics. He has free will. He is a supernatural intelligent Being, a supernatural Creator.

The second phase: Christians hold that God is omnipresent, omnipotent, omniscient, and just, and that in those capacities he controls his creation, supervises human beings, rewards those who are righteous (those who keep his laws), and punishes others who are unrighteous (those who go against his laws) like humans do.

The atheist reasons: 'If God exists and is just and has those capacities attributed to him by the Christians, then the happenings—the injustice and evils—in the world are not supposed to be. That is, the strong trample upon the weak, the rich oppress the poor, the wicked maltreat the innocent, and fate favours the lazy and the dishonest, while the hard-working and the honest are hardly favoured. And God, described as the highest moral excellence, seems to sit idly by, allowing such unjust events.

'In that situation, there is no God,' concludes the atheist. I believe the atheist's reasoning here is founded upon ignorance.

God, for sure, exists, and he rewards and punishes individual human beings accordingly. The matter is that the atheist, being an ordinary human and being ignorant, relies upon appearances, which are illusory and lack spiritual reality, to assess God's dispensation of justice. God's ways are not the ways of human beings (Isaiah 55:8). God's peculiar essence enables him to see the reality in everything beyond the manifestations to a human's physical senses. While human beings, being worldly, judge appearances, God, being Spirit and omnipresent, omnipotent, and omniscient, sees beyond appearances to see reality and truth in everything and judges the heart (not appearances) of every human being. That condition enables him to correctly judge, reward, and punish individual human beings accordingly in any situation and at the appropriate times.

When Jesus was asked, 'Does God bestow rewards for what other men have done?' he replied as follows:

Men never know what other men have done: this life is such seeming life. One man may seem to do a mighty work and be adjudged by men as worthy of reward. Another man may seem to be a failure in the harvest fields of life and be dishonoured in the face of men. Men do not know the hearts of men, God only knows the hearts of men, when the day is done, He may reward with life the man who fell beneath the burdens of the day, and turn away the man who was the idol of the hearts of men.' Jesus illustrated that with the parable of the workers in the vineyard. (*The Aquarian Gospel of Jesus the Christ* 143)[5]

Further illustration of God's manner of dispensation of justice is brilliantly set out, though tersely, in a poem by Ralph Waldo Emerson: 'There is always some levelling circumstances that puts down the overbearing, though no checks to a new evil appear, the checks exist, and will appear. The dice of God is always loaded'—meaning that there are always checks and dispensation of justice through God's laws. Nature [God] always balances its books.

Diligently, I have considered the atheist's view that God does not dispense justice and have found that, contrary to the atheist's opinion, God does unfailingly reward and punish human beings according to each person's moral conduct. The fact is that the atheist wrongly assesses

---

[5] Levi H. Dowling, *The* Aquarian Gospel of Jesus the Christ: *The Philosophic and Practical Basis of the Religion of the Aquarian Age of the World and of the Church Universal* (1908).

God's perfect dispensation of justice; God, unlike human beings, sees the reality in everything and acts according to facts.

So let us not be unmindful of karma—God's law (nature) is a strict accountant: 'Whatever a man sows that must he reap.' That is a spiritual law of God, and it never fails.

The reasons for the atheist's belief that God does not exist therefore hold no water. God is Spirit and therefore cannot be seen or touched. He is the first, the unmoved mover (for he is the cause of himself). He is that that has to be, the first which 'cannot not exist', a Source that is not contingent upon something else, but only upon itself, to be in being. That is the reasoning of a scriptural philosopher.

If, in searching for what or how God is, the atheist finds not the answer, then it is the atheist's defective senses that have failed. God, being Spirit, can only be found in or experienced through the spiritual instrument that is *faith*.

I have gone far into this subject of whether God exists or not in order to pierce the veil of misunderstanding and ignorance that blocks the atheist's vision or insight into the spiritual realm of reality. Further, I have revealed to the atheist that the invisible energy or force which he or she readily accepts as the source of life (call it the Big Bang or evolution), that which he or she acknowledges in science and recognises in all natural elements of the world, is of and about God.

The above analysis clearly establishes that none of the likely roots of atheism holds water. Atheism is an absurd and totally unsubstantiated concept that lacks reality. God exists. 'Only the fool has said in his heart, "There is no God"' (Psalm 14:1).

So far, I have challenged Tai Solarin's opinions in the preface he wrote for Anene Obianyido's book *Christ or Devil?* I will now tackle Obianyido's opinions in the following chapters.

ACKNOWLEDGEMENTS
OF *CHRIST OR DEVIL?*

From his acknowledgements to the final chapter of his book *Christ or Devil?*, Anene Obianyido incessantly attacks Jesus the Christ, Christianity, and God in the most discourteous, uncivil manner, using unrefined, uncultured insulting words and expressions.

For that I intend to pay him back in his own coin; I intend to give him the length of my pen by fiercely challenging him, using words and expressions as wild as his whenever I see a need for it.

For the same reason given in the preceding chapter concerning Tai Solarin's attacks against Jesus the Christ, Christianity, and God, I will introduce the points Obianyido raises in his book under the subheading 'Obianyido', and my replies to the points under the subheading 'Reply'.

Here, again, we go.

OBIANYIDO: I was surprised that my severe criticisms and heretical write-up about Christ and Christianity was read and typed by a Christian. He is a gentle character and such a devoted Christian.

From the members of my family, my wife in particular, I expected violent opposition to my anti-Christ manuscript.

I was surprised that no scene was created. My family did not disturb me and my new faith. I feared my wife most: she had access to my script but did nothing to it. In appreciation I am thankful to every one of them.

REPLY: Let me start with Obianyido's claim to 'my new faith'. Throughout his book, he demonstrates interest in two opposing faiths: atheism and indigenous African religion. Which of the two are we to consider as his new faith? Tai Solarin, unlike Obianyido, in the preface he wrote for Obianyido's book *Christ or Devil?*, boldly and clearly declared his faith as atheism: 'I am an atheist,' he says. Why has Obianyido, throughout his book, sandwiched his 'new faith' between atheism and indigenous African religion? Why is his faith kept under wraps?

The Igbo (a tribe in Nigeria) have a proverb that says, 'Oma akwa awu aru malu onweya.' The English translation is: 'One who bathes with his or her dress on has something he or she recognises as nasty about his or her body to be veiled from others' view.'

Whatever Obianyido's new faith is, and whatever is nasty about this new faith, can easily be discovered by my readers before *In Defence of Jesus the Christ* is read through.

Obianyido entertained fear about the safety of the manuscript of his book. Conscious of the perversity and profanity of his manuscript, he feverishly feared that his relations, all Christians, would react adversely to it or destroy it. Contrary to his fear, the manuscript survived. His relations treated it civilly. He in turn appreciated their magnanimity by thanking them. Good of him!

By implication, Obianyido inadvertently recognises the virtue, the good, in practical Christianity. But he foolishly, defiantly went on opposing Christianity. Thus, he continued to cheat his conscience!

There are people of some other faiths who would not have shown such tolerance as did those Christians. One of such faith that comes readily to mind is Islam. The memory of the events surrounding Salman Rushdie's book *The Satanic Verses* is still green and with us.

Obianyido's wife displayed a highly recommendable Christian principle by her behaviour towards her husband's profane manuscript against Christianity. Incidentally, her conduct towards her husband's attitude agrees, to a far extent, with the wisdom imparted by Jesus the Christ to Ruth. The story of Ruth appears in the book *The Aquarian Gospel of Jesus the Christ*. It is very interesting and richly instructive, and falls almost on all fours with what took place between Obianyido and his wife. I, therefore, find the story apposite to the case of Obianyido and his wife, and have lifted it from *The Aquarian Gospel of Jesus the Christ* to present it here:

> And Ruth was distressed. Her husband was Asher-Ben. Now Asher-Ben was a Pharisee of the strictest mien and fought and regarded Jesus with disdain.
>
> And when his wife confessed her faith in Christ, he drove her from his home.
>
> But Ruth resisted not; she said, 'If Jesus is the Christ, he knows the way, and I am sure he is the Christ.
>
> 'My husband may become enraged and slay my human form; he cannot kill the soul and in many mansions of my Father's land I have a dwelling place.'
>
> And Ruth told Jesus all; and then Jesus said, 'Your husband is not willingly at fault; he is a devout; he prays to God, our Father-God.
>
> 'His zeal for his religion is intense; in this he is sincere; but it has driven him insane, and he believes it right to keep his home unsullied by the heresy of Christ.

'He feels assured that he has done the will of God in driving you away.

'Intolerance is ignorance matured. The light will come to him someday, and he will repay for all your heartaches, grief and tears.

'And Ruth, you must not think you are free from blame.

'If you had walked in wisdom way, and be content to hold your peace, this grief would not have come to you.

'It takes a long time for Light to break into the shell of prejudice, and patience is the lesson you have to learn.

'The constant dropping of water wears away the hardest stone.

'The sweet and holy incense of godly life will melt intolerance much quicker than the hottest flame.

'Just wait a little time, and then go home with sympathy and love. Talk not of Christ, nor of the kingdom of the Holy One.

'Just live a godly life; refrain from harshness in your speech, and you will lead your husband to Light.'

And it was so. (*The Aquarian Gospel of Jesus the Christ* 77:4–22)

That path of wisdom which Jesus the Christ prescribed for Ruth to follow is very similar to the one taken by Obianyido's wife concerning her husband's heretical manuscript. That shows the wife to be a practising Christian.

Obianyido, although flabbergasted at his wife's gentle, noble attitude and full of praises for her, was unlike Ruth's husband in that he stubbornly did not turn back from attacking Jesus the Christ, Christianity, and God; he went ahead and published his heretical book, which I am today challenging.

OBIANYIDO: This book, *Christ or Devil?*, is my first attempt at writing a book of this nature.

REPLY: Obianyido, by that statement, gives the impression that he has written books or a book before *Christ or Devil?* He makes no mention of any such book(s).

I can categorically say that I know of no other book(s) published by him before or after this one I am challenging; I believe that *Christ or Devil?* is his first attempt at writing a book (of any nature). No wonder the entire foundation of the book is weak and wobbly!

The idea of telling his readers that *Christ or Devil?* is his 'first attempt at writing a book of this nature' is odd and uncalled for. It is a plea to his readers to deal with the book softly; he solicits for sympathy and suggests that his readers be nonjudgemental about the weakness of the book. That instantly betrays his fizzy feeling and fear that the book is below the mark, the contents, for the most part, false. Therefore, the plea is defeatist and the book apologetic ab initio. That is to say, the book is already seen by him to be amateuristic and unreliable in fact and quality. And it turns out in the end to be so, by my evaluation.

One has got to read the book with circumspection, with a good measure of misgiving. It is a path to be walked with measured steps, bearing in mind that it is the author's 'first attempt at writing a book of this nature'.

Given that the book is his first attempt at writing a book of this nature, are his readers to take in, without question, whatever rubbish is given in the book? The book, according to Obianyido, is 'dedicated to all freethinkers'. Every freethinker who disagrees with any issues in the book is invited to exercise his or her freedom in approving, criticising, or censuring his book, his call for sympathy notwithstanding. In the first place, it is unnecessary that his readers be told in advance that the book is the author's 'first attempt at writing a book of this nature'. The book's quality is to be allowed to speak for itself and show the book's worth. By its fruits the readers are to know all about the book.

In Defence of Jesus the Christ, challenging Obianyido's book, cannot be gagged. It will spare no point in his book, however minor, so long as it is detected, that contradicts what is acceptable as scriptural and/ or spiritual fact, or that amounts to groundless criticism of the Christ, Christianity, or God. Otherwise, it would appear as if my book were colluding with his or condoning the unwarranted castigations of the Christ, Christianity, and God.

There ends my challenge to the acknowledgements section.

My next chapter will be about the contents of the introduction to Anene Obianyido's book *Christ or Devil?*

INTRODUCTION TO
CHRIST OR DEVIL?

OBIANYIDO: An atheist friend of mine declined an invitation to a television debate on whether God exists or not. Refusing the invitation, my atheist friend said, 'In a society where attitude of Christians is what it was in Renaissance Europe, it would be suicidal for me to participate in an open debate on God or Christ.'

After the decline, another atheist friend, a bolder one, accepted the invitation next time and did excellently well in the presentation of his disagreement with the Christian concept of God.

REPLY: How fussy Anene Obianyido is, worrying over a trivial matter—a television debate on whether God exists or not.

According to him, his atheist friend won the debate against the Christian, i.e. he proved the nonexistence of God. His claim was made with joy.

We, Obianyido's readers, are not presented with the facts of the debate. So we are left to rely on his biased and prejudicial conclusion. He made himself the judge and the jury of the debate. But we must not forget that he has a vested interest in atheism, which said interest must have affected him and influenced his assertion that the atheist friend of his proved the nonexistence of God.

Whatever may be his opinion about the result of the televised debate, one important fact emerged at the end of the debate. Remember, his atheist friend who declined the invitation did so because he entertained some forebodings and apprehensions that the debate would turn into a scene similar to the Roman gladiatorial arena—violent. That prognostication came to nothing as there was no violent reaction from the Christians after all. The friend of his realised then that he had been afraid of nothing but his own shadow!

Atheists are always jittery whenever they hear the name of Jesus the Christ, Christianity, or God being spoken of. A throwback: Obianyido shivered to his bones fearing that his manuscript would be destroyed by Christians. This has been mentioned early in *In Defence of Jesus the Christ*. I suppose that earlier incident about his heretical manuscript and his family and this later one concerning the television debate add up to demonstrate the genuine Christian qualities of tolerance, gentility, civility, and civilisation.

What seems unclear about this man Obianyido is that his attitude is negative about God (he does not believe in God), but at the same time he pretends to be very passionately obsessed with indigenous African religion. Does he not realise that indigenous African religion is based on theism (deity)? Again, why has he not, like Tai Solarin, declared atheism as his faith? Why is he hiding his faith?

Judging by the information in his book, all his friends are atheist. If he is not already an atheist, I am sure he is imperceptibly being sucked into the atheistic vortex. Tai Solarin, the author of the preface of *Christ or Devil?*, and the two other friends of Obianyido's—the one who declined the invitation to a television debate on whether or not God exists, and the other who accepted the invitation the next time—are all atheists. Obianyido must have many other atheist friends. 'Tell me who your friends are, and I will tell you the sort of person you are' is a saying.

No one, therefore, who calls Obianyido an atheist will be far from that target. He has not yet gathered sufficient courage to break his mould, come out into the open, and confess atheism as his faith. His show of interest in indigenous African religion is deceitful and hypocritical.

Obanyido's faith has been in flux. Originally, he was an adherent of an indigenous African religion (he was born into it, I surmise). Next, he shifted to Christianity. Amazing! He seems at the same time to be casting a longing, wistful, furtive glance at atheism, if he has not already embraced atheism. He is like a wife prospecting for a husband. Or is he merely having a merry-go-round? His fickle, capricious mind, being unstable, oscillates this time between the choice of atheism and indigenous African religion. No one is certain on which side his pendulous mind is to anchor for good.

OBIANYIDO: My book *Christ or Devil?* is an attempt to lead the readers through the mental path I have trodden to reach my present conviction that Christianity, as a foreign religious culture, and as it is practised in my country, constitutes a corrupting influence on African's rich traditional value system.

REPLY: I have read through *Christ or Devil?* by Anene Obianyido. I am of the strong opinion that the view that the 'mental path' he has 'trodden' led him to a wrong conclusion—he arrived at a mirage.

Any of his readers who follows that path is most likely to fall off a mental precipice of abject ignorance.

To give adequate reasons for my conclusion, I need to highlight Obianyido's points against Christianity, then deal with them. He complains about how it is practised in his country; he complains that it is a foreign religion and that it 'constitutes a corrupting influence on Africa's rich traditional value system'.

That allegation is wrong. It gives the impression that indigenous African religion with its traditional culture was in an ideal state, socially speaking, before Christianity was introduced to Africa. The truth can only emerge if the precepts and practices of indigenous African religion, with its traditional system (before the advent of Christianity in Africa), is juxtaposed with Christian precepts and practices. Then their respective moral and social worth is placed on a social and moral scale to determine which of the two faiths has greater weight in terms of moral and social values. Personally, I believe the Christian faith will outweigh those of the Africans.

Christianity has, since its inception in Africa, been instrumental to the abolition of many evil practices of indigenous African religion and culture. It brought about the abolition of burying human beings alive with deceased kings or chiefs. It stopped the killing of twins or triplets; in some cases, their mothers also used to be killed. There are many other evils of indigenous African religion and culture which Christianity checked. Among these other evils is the killing of those suspected to be witches and the practice of the Osu system (a caste system of social divide). These last two still have a faint presence; they have not been effectively eradicated. Due to ongoing pressures from various social bodies and governments being championed by Christianity, those diabolical practices are suffering a slow death. Peter the apostle spoke against the caste system (Osu) in his time (Acts 10:28).

Obianyido himself mentions in his book some of the evils of Africa's indigenous religions and cultural practices and goes further to say that some of them have been checked. I find it odd that he falls short of saying who or what was responsible for the checking. He does not know who or what brought about the checking. He has forgotten that Mary Slessor, a Christian, popularly known as the Queen of Calabar (in Nigeria), played a major part in stopping the killing of twins.

Jesus the Christ found some of the traditions of the Jews (into which religion he was born) unworthy before God. He took on the daunting task of making all necessary changes thereto. He made changes to the

Jewish tradition/scriptural laws given by Moses, their prophet, in order to place the laws within the correct current conditions for serving society and pleasing God (Matthew 5). He amended the condition for the application of the Sabbath (Matthew 12). He condemned the Pharisees' giving of preference to traditions over the laws of God (Matthew 15).

All I am proposing is that, where necessary, changes be made to religion and culture/tradition. Obianyido's view that Christianity 'constitutes a corrupting influence on Africa's rich traditional value system' is in indirect opposition to the changes needed to Africa's religions and traditions. His idea is short-sighted and lacking in wisdom. Christianity seeks to make necessary changes to African indigenous religion and culture/tradition to improve these things by raising the moral and social standard to a level appropriate for serving God through serving humanity.

Naturally, every reasonable person or religion aspires to the making of necessary changes for higher social standards. Any such move can sometimes go astray as a result of ignorance of the correct course to follow. The propensity to advance to a higher and better moral and social standard entails adoption of and adaptation to new, better ideas either internally generated or externally copied. Africans are not to be excluded from such an urge.

And, of necessity, the foreign ideas reasonable people of any race or nation pick as the building blocks for the necessary changes to their systems are ideas they want but lack, or those they find better than what they have locally; the foreignness of the ideas does not matter. Obianyido suffers from xenophobia and hates foreign ideas.

From the beginning of social history, nations, races, and tribes have engaged in social intercourse. In the course of such exercise, concepts, cultures, religions, and so on, were all the time being copied from one another among developed, developing, and underdeveloped nations. Africa cannot run away from that practice.

I do not believe genuine Christianity is simply against the indigenous religions and culture of Africa. Rather, I think that Christianity only seeks, and rightly so, to influence indigenous African religion (and culture) to strip itself of the practices that are inhumane, destructive, and inimical or menacing to humanity and, therefore, against God.

In such a circumstance, indigenous African religion and culture can borrow, where need be, good religious principles from any foreign religions to enrich it and improve its social and moral contents.

At the same time, I consider that total abandonment of indigenous African religion and culture for foreign religions or culture without good reasons(s) may not be an ideal option.

So, nations, races, and tribes can stick to their social practices so long as the practices are not in conflict with morality—social justice and respect for God.

Culture with religion is a living creature: it grows with time and tends to conform to circumstances so as to update itself in the service of humanity. 'A state without the means of some changes [necessarily for the better] is without the means of its conservation' (Edmund Burke, 1729–1797). Lack of enough room for essential changes to Africa's indigenous culture and religions was a factor, among others, that caused the destruction of indigenous African culture and religion. Africa's indigenous culture with its religion could therefore borrow from the practices of any good foreign religion for the necessary improvements of itself.

Great Britain, France, and Germany, to mention a few, had their respective indigenous religions and cultures influenced by Christianity. This was not seen to corrupt their cultures. Christianity was presented to other countries and races. Papua New Guinea is an example. Papua New Guineans took from Christianity what they saw necessary while retaining some of their indigenous culture and religion, such as their traditional burial ceremonies.[6]

In those countries named above, Christianity was not seen as having a corrupting influence on their social systems. Why is Obianyido alleging that Christianity 'constitutes a corrupting influence on Africa's rich traditional value system'? Obianyido is in favour of having atheism in Africa. Will the introduction of atheism into Africa not constitute a corrupting influence on Africa's rich traditional value system'?

Now we step into his second point: 'the wrong manner in which Christianity is being practised in my country'. This notion of Obianyido's can only be construed to mean that he is not against Christian practice—it is good. He is only against the manner of the practice of Christianity in his country (he is from Nigeria). In other words, he welcomes Christianity. That is quite OK with me. But then why has he been attacking Christianity? The answer is that he is a confused man! The only obvious reason for his condemnation of Christianity is that it is a foreign religion.

That reason is a senseless base. Religions are to be assessed on the merit of their teachings and the practice of their precepts. Christianity wins my unflagging support where assessment of religion is based on social and spiritual values.

Africa may have a 'rich traditional value system', but that is not all there is to the matter: I am talking comparatively. 'Nothing is good or bad, otherwise by comparison.' When Africa's rich traditional value system is compared with the Christian principle, the ugly difference appears. The indigenous religions and traditions of Africa have been found to be full of social evils, and in that respect, Christianity is far better. Africa, therefore, needs radical changes and must not remain ossified in evils. Sticking to an African indigenous religion and tradition that is replete with evils, and rejecting foreign religions that have better social

---

[6] A. L. Crawford, *Aida, Life and Ceremony of the Gogodala* (Bathurst, Australia, National Cultural Council of Papua New Guinea, 1981).

values, as Obianyido seems to suggest, is narrow-minded dogmatism. Africa should borrow better principles from foreign religions for the refurbishment of its own religions.

OBIANYIDO: I have, to the best of my limited ability, looked hard at the Christian religion, i.e. its historical growth and its contemporary role in a developing country like ours, to see what it offers in the sphere of moral educational value and indigenous cultural evolution, and found it wanting.

REPLY: Hang on! Does Obianyido, a disciple of morality in schools, not condemn religious education? (Refer to Chapter 10 of *Christ or Devil?*) Here he complains that Christianity does not offer 'moral educational value'. What is Christianity precisely about? The Ten Commandments, the Sermon on the Mount, other teachings of Jesus the Christ, and the teachings of his disciples and his apostles are of moral educational value, are they not? Can Obianyido understand that?

OBIANYIDO: I wish that no one will quarrel with my right to hold the views expressed in this book *Christ or Devil?*

REPLY: Everyone, Obianyido included, has a right to express contrary views to another's. If that means quarrelling with Obianyido, so be it! No true Christian will disturb his right to free expression, even where such expression flies in the face of the teaching of Christianity.

The acknowledgements section of *Christ or Devil?* praises the Christians who tolerated his vile and venomous criticisms and attacks against Jesus the Christ, Christianity, and God. About the television debate he discusses, there was no violent reaction against his atheist friend who took part in the debate for postulating that God does not exist. Why does Obianyido here want further proof to ensure his safety? Says the Bible, 'This generation is an evil generation; it seeks a sign, but no sign shall be given to it except the sign of Jonah' (Luke 11:29). The tolerance by the Christians concerning Obianyido's heretical manuscript, and the peaceful response of the Christians to his atheist friend who went on television to deny the existence of God, are both signs sufficient to assure him of his safety, even though he holds strong opinions against Jesus the Christ, Christianity, and God, as expressed in his book.

At the same time, although no one would quarrel with him for holding his opinions, he should not expect to get away with it when, in exercising his freedom of expression, he unjustly steps upon someone else's toes. The victim would react and challenge him in order to keep the facts straight and clear, or in such a manner that would make him lift his weight off the person's toes.

The primary task of *In Defence of Jesus the Christ* is not to do unwarranted damage to Obianyido's freedom of expression, but to beat to size any matters in his book considered inconsistent with what is held to be correct. 'Everyman has a right to utter what he thinks truth, and every other man has a right to knock him down for it' (Samuel Johnson).

Given Obianyido's admission, in expressing his opinions against Christ, that he 'hopes to stimulate intellectual discussion in the relevance of Christian religion to the developmental need of the second and third countries, with particular reference to Nigeria', I feel compelled to share in the discussion.

To do that, I hope to muster all available facts and opinions known to me that are in favour of, or against, his opinions. On those principles will I found my book *In Defence of Jesus the Christ*.

WHAT IS RELIGION?

(CHAPTER 1, *CHRIST OR DEVIL?*)

OBIANYIDO: Early religion only meant to me the belief in Jesus Christ born by the Virgin Mary, who conceived him by the power of the Holy Ghost, making him the Son of God. I now have a contrary opinion and reject all that.

Also, I object to the fact that Jesus came to the world only to forge a link between humankind and God. Nor do I accept that his death has washed away our sins.

REPLY: The foregoing two paragraphs are loaded with important, moot points about Christian beliefs, to wit:

(a) that the Virgin Mary conceived Jesus by the power of the Holy Ghost;
(b) that Jesus (Christ) is the only Son of God;
(c) that Jesus (Christ) came to the world to forge a link between humankind and God; and
(d) that the death of Jesus (Christ) has washed away our sins.

Anene Obianyido has contrary views to those Christian beliefs and rejects all said beliefs instantly. Oddly enough, he expects his readers to agree with him when he has given no particular reasons for his opinions.

Nevertheless, his opinions are reflective of important scriptural and spiritual issues. They have, from the long-distant past to the present time, been recurring subjects for debate among philosophers, theologians, historians, and other classes of people (nonprofessionals) with divergent views.

The four issues raised by Obianyido are to be discussed one after the other:

Whether the Virgin May Conceived Jesus by the Power of the Holy Ghost

There is this wrongly conceived notion which is almost universal among present-day Christians: they rest their belief that Jesus is the Son of God, I guess, on their wrong doctrine that his mother, the Virgin Mary, conceived him by the power of the Holy Ghost without Joseph in the picture.

This belief is highly controversial. I join Obianyido in rejecting it, without hesitation. I want to give time and space to offer enough my reasons for disagreeing with those Christians. My discussion of the subject is to centre on whether Joseph played a biological part in his wife's conception of Jesus (whose other name is Emmanuel). Essentially, we need to search through the Holy Bible in our quest for the right answer.

In the New Testament, on several occasions, Jesus Christ calls himself the Son of Man. See Luke 7:34, 17:22, and 22:69, and Matthew 9:6, 11:19, 12:8, 32–40, 13:14, and 16:27. He was not wrong: he was, earthly, the son of Joseph.

Mary, Jesus's mother, acknowledged Joseph, her husband, as the son's father whose ancestor was David (Luke 18:38–39; Matthew 9:27).

The gospel of Luke tells of Jesus's parents (Joseph and Mary) going to Jerusalem with their son for Festival (Luke 2:41–48). Verse 48 is particularly informative. It says that Jesus's mother said unto him, 'Son, why has thou thus dealt with us? Behold thy father and I sought thee sorrowing.'

The father in the context refers to no other person than Joseph, the husband of Mary, Jesus's mother.

Jesus himself recognised Joseph as his earthly (biological) father. This is why he employed the description 'heavenly Father', to distinguish his earthly father, Joseph, from God, the heavenly Father (Matthew 18:10).

The people of Jesus's era recognised Jesus as the son of the man Joseph when they asked about Jesus, 'Is this not the carpenter's son?' thus referring to Joseph by his trade, for he was indeed a carpenter (Matthew 13:54–56).

The prophecy about the birth of Jesus declared that Jesus would be born in the lineage of David. Here, I ask, is Joseph not a descendant of David? Is he not of the lineage of David?

We are nowhere informed in the Bible that Mary, the mother of Jesus, or the Holy Ghost was of the lineage of David (but that Joseph was is clear in the Bible), nor does the Bible tell us that Joseph was the adopted father of Jesus—a rumour timidly being spread as a counter to the fact that Joseph biologically fathered Jesus.

Additionally, Jesus was a Jew, and in Jewish custom and tradition, lineage is paternal, not maternal. I have mentioned these facts because some present-day Christians, in order to sustain their wrong teaching that Joseph was not the biological father of Jesus, always rely on either the perplexing story about Mary's conception of Jesus by the power of the Holy Ghost or on their contrived adoption idea, or both (the two unsubstantiated and unsustainable grounds), to deny credit to Joseph as the biological father of Jesus.

And Joseph was of the lineage of David (Matthew 1:1–20; Luke 2:1–5, 3:21–31; John 7:41–42; Romans 1:3–4). Therefore, Jesus stemmed from Joseph.

Read Revelation: 'I, Jesus have sent my angels to testify unto you these things in churches. I am the root of the off-spring of David, and the bright and morning star' (Revelation 22:16). Connect that to Romans 1:3–4, which reads, 'Concerning his son Jesus Christ our Lord, which was made of the seed of David according to the flesh; and declared the sons of God with Power, according to the spirit of Holiness'. What does the passage teach us?

I understand the passage to mean that Jesus was born in the lineage of David (the ancestor of Joseph, the biological father of Jesus) as a 'flesh and blood' human being, but by the power (authority) of the Holy Ghost, the incarnated spirit of the baby (Jesus) was declared to be holy (i.e. the Christ, the Son of God).

That bit of Bible history seems to me to shine a light upon how the belief that Mary conceived Jesus by 'the power of the Holy Ghost' without Joseph (as the biological father) in the picture became part of the Christian concept of Jesus's being 'conceived by the power of the Holy Ghost'. I guess that Christians misunderstand the portion of the Bible in question and, as a result, misrepresent it.

It seems to me that the only part played by the Holy Ghost in the entire event was in the announcement in advance of the event by the angel of God, i.e. that the incarnated spirit of the baby Jesus was declared to be holy—that is, as the Christ, the Son of God—by the Holy Ghost.

Let us further consider the issue of whether Joseph was involved in the conception of Jesus. Be mindful of this from the book of Acts in the New Testament: 'And when he had removed him, he raised up unto them David to be their king; to whom also He gave testimony, and said, I have found David the son of Jesse, a man after my own heart, who shall fulfil all my will. Of this man's seed had God according to His promise, raised unto Israel a Saviour, Jesus' (Acts 13:22–23).

To cap that, read, 'Philip fined Nathanael, and saith unto him, "We have found him, of whom Moses in the law, and the prophets, did write, Jesus of Nazareth, the son of Joseph"' (John 1:45). That's amazing! I ask, what can be clearer in determining the true lineage of Jesus than that passage, and another, Luke 3:23, which, together with the foregoing passage, categorically directly links Jesus (as the son) to Joseph (as the biological father)?

To make my discussion easy to follow, I shall call the above references group A.

In the same book, the Bible, we have group B, with references that seem to make suggestions contrary to those of group A. Group B gives the impression that Jesus (who became the Christ) was God's direct Son or the direct Son of the Holy Ghost. That seems to say that God the Father or the Holy Ghost fathered Jesus, leaving Joseph out of the conception scenario.

After the baptism of Jesus, a voice (no doubt God's) from heaven said, 'You are my beloved son, and I am fully pleased with you' (Mark 1:11). Jesus said, 'I must be about my Father's business' (Luke 2:49), 'for my Father has given me this command' (John 10:18). 'For it is my Father's will that all who has seen His son and believes in him should have eternal life' (John 6:40). 'Mark my word … I will not drink wine again until the day I will drink it new with you in my Father's Kingdom' (Matthew 26:29). 'My Father, if it is possible, let the cup of suffering be taken away from me' (Matthew 26:39). 'My Father did. And now He offers you the true bread from heaven' (John 6:32).

Put the two groups (A and B) next to each other to find that each appears to contradict the other. The seeming contradiction prompts the important question: given that both groups are in the same book, the

Holy Bible, is the Bible confused, or is it contradicting itself? My answer is no. The Bible is not confused, nor is it contradicting itself.

How can such be the case? The group A references are about Jesus as a human being (flesh and blood), who became the Christ, and about Joseph as the earthly biological father of Jesus. The group B references are about Jesus, the aspect of God, the Christ, the Son of God, which Jesus became, and about God as his heavenly Father, spiritually speaking. In the foregoing circumstance, the Bible is not contradictory, nor is it confusing. It is misunderstood because of the unclear construction of the expression telling the story of the conception.

The preceding analysis is an attempt to establish that the conception of Jesus by his mother, Mary, was not done by the power of Holy Ghost alone; it was a biological conception, and Joseph, the husband of Mary, was the person most likely responsible, as a physical agent, for the conception.

No matter how clear the analysis leading to the established conclusion that Joseph was Jesus's biological father is, present-day Christians may not be prepared to accept it. The likely reason is that acceptance of it will cause casualties in their religion. Followers are likely to falter, losing confidence in the teachings of the faith, and some will abandon ship, that is desert the religion altogether.

Imagine this: 'Clergy who deny the Virgin birth or body resurrection of Jesus Christ will be tried as heretics, under a new measure voted on yesterday at the General Synod of the church of England.'[7]

Such a disciplinary measure may apply only to those within the fold of the synod. At least I hope so.

The policy is likely based on the fear that doubting the teaching of the Church of England or its interpretations of the Bible, or expressing any

---

[7] Ruth Gledhill, 'Church Aims to Put Clergy in the Dock with Modern Heresy Trials,' *The Times*, February 15, 2005, 4.

opinion contrary to the church's, will drain the lifeblood of the faith. I think that to take any drastic measure against Christians outside the fold of the synod would be a wrong scriptural and spiritual attitude. Whether or not any opinions contrary to the church's are correct or not, it is better that Christians be allowed the right to their personal convictions and opinions. Otherwise, their opinions may be suppressed and yet not eradicated.

Is it not better that in a confusing circumstance, a church muster evidence or proof enough to convince the doubting Thomases among the Christians that the doctrines and teachings of the church are based on truth? Did Jesus the Christ, when faced with a somewhat similar situation, not take steps to convince doubting Thomas (one of his apostles) of his resurrection and appearances (John 20:24–29)?

Obviously, any measure taken against anyone without the fold of the synod on account of one's conviction and opinion will seem an ugly backward march to about the 1500s in Europe, when the Roman Catholic Church was muzzling and gagging the members of the faith with threat of inquisition and death for daring to question the church's doctrines or for expressing opinions contrary to those of the church. Any such measure will be potentially counterproductive.

Christians who question or doubt the teachings of their faith are, no doubt, searching for truth. That attitude is natural and expected. It is wise to understand that opinion arrived at through personal reasoning and conviction is by nature an authority and law unto itself. It cannot be crushed, nor does it capitulate to unclear teachings or doctrines. Where force is applied against convictions personally reasoned out, people who possess such convictions are most likely to openly reject the force and make up their minds to face the consequences. The schism in the early Roman Catholic Church between the church (the Pope) and Henry VIII of England is a classic example.

Alternatively, such doubting Christians may, under pretence, calmly submit to and accept the teachings being forced upon them in order to avoid the pain of force. That means a person in that situation will be professing one thing openly but secretly harbouring quite a different opinion that aligns with his or her personal conviction.

In a situation of this nature, the very teachings and doctrines of Christianity will make no real impression on the person concerned. Consequently, the chance of truly spreading the intended gospels will be lost.

For that reason, the use of force or threat to advance a cause is not a reasonable option vis-à-vis the use of rational means such as explaining, that is arguing with convincing information. Otherwise, gagging Christians or intimidating them about doctrines and teachings may simply force uncertain concepts down the throat of the reluctant Christian. The concept will not digest but will reduce the Christian to a blind follower—a zombie!

Airing one's views about the teachings or doctrines of any church is not, therefore, a matter that should provoke witch-hunting of the wrong, irrational practice of the far-gone Roman Catholic Church of the Middle Ages in the wake of Christendom.

Returning to our subject, the story of the Virgin Birth should not be guzzled raw as it is presented without question when one is in doubt. To lean on the somewhat cryptic expressions the 'angel of God said to Mary, "And behold, thou shall conceive in thy womb, and bring forth a son, and shall call his name Jesus"' (Luke 1:31) and 'When his mother Mary was espoused to Joseph, before they came together, she was found with a child of the Holy Ghost' (Matthew 1:18), among other unconvincing, unclear statements, to conclude that Jesus was conceived by his mother by the power of the Holy Ghost and that therefore he was born as a direct Son of the Holy Ghost or God, when there are doubts surrounding the story, is unsafe.

Obianyido, therefore, rightly questions the Christian claim to the Virgin Birth by the power of the Holy Ghost. I, too, question that belief. The reasons for my disbelief have earlier been given.

I am pretty sure that some Christians of today who readily accept that Jesus was conceived by his mother by the power of the Holy Ghost will tend to ask, 'Do you mean that God, the Almighty, could not make it happen that Mary conceived by the power of the Holy Ghost, without more?' To that somewhat reasonable question, my immediate answer is 'no'. That I do not mean. But I do not doubt the ability or the prerogative of God to do anything he desires to do since I believe he is omnipotent, omnipresent, and omniscient. Yet, I postulate that God does not contradict himself or his laws. Human beings, for sure, by natural law of God need the mating of man and woman for pregnancy to materialise. By that I mean that a woman needs to receive a man's semen to conceive—and nowhere in the Bible is it suggested that Mary the mother of Jesus was a hermaphrodite. Besides, the Bible supports me.

To come at this from a different angle: Do not ask about the meddling by science where insemination is performed to produce babies, because that does not subtract from the law I just mentioned, as long as insemination means the blending of the male's substance (if you like, semen) with that of the female.

I am of the view that Joseph and Mary (the mother of Jesus) mated, and this resulted in the conception of Jesus. My points on that issue have been made. The references from our group A, above, strongly support that fact that Joseph biologically fathered Jesus. Why do we need to look at the matter from weaker angles? Why need we reconstruct the obvious and transparent facts, evidenced in the Bible, in order to give the Holy Ghost, the credit he has never asked for? The Holy Ghost never played a part in the conception of Jesus, except that the angel of God declared that a holy baby was to be conceived by the power of the Holy Ghost. Mary would be blessed with a holy baby.

The angel of God, for his part, and given his status, capably knew in advance that Mary, who then was a virgin and was espoused to Joseph with a view to marriage (wedding), would conceive a holy baby for Joseph before their wedding/marriage, and told Mary of the event to come. Mary later conceived as she was told (Matthew 1:18–21; Luke

1:27–35). All these messages were about the spiritual ability of the angel of God and the Holy Ghost to have knowledge of events well in advance, i.e. before the events happened. Joseph became aware of the pregnancy later. The saying is 'A virgin will conceive', not 'has conceived'.

Do not forget that the same angel of God made a similar declaration to the priest Zacharias and his wife Elizabeth about Elizabeth's going to have a baby at her old age. The baby was John the Baptist (Luke 1:11–13). In each of the two events, the angel of God was able to say in advance the nature of the spiritual work the expected baby would do.

In my attempt to present Joseph as the biological father of Jesus and, at the same time, see off the Christians' claim that Mary conceived Jesus by the power of the Holy Ghost, I am confronted by this sticky portion in the Bible that suggests that Joseph knew nothing about the pregnancy of his lover Mary until later, and that when he possessed the knowledge of it, he wanted to hide Mary away, not wanting to make a public example of her. It is that sticky point that seems to say that Joseph was not responsible for the conception of Jesus that I want to deal with next.

About that, I contend that Joseph did mate with Mary but possibly did not know of the pregnancy earlier, finding out about it later. He was not expecting that to happen before their marriage or wedding. He became so embarrassed and panicked that he wanted to hide her from public view, I surmise.

I highly suspect that Joseph at that time belonged to the Essenes sect of Judaism. The sect was made up of very strict Jews who lived in communes. A few of them were married, but most of them were monastic celibates. It was one of their strict rules that celibates must go through the approved marriage (wedding) ceremony before attempting to procreate (to produce offspring). Joseph and Mary, who were betrothed but had not yet wedded, had an ethical misadventure by the pregnancy. So Joseph failed to uphold the strict standard of behaviour set forth by the sect the Essenes.

As I said earlier, Joseph, being confused, wanted to hide Mary or put her away. The angel of God, perceiving Joseph's intention and also foreseeing from the incarnated soul of the conceived baby that Jesus was holy (Romans 8:29), instructed Joseph in a dream to disregard the worldly rules and tradition of his sect the Essenes and take Mary as his wife.

By that explanation, the final obstacle in my attempt to prove that Joseph fathered Jesus has, I hope, been cleared!

The Christians who insist that Joseph had nothing to do with Mary's conception of Jesus are, on balance of probability, wrong. They likely rest their claim on their misunderstanding of some information in the Bible (information they are unable to correctly piece together about the story of the angel and the power of the Holy Ghost), or they rely on their concern with the Holy Ghost as a garb on Jesus so as to make him a special Son of God.

That position, the status of 'special Son of God', describes the divine level which Jesus attained, earned, and sustained in his earlier incarnations and demonstrated in this, his last one we are dealing with. It was not necessary for his mother to have conceived him by the power of the Holy Ghost for him to earn the title 'special Son of God', the Christ—'My son in whom I am well pleased' (Matthew 3:17).

That my conclusion that Joseph, not the power of the Holy Ghost, was biologically responsible for the conception of the baby Jesus by his mother, which I reached through logical and scriptural paths, is certainly a bitter pill which some headstrong Christians will find hard to swallow even with wrenched faces. Does that matter? Does truth care?

With hesitation, I argue that if, by the way it is granted, Mary conceived Jesus by the power of the Holy Ghost, then Jesus was not of the lineage of David as prophesied, and he did not become a righteous individual by his moral efforts and his spiritual conduct, but as a result of a predetermined state foisted upon him by the Holy Ghost. In that case, he would have acted like one who was designed for righteous conduct.

How could he then, in a situation like that, have asked us to follow his teachings and conduct if he had the huge advantage of the Holy Ghost's blessing? He taught that if we believe his teachings and accept him, we will do the works he did and even more (John 14:12). That means he rose from human to become the Christ.

Jesus was born like everyone else, a human being. By his personal efforts, his self-controlled conduct along the path of righteousness, from his past incarnation, he pleased God by his faith to become the Christ, 'the special Son of God'.

The idea of the Virgin Birth by the power of the Holy Ghost, making Jesus the special Son of God, is in doubt most likely, as it is unsubstantiated.

I, therefore, share with Obianyido the doubt he entertains about the power of the Holy Ghost and the Virgin Birth.

Some Christians and non-Christians have openly questioned the Christian notion of the Virgin Birth. Others, mainly Christians, are timidly contented to retain their doubt secretly, allowing it to be rumbling in their heads for fear that openly posing the question about the matter will betray them as nonbelievers in Christianity. I am of the opinion that people should question whatever is unclear to them so as to get to the truth.

The pillar that should hold genuine Christianity up is not the alleged Virgin Birth/power of the Holy Ghost, but the truth which Jesus Christ, above other human beings, taught and about God and practised himself.

Another issue raised by Obianyido: He rejects the Christian belief in Jesus Christ, born of the Virgin Mary, who conceived by the power of the Holy Ghost, making her child the Son of God. Bear you in mind, we have already separated Jesus (as a human being) from the Christ (as an aspect of God, the Spirit or Son of God) and established that he was the son of the man Joseph. Obianyido's question is about Jesus the Christ, not about Jesus the human being (as I understand the question). That fact makes his question a spiritual one.

Personally, I believe God has no child in the sense that we recognise earthly sons and daughters. It is unimaginable to conceive Jesus as the Son of God without more, even with the Holy Ghost episode considered, when in detail we look into what the term *earthly son* means. God could not have been biologically involved in the conception of Jesus. Therefore, God is not Jesus's earthly father, but Joseph was. That is vividly clear. To think otherwise is sacrilegious! Call a spade a spade, not a digging tool!

But through creation, we are all the children of God. We can become special or spiritual children of God by faith through serving God righteously. To do that, one has to recognise the presence of the Christ in oneself, for the Christ is in every human being (1 Corinthians 3:16; Colossians 1:26–27; Galatians 1:15–16), lying latent until one awakens the Christ by faith and allows it to take over and live, in full, one's life for oneself.

Jesus did just that in the course of his many incarnations, and in the end he experienced full manifestation of the Christ, the essence of God in his life. Thus he became the special Son of God—"'My beloved son, in whom I am well pleased", said a voice [God's] from heaven' (Matthew 3:11).

Let me make this conclusion clearer: Jesus was born a human being who had purified himself during his previous incarnations. He did that by surrendering his lower self (his selfhood, his worldliness, his worldly lusts) to his higher self (his inner self, the Christ in him) so the latter might live his life for him, i.e. function as his life for him on earth. As a result, Christhood shined through him, making him the Christ, the special or spiritual Son of God.

The spiritual alchemy that transformed Jesus, a human being, into a spiritual being, the Christ (the Son of God) is perplexing, yet it is a very, very important scriptural subject.

John 1:1 has this: 'In the beginning was the Word, and the Word was with God, and the Word was God—And the Word was made flesh, and dwelt among us.' This refers to Jesus, no doubt. I have attempted to explain the transformation, yet the matter seems to remain confusing.

Here, I give it another try: God incarnated in flesh the Word, the Christ (the Son of God), manifested through Jesus (a human, flesh and blood). That is to say, Jesus in his righteousness surrendered his humanhood to the Christ in him and, by faith and the grace of God, became synonymous with the Word, the Christ, the Son of God. And the Word lived in the flesh as Jesus the Christ in our world.

What a mystical union of Jesus and the Christ!

To continue discussing the same issue, we go over to the book *The Aquarian Gospel of Jesus the Christ*, which offers a more detailed account of the events of Jesus the Christ than our popular New Testament. In the book Jesus says,

> All men are sons of God [all human beings are children of God; this is clearer] by birth [by creation]. God is the Father of all races; but all are not sons [children] of God by faith.

> He who attains victory over self is the son [child] of God by faith, and he who speaks to you has overcome and he is called the son of God, because he is the pattern for the sons of men [human beings].

> He who believes and does the will of God is the son [child] of God by faith. (*The Aquarian Gospel of Jesus the Christ* 139:1–8)

The foregoing explanation corroborates my earlier analysis on the fact that Jesus, a human being, became the special/spiritual Son of God by faith, i.e. he surrendered himself to the Spirit of God (his inner self), showing he was a mystic.

That mystical transformation earned Jesus the title 'the Christ', meaning 'the Anointed One', the Son of God. In that circumstance, the name Jesus the Christ (Jesus Christ for short) became coterminous with the expression 'the special or spiritual Son of God'. In other words, the Word—i.e. Christ—was made flesh through Jesus (a human being), who lived in a physical world (John 1:1–14).

Following the preceding analysis, we arrive at the fact that Jesus became the Christ. This means that when we talk of Jesus, we refer to or mean the Christ, the special Son of God, by faith.

On that basis (of Jesus becoming the Christ, i.e. synonymous with Christ), Jesus was able to say, 'Before Abraham I was' (John 8:58). That means the Christ he became had been with God before Abraham came into being; he had been with God as an aspect of God in the creation of the world and all therein. It means at the time of his making the claim that he had become the Christ, he was speaking as the Christ, not as Jesus, the flesh and blood. I refer to the Bible to support what I have just said. Notwithstanding that Jesus knew he was universally well known as Jesus, he went on to ask his disciples, '"Who do men say that I the son of man am?" And they replied, "Some say that thou art John, the Baptist; some Elias and others Jeremiah, or one of the prophets." He went on and asked them, "But who say ye that I am?" And Simon Peter answered and said, "Thou art the Christ, the son of the living God"' (Matthew 16:13–17).

It is amazing that Peter used the expression 'the Christ' to indicate that Christ is a title and not the name of a person, Jesus. Also, the intelligent answer shows the depth of Peter's spiritual knowledge about the Christ as the Son of the living God, into which Jesus mystically transformed, making him Jesus the Christ, the likeness of God. Peter could have said, 'Thou art Jesus' (because he knew his name to be Jesus). He did not; he would have been wrong if he had done so because Jesus had become the Christ. Peter distinguished Jesus as a human being from the aspect of God that manifested through Jesus, the flesh and blood, as the Christ.

Again: Jesus the Christ did ask the Pharisees, 'What think ye of the Christ? Whose son is he?' (He did not ask 'What think ye of Jesus?') They answered, 'The son of David.' They were wrong; they were thinking of Jesus, the flesh and blood, the son of Joseph whose ancestor was David.

Because they were wrong, he then asked them, 'How then doeth David in spirit call him Lord, saying, "The Lord said unto my Lord, sit thou on my right hand till I make thine enemies thy footstool"? If David then call him Lord, how is he the son? And none of them could answer that puzzling question' (Matthew 22:41–46).

It will be interesting and informative to learn why Jesus made the statement 'Before Abraham I was.' Jesus had a spiritual lesson to teach when he set up that perplexing claim of having existed before his ancestors. He intended to explain the spiritual status of the Christ, as well as his synonymous relationship with the Christ, the Son of God. He wanted to show that he was the Christ.

In the statement quoted as David's, the first 'Lord' refers to God; the second refers to the Christ, which tittle Jesus earned and which thing he became. And the Christ is the spiritual Son of God, the special Son of God, which Jesus became by faith.

The arrangement of David's statements distinguishes Jesus as an ordinary human being, the son of Joseph (David's descendant), from Jesus the Christ, the spiritual as well as the special Son of God who had been with God before all creation and, therefore, before Abraham was created or born.

David recognised the Christ as an aspect of God, the spiritual Son of God who had always been with God before creation. He also recognised that in such a situation, the Christ was higher than himself; hence he called him 'my Lord'.

Jesus recognised that since he had become the Christ who, as a spiritual Son of God, had been with God before creation, he therefore had come before Abraham and was greater than David.

I hold Jesus the Christ in the highest esteem, not on account of the story of the power of the Holy Ghost, but because of his unique spiritual personality: throughout his mission, he demonstrated the Christ, the aspect of God in him, outwardly (the Word made flesh and dwelling among us). He therefore deserves an enormous amount of love and the most tremendous praise, and the divinity accorded him as the spiritual Son of God, by faith.

Next issue: Obianyido rejects the idea that Jesus the Christ is the link between humankind and God. Is he correct?

The knowledge we gathered from our earlier analysis showing that Jesus became the Christ (the Son of God) favours a brief answer to the question of whether Jesus the Christ is the link between humankind and God. Since Jesus the Christ has been proven to be the Son of God, it goes without saying that Jesus the Christ is well positioned and qualified as a link between humankind and God. Simple.

What of the other issue where Obianyido doubts that the death of Jesus the Christ washed away our sins?

That expression 'his death washed away our sins' is used in a figurative sense. It needs explanation, therefore. To take it in just as it is will mislead; it must be considered in the circumstance in which it was used. All the events that accumulated to cause the death are important. In this case, all that the expression seeks to say is that Jesus died or met his death as a result of his helping us to embrace his teaching that righteousness does away with sins and earns the actor eternal life in the kingdom of God. The expression is like saying that Nelson Mandela of South Africa gave up his freedom or pleasures so as to gain freedom for his fellow black South Africans.

In our particular case (about Jesus the Christ), it is not that his death automatically, without more, washed away our sins, as misguided Christians are inclined to conceive. The washing away of one's sins takes effect only when the sinner accepts the teachings of Jesus the Christ (which teachings resulted in Jesus's incarceration and eventual death) and puts them into practice so as to gain God's favour, which means forgiveness of sins and consequent eternal life in the kingdom of God.

That condition is the reason Jesus Christ said to Nicodemus, 'You must be born again'—for his sins to be forgiven, so he could earn the kingdom of God. That is to say, the washing away of our sins happens only after we have put the teachings of truth (which cost Jesus his life) into practice. See John 3:1–21, verse 21 in particular.

Look at 1 Peter on the same matter (1 Peter 1:3–25), which talks of being born again by living out the good news, which is about God. In short, it is the acceptance of the laws of God (as revealed to us by Jesus the Christ) and the practising of them that washes away our sins.

When we stand upon the foregoing crystal-clear interpretations, we find it alarming and disturbing that some Christians incorrectly interpret the expression 'His death washed away our sins.' They teach that the sins of one who confesses that Jesus the Christ died for our sins and then accepts to be baptised in his name, without more, are washed away. I disagree, and ask, what is the meaning of 'you must be born again'? I believe it means that you must change from unrighteousness to righteousness in order to earn the kingdom of God, which Jesus Christ, John the Baptist, and the disciples and apostles of Jesus Christ made their core teaching.

Another, related idea by some Christians is that God, to save sinners, gave his only begotten Son, Jesus the Christ, to be sacrificed—I know not by whom or to whom! I vehemently disagree with that information; I very much oppose it. It is an embarrassing scriptural teaching and equates with blasphemy! God could not have, on any account, on behalf of sinners, given His only begotten Son to appease himself. God is not wicked! To accept the information is rash. Concerning the matter, I think the teachings of the Bible have been misunderstood and misinterpreted. Or there could be some adulterations, alterations, or interpolations somehow, in respect to the original text.

Jesus the Christ was not sent to be sacrificed because of the sinners, but to redeem the sinners. In doing so, his mission clashed with the ambition, the stupid reasoning, of the wicked world, who as a result killed him (only his body, of course). He died a martyr, no doubt.

At the beginning of my reply to Obianyido's rejection of the four Christian beliefs, I assigned each a letter of the alphabet those beliefs, highlighting them as (a), (b), (c), and (d). In my attempt to find adequate answers to his assertions, I examined each of them.

To begin with, I observed that the issues Obianyido talks about have for long been bubbling in the minds of many Christians and some non-Christians. Some Christians have become so bothered about the uncertainty of some of the beliefs and have openly been questioning the claims being made by some other Christians.

Having considered the importance of the issues in the matter of religion, I allotted much time and space to them, intent on giving detailed treatments and presenting my findings, the most likely answers to each of them.

Inspired, I went through a long, winding, rugged road with spiritual guidance (I believe) and arrived at the following answers:

   (a) Jesus (as flesh and blood) was born the son of earthly parents, Joseph and Mary. Joseph was the biological father.
   (b) Jesus the Christ (heavenly) is by faith the spiritual Son of God, for he pleased God by representing God's law on earth as the Christ.
   (c) As the spiritual Son of God, Jesus the Christ is in a good stead, and spiritually qualified as a link between humankind and God.
   (d) For teaching us (the world) the laws (of God) that govern the life we live that will lead to forgiveness of sins (washing away our sins), he incurred a worrying amount of opprobrium and enmity from the wicked world, who eventually killed him.

His death does not simply 'wash away our sins'; we must accept and practise his teachings for our sins to be washed away.

His death signifies the death of our sins; his resurrection signifies the rising of our righteousness—the giving up of sins (Romans 6:3–10).

The washing away of our sins reminds me of the present-day Christian idea of Good Friday.

The New Testament has it that Jesus was arrested, tried, tortured, derided, crucified, and buried on a Friday. On the third day (Sunday), he rose from the dead.

Some present-day Christians annually commemorate the day, seeing it as a time for celebration, festivity, and thanksgiving to God. Why? According to Christians, the particular Friday is good because Jesus gave himself up (or God the Father gave him up) to be killed so that our sins could be washed away (i.e. forgiven) by his blood!

I am not at all comfortable with that conclusion. Humanly speaking, there is nothing good about that Friday. To me the name 'Good Friday' is a misnomer. The idea of Good Friday is a wild, blind, undisciplined scriptural philosophy. The philosophy is based on selfishness and pleasure derived from the suffering of someone else—a state adjunct to sadism. There is no moral justification for that. No measure of benefit derivable from the suffering of an innocent person, even where the person voluntarily surrenders himself to be tortured, justifies any degree of joy by another person. I personally see the day Jesus was punished, killed, and buried for our sins as a gloomy day for our reflection and mourning!

Jesus, his disciples, and his followers found nothing good about that miserable Friday. The pathos of the events of that Friday made Jesus feel forlorn; he cried that God had forsaken him (Matthew 27:46). His disciples were offended and sorrowful about the happenings (Matthew 26:31–75, particularly verses 31, 37–38, 51, and 75). Consider Matthew

16:10 and John 16:20—and Matthew 9:15 and 17:23, too, if you like. The idea of naming that gloomy day *good* is misconceived.

From that perspective, I view that the Friday in question deserves to be annually remembered and called 'Bad Friday', and the Sunday, the day Jesus rose from the dead, be annually remembered and be called 'Good Sunday'—a day of thanksgiving to God, a day of rejoicing.

I am no fan of Good Friday, although I staunchly believe in Christianity. I do not, like a sheep, follow the crowd without good reason.

If any fans of Good Friday would be good enough to prove me wrong (let's avoid making a mockery of truth), I would humbly change my mind, apologise, and accordingly accept that I was wrong. Jesus's death signifies the death of our sins; his resurrection signifies the rising of our righteousness—the giving up of sins (Romans 6:3–10).

OBIANYIDO: The circumstances around me in my secluded rural environment in Nigeria then, during the early white missionary days, strengthened my belief in all about Christianity. At that time, the only source of education was through the white missionaries—the Roman Catholic Mission (RCM) and the Church Missionary Society (CMS). Both were particular about having Christian religion in the curriculum of their schools.

The then white Christian missionaries called the indigenous African religion pagan, which equates with Satan-worshipping; they frowned upon the cultural activities and the traditional ceremonies associated with such religion.

The missionaries used a cross and colourful pictures of a long-nosed white man nailed to the cross to promote Christianity and to condemn indigenous African religion. I imagine the white missionaries were relations of Jesus because of their resemblance to the image of Jesus on the cross. I was constrained, judging by the dress, colour, physical features, and manner of the missionaries, to conclude that the missionaries were not of this world.

The members of my village were in the same confused state as I, a state born of relative primitive ignorance. We were all charmed and mesmerised by the Western products reaching us through the white missionaries.

The primitive ignorant villagers, I included, were amazed at the time to hear the gramophone as talking iron or spirit.

REPLY: Obianyido paints a woeful and miserable picture of his primitiveness and that of the members of his village. Only their unfortunate circumstance, i.e. their primitiveness, their ignorance, and their fate, brought that upon them. Their ruinous ignorance led them to mistake things and see things wrongly.

Obianyido's tale sounds like *Alice in Wonderland*. Says Plato, 'Lack of knowledge is the cause of misfortune; it is certainly a fatal bar to success in anything.' So, about their illusions, those people have only themselves to blame. One can only guess that the white missionaries might have taken advantage of their ignorance and easily persuaded them to accept them and their teachings, which teachings, even then, had a good measure of moral and social benefit to offer.

Another issue: Obianyido complains that the white missionaries called the indigenous African religion pagan. To that idea, he personally adds, 'That equates with Satan worship.' Here he displays his ignorance of the meaning of the word *pagan*.

A pagan is a person whose beliefs and practices do not belong to any of the main religions of the world (Christianity, Judaism, Islam, etc.). Paganism was in existence long before those main religions.[8]

---

[8] 'Pagan', *Collins Cobuild English Dictionary* (1993).

If my definition of *pagan* is accepted (I have no doubt it is acceptable), it means being a pagan does not equate with worshipping Satan. It may mean worshipping God wrongly out of ignorance. Satan is thought of as the chief opponent of God. Since a pagan worships God (or gods) in wrong ways, the idea that pagans worship Satan, which Obianyido added, is to be thrown way!

I will not hesitate to accept that indigenous African religion fits into the frame of the definition given by the English-language dictionary earlier named. Though the main religions call indigenous African religion pagan, if by way of comparison we stretch the argument and consider the contents or precepts and practice of paganism and juxtapose these with those of Christianity today, we are bound to find very little difference. The two are almost the same except in name.

To do the comparison meaningfully, we must rely on what we have learnt from some books on religious history. *The Fabulous First Centuries of Christianity*, by Vance Ferrell, is one such book.

At the tail end of Chapter 15 of *In Defence of Jesus the Christ*, I will attempt to show the similarities between paganism and later Christianity. Until then.

OBIANYIDO: Emil Ludwin, a white man, said, 'How can Africans conceive God? How can this be? Deity is a philosophical concept which savages are incapable of framing.' That is unacceptable.

REPLY: Concerning the point Obianyido mentions as a response to what Ludwin said, I assume that God in that context is the Christian mode of worshipping God. Otherwise, I am ready to challenge Ludwin.

Africans conceived of God and worshipped him in their own peculiar way before they were introduced to the Christian mode of worshipping God.

Since what Ludwin said relates to the Christian way of worshipping God (I surmise), I agree with him. The account given by Obianyido in his book *Christ or Devil?* concerning the primitive, ignorant, backward state of his community at the time Christianity reached them supports Ludwin's observation.

Obianyido's account suggests that he accepted Christianity without understanding in detail what it was all about. For that reason, he later rejected it, at the time he became educated and thought he had gained better knowledge of the Christian God (the mode of worshipping God by Christians). So, his U-turn gives him away as 'untutored', unable to conceive the Christian God at the time of his acceptance of Christianity. Considering this, what then does he find wrong with what Ludwin said? Why is he blowing the whistle or crying foul about Ludwin's opinion? He is just a petulant person.

Obianyido is merely hypersensitive about anything said that sounds derogatory to his race, be that thing a fact or not. There is nothing seriously wrong with Ludwin's opinion except that it looks like it is couched in a rude, raw framework. Ludwin was then not sober. He said what he observed with an air of pride and superiority over Africans, and in so doing he displayed extreme arrogance. In short, he treated Africans in a cavalier fashion. Though he was thoughtlessly lacking in civility, there were fruits of sense beneath his opinion. To understand an outlandish religious concept of the Christians and their mode of worshipping God, in those early days, Africans needed some degree of upgrading in scriptural knowledge and Western education—the use of the European language as a vehicle to carry them through.

OBIANYIDO: I came to know of other religions besides Christianity later. Before then I had believed every word said in favour of the white man's God.

I acquired knowledge of those other religions from traders who told me of Islam in the northern part of Nigeria. And from former servicemen I learnt of Hinduism at Lagos, the former capital of Nigeria, where I went for further education and employment. I learnt of more religions such as Buddhism and Confucianism. Becoming aware of all these other religions stirred me into querying the impression which the white missionaries were wont to convey that Christianity was the only religion and that traditional African faith failed to qualify as a religion.

I learnt from Professor Bolaji Idowu that to the Western world, indigenous 'Africa was barren of culture, or any form of social organisation. if anything in her could be called religion at all, it could only be because in Africa the Devil in all his abysmal grotesque and forbidden features, black, blackest of aspect, armed in the teeth and horns complete, holds sway.'

Bolaji Idowu said that 'religion is something resulting from the relationship which God established from the beginning of human life between Himself and man.'

J. B. Pratt saw religion as 'the serious and social attitude of individual or communities towards the power or powers of which they conceive as having ultimate control over their interest or destines'.

With that knowledge gathered from those opinions, I became satisfied that African faith qualified as a religion. I am now asking whether the African traditional religion has any prospect?

REPLY: Obianyido is overly emotional about, and hypersensitive to, any opinions given against Africa by white foreigners. That is the reason he has given much attention to Professor Idowu's personal observation about the Western world's view of African social life.

Before I continue, I want, first, to comment on Professor Idowu's definition of religion. I disagree with him and view that God played no significant part in setting up religion. It was humankind that established religion. Religion resulted from humankind's efforts to learn the laws of the invisible almighty force/authority/energy behind the creation of the universe and all therein, including the ever-occurring events within it, so as to obey the laws and bring peace, harmony, and progress between humankind and the Creator. That is that.

Next, we go to another of Professor Idowu's observations about Africa. According to Obianyido, he learnt from the professor that, to the Western world, Africans lacked any form of social organisation, whether cultural or religious. I doubt that the Western world entertains such a view. But let's grant it to be the case for the sake of discussion.

In that context, the Western world miserably lacked knowledge of the meaning of 'social organisations', and following that, they stupidly conceived that a race, no matter its stage of development or civilisation, could exist without social organisation. By nature, human beings are social and gregarious. Even animals, including birds and ants, are by nature instinctively inclined to organise socially in order to promote their interests and to preserve their progeny. Therefore, I cannot understand why the notion that Africa is devoid of any form of social organisation should arise.

If it were true that the Western world entertains such a notion ascribed to it by Professor Idowu, I would put the Western world's assertion down to a wrong assumption of superiority over Africans. And the assumption made idiots of those of the Western world who were involved!

Africa, long before Western civilisation reached its shores, had pronounced social organisations. The fact that African social organisation never conformed to that of the Western world did not make Africa's social organisations nonexistent then. Africa's organisations related to social activity, such as culture and religion, were peculiar to Africans though strange to the Western world at the time. So, these types of organisations had been in existence from time immemorial. Some such very early social organisations or activities are still extant and strong. Those of the Western world who failed to observe the social organisations in Africa might have been suffering from the veil of ignorance.

History has it that indigenous African religion suffered for many years as it was pounded severely by the foreign religions that invaded its domain. That might have prompted Obianyido to ask whether traditional African religion has any prospect.

One wants a functional crystal ball to be able to answer that enigmatic question. It has been many decades since foreign religions, particularly Islam and Christianity, had their grim grip on Africa after having dealt its religion a next-to-knockout blow. Consequently, any crystal ball is likely to find the phenomenon of indigenous African religion too dusty and hazy to see through to determine the right answer to the question posed by Obianyido.

Even then, I am to a tiny degree optimistic that indigenous African religion is not completely dead; it may have fallen in swoon, so to speak. For that it wants the moral kiss of life for its resuscitation. Obianyido pretends to be enthusiastic about the revival of indigenous African religion. Unfortunately for Obianyido, his atheistic mouth, with its rash and godless lips, lacks the quality and capacity to administer the necessary kiss of life.

If there is any possibility of indigenous African religion coming back to life, the necessary kiss of life must have to come through calculated socio-moral changes in the practice of religion. It will not matter that the ingredients for the changes are from a foreign religion like Christianity, provided the changes are the best for humanity and for service to God.

ORIGIN OF CHRISTIANITY

(CHAPTER 2, *CHRIST OR DEVIL?*)

OBIANYIDO: Jesus Christ broke away from Judaism to form Christianity and was punished for that by the Jews.

Judaism is based on the wild claim that the Jews are the chosen people of God. Yet their social and political life was up and down as they were many times conquered by one nation or the other—Babylon, Assyria, Persia.

It was during this turbulent period of Jewish history that the man Christ and his new religion were born. He therefore preyed upon the Jews, who then were victims of social and political catastrophes.

In the traumatic state of the Jews, always under threat and pressure by their neighbours, their Jerusalem, where they believed their God lived, was taken from them. As a result, they pinned their hopes on a Messiah who would come from one of the sons of David. Christ, a clever mystic trickster, messianic pretender, and egocentric dreamer, being credited with brilliant feats, was seen as that Messiah.

REPLY: Anene Obianyido's notion that Jesus Christ broke away from Judaism to form Christianity is incorrect; it is a farce. The fact is that

Jesus was born of parents, Joseph and Mary, who were Jews. It follows then that he was born into Judaism as it was his parents' faith. Despite this, his spiritual mission was not attached to any particular religion.

Jesus's missionary outlook was universal, and respected no faith. He was rather bent on correcting what he saw in the Jewish religion and, in fact, other religions as an odd and unrighteous manner of serving God. On those grounds, he criticised the misguided and unwholesome religious practices of the Jews. He gave the parable of the Good Samaritan to show that what matters most in earning the kingdom of God is the conduct of individuals, not the belonging to any religious sect (Luke 10:30–37).

His campaign was one of the reasons he fell into conflict with the authorities of Judaism—the Pharisees, the scribes, the elders of the Jewish religion, and the Jewish priests. Some of the Mosaic teachings, Jesus reinterpreted to give them facelifts to be in tune with the correct spiritual facts. He did not come to destroy the law but to fulfil it, i.e. give it a meaningful interpretation for the seekers of the kingdom of God to follow (Matthew 5:17–18).

The teachings and the corrections slowly coalesced into the corpus of spiritual teachings and principles we, today, call Christian doctrine. Jesus's followers who were helping in the dissemination of the doctrine (teachings) later crystallised into what the people of Antioch nicknamed Christians (Acts 11:26). So Jesus Christ did not intently go to form a religion (Christianity). He did not break away from Judaism, and therefore he never was attached to it to the exclusion of other religions. As I previously mentioned, he aimed at teaching every people, every religion, what mattered in serving God correctly.

The Bible bears witness to the claim that Jesus never abandoned Judaism—yet he did not stick to it to the exclusion of other religions. He was simply universal as far as religion was concerned. For his attendance at Jewish places of worship, refer to Mark 3:1; John 8:1–2; and Matthew 21:12–13. Long after his death, his disciples and his apostles continued to attend the Jewish synagogues and temples (Acts 6:9; 17:16–17). Jesus

Christ, therefore, did not set up his own religion. What he did set up was a church which he asked Peter to continue as the leader so as to help spread his teachings and keep them alive.

Church in those classical days meant a body spreading the ideas and teachings of their religion. Today, the word *church* has taken on a connotation as a religion with buildings for worshipping God.

What about this? Here and there in the Bible, we read about the Jews as 'the chosen people' of God. It is 'the God of Israel', 'my people Israel', and so on. Obianyido queries the notion of God favouring the Israelites. There are many people today, including some Christians, who, like Obianyido, want to know why.

As it did for Obianyido, the matter perplexed me, I confess. But that was the very first time I had knowledge of it. Later, I investigated the question. The Bible obviously informs us, in various verses, of the special relationship between God and the Israelites as a race, but in no way does it clearly let us know why, when God is the Creator of all races. That situation makes the question a conundrum.

As I mulled over the subject, two possible ideas flew into my mind:

First, the Old Testament cultivated that phenomenon of God being for the people of Israel and the people of Israel being for God, as God had chosen.

I guess the idea came through the Jewish prophets and the elders of the Jewish religion. That is, by the prophets' and the elders' propaganda, God was conceived as belonging to the Jews and was localised within the native land of Israel. In other words, they monopolised God and gave him a local name, Yahweh. In such a situation, Yahweh belonged to them and they belonged to Yahweh.

While the Israelites were in exile in, say, Persia (a foreign land), under bondage, and were suffering, their conceived local God (Yahweh) could not help them. They seemed then to have reflected and found that the reason was that their Yahweh was localised and had no domain in, and no authority over, the foreign lands where they were living in bondage. Following that reflection, the idea of a God whose authority went beyond the Jewish land to all foreign lands began to float and smoulder in their minds.

The wake of the New Testament era, with Jesus Christ's spiritual philosophy, uprooted the practice of monopolisation and localisation of Yahweh (God). It follows that during the new era, thanks to the brilliant teaching of Jesus the Christ, the smouldering ember in the minds of the Jews (the Israelites), fanned by the spiritual philosophy of Jesus the Christ, burst into flame. The teaching of Jesus Christ, like a gust of wind, swept through Israel to foreign lands and brought the concept of a universal God into the mind of the Jewish community.

In practice, Jesus the Christ socialised with Jews and non-Jews. He associated with the Samaritan woman he met at Jacob's well (John 4:6–29). With the parable of the Good Samaritan (Luke 10:30–37), he illustrated that the Gentiles and other races, besides the Jews, are all acceptable to God. He taught his disciples not to discriminate against any race or nation. He sent his disciples to go and preach to all nations (Matthew 28:19–20).

Let us go further. In consulting *The Aquarian Gospel of Jesus the Christ*, we discover that it reads as follows:

> Now in the evening Jesus and the mother sat alone, and Jesus said, 'The Rabbi seems to think that God is partial in His treatment of the sons of men; that Jews are favoured and are blessed above all other men. I do not see how God can have His favourites and be just. Are not the Samaritans and Greeks and Romans just as much as the children of the Holy One as are the Jews? I think the Jews have built a wall about themselves, and they see nothing on the other side of it. ... It surely will be well if we could break these barriers down so that

the Jews might see that God has other children that are just as greatly blest. I want to go from Jewry land and meet my kin in other countries of my Fatherland.' (*The Aquarian Gospel of Jesus the Christ* 17:13–20)

As a result of the activities of Jesus the Christ, the concept of God, for the Jews, only became consumed in the flame of the universality of God, as taught by Jesus the Christ.

God is no respecter of persons, races, or nations (Romans 2:11). He is God of all nations and races (Romans 3:39–40).

Second, the Jewish cliché, their common expression that God belongs to the Israelites, or that the Israelites are God's 'chosen people', found here and there in the Holy Bible, could have been founded on the assumption that the Jews (as a race) were the first to discover God, to recognise the monotheism of God, and to conceive and see God as one and only one God, the Creator of the world and all therein, the only power in Creation. That situation might have earned them a close and special relationship with God.

Of the two likely reasons for that cliché, 'the God of Israel' and so on, the latter seems to me the better, stronger, and more correct, if it is found true that the Jewish race was the first of all the races to have a comprehensive knowledge of God.

Again, if that be so, one can take the second reason as one that demystifies the perplexing question posed by Obianyido.

Whatever the case might be, it follows that it was the teaching of Jesus the Christ that helped to release Yahweh from the grip of the local Jews, who later saw God as a universal God—God for all races.

Except for the sake of satisfying my curiosity, which pushed me into the exploration of why the Bible claims that the Israelites have a special relationship with God, the subject is not part of the serious business of *In Defence of Jesus the Christ*.

Next to be looked into is Obianyido's allegation that Jesus Christ preyed upon his people, the Jews, taking advantage of their suffering as victims of social and political catastrophes perpetrated by their neighbours. This view of Obianyido's is blind. Obianyido is unable to see Jesus Christ's mission for the world. His mission was not political but spiritual. Speaking to that dichotomy, Jesus Christ said to the Pharisees, 'Render, therefore, unto Caesar the things which are Caesar's and unto God, the things that are God's' (Matthew 22:15–21). His mission was geared towards one sharp point: 'For I am not come to call the righteous, but the sinners to repentance' (Matthew 9:9–13; Luke 5:27–32).

The sinners include sinners among all races and nations, and enemies of the Jews (Matthew 24:14). In his activities, Jesus addressed, besides the Jews and non-Jews, the Gentiles and the Samaritans (John 4:3–29; 39–42). Was he, by so doing, also preying upon all races and all nations? Obianyido has this question to ponder over.

And, if according to Obianyido, Jesus Christ's mission took place during a turbulent period in Jewish history, how could that have made the mission political? Mere coincidence in time or accidental timing of the two separate historical events does not make Jesus Christ's mission political. The fact that Jesus the Christ's mission was clearly spiritual separates it from politics and shows the coincidence of Christ's mission and politics in time to be a mere historical accident. Obianyido talks rubbish, therefore.

I intend to detail Jesus Christ's mission later, in the final chapter of *In Defence of Jesus the Christ*.

Overall, I assert that the rude, rash, and barbaric manner, lacking in all shades of decency and civility, employed by Obianyido to describe and discredit Jesus the Christ and his mission borders on absurdity. Such an attitude, per se, is vacuous and belongs to the era of long-past unpolished journalism.

CHRIST

(CHAPTER 3, *CHRIST OR DEVIL?*)

OBIANYIDO: Philip Graham described the business of Christianity as 'the tragic result of Christ's megalomania'. I agree with him.

What bothered me and prompted the writing of my book is that those results are more evident in backward and underdeveloped countries who require every bit of their mental and material resources for their much-needed development.

REPLY: The word *megalomania* means 'a mental disorder characterised by delusions of grandeur, power, etc.' According to Anene Obianyido, that is the expression used by Graham to qualify Jesus the Christ. For Graham to conceive of such an insulting notion about the divine personality of Jesus the Christ, his state of mind must have gone beyond delirium and approached the vicinity of insanity. Indeed, I consider his utterance as a signpost pointing to insanity.

'Insanus omnis furere credit ceteros' (Every madman thinks everybody else is mad). That is likely so. It is correct to say that a mentally sound and sober person can distinguish correctly from one who is mad and others who are sane by what the suspect (the insane) says or does.

As for Obianyido, who readily agrees with Graham's stinking vomit, he seems to have no choice: nature inclines things to their liking. 'Like attracts like' goes a saying. Obianyido has to think like Graham.

The Igbo tribe in Nigeria has a proverb that says, 'Anaghi ama mbido ala.' The English translation is 'It is hard to determine the inception of insanity.' I agree with that, but I wish to add that some cases escape being 'hard'. If what Obianyido quoted belongs to Graham, then Graham's problem is a case of madness that has escaped the 'hard'. His utterance gives him away as mad. How could he have said what Obianyido ascribed to him, when he must have known fully the divine personality of Jesus the Christ and of Jesus the Christ's teachings on compassionate love, his humility, his miracles that helped people with problems, and his matchless good moral character—in short, his excellence in all virtues? In such a case, if Graham was not mad at the time he made the statement, then he was on the threshold of madness.

It may be necessary for my readers to hold off giving their opinions on the issue until they have gone through my book and, perhaps, other reliable sources (if they so choose) for what is known about the divine personality of Jesus Christ. I have no doubt that Graham's assertion and the fact of the personality of Jesus Christ will manifest. I hold that Graham had no grounds for his insulting and prejudicial view.

Now we come to Obianyido's view. About that, the first point that strikes me is that he seems a despondent materialist who, to a large extent, is bereft of spiritual values. He thinks only of material progress and does not consider that any progress in any society without virtue turns sour and worthless sooner or later.

He is bothered that undeveloped and underdeveloped countries are not making material progress, according to him, because they embraced Christianity. Is that not nonsensical? He is simply imprudently posturing and playing to the gallery. He is very pedantic and thinks he is a polymath or a keeper of wisdom for African communities. Is he suggesting that what stops Africa, Nigeria in particular, from making material progress is Christianity? What a sightless bit of reasoning!

Are the European countries he compares to Africa not Christian countries? And yet they are making tremendous material progress. He is always making illogical detours from common sense, intent on finding weapons, so to speak, for attacking Jesus Christ, Christianity, and God.

Criticising Christianity, Obianyido uses the expression 'what bothers me' so as to be seen as a protagonist championing a fight for material progress in Africa, so as to ingratiate himself with Africans. That is a crooked way of looking for undeserved fame. Surprising! He is too soon, too oblivious of the fact that whatever measure of initial education given him by the Christian missionary school, the school rescued him from the snare of want of education while he was in his 'secluded rural environment' wallowing in lack of knowledge.

What else do backward and undeveloped countries want as a means of development apart from education? And it was the white Christian missionary school that initiated Obianyido into education. Now, imagine his disrespect for, and ingratitude to, the white Christian missionary to whom he owes the little measure of his education. See how he deals treacherously with Christianity. Surprising!

No less surprising is the fact that he uses an expression such as 'the primitive ignorant villagers, myself included' to describe his state of civilisation and that of his fellow Nigerians at the time when the white Christian missionaries reached Nigeria (see Chapter 1 of *Christ or Devil?*). Expressions of that sort taste sugary to him only when they proceed from his lips (or pen, if you prefer). When Emil Ludwin used a similar description of Africans, Obianyido became furious. He boiled over, foamed up, and exploded and was unable to work out Ludwin's reason for doing so (see Chapter 4 of *In Defence of Jesus the Christ*).

According to Obianyido, 'The backward and undeveloped countries require every bit of their mental and material resources for their much-needed development.' Apparently, they do not need Christianity (religion) because Christianity produces 'tragic results' and handicaps development, he reckons. He is very wrong; he is a dimwit to have conceived that. The backwardness of Africa in all facets of its history is not to be attributed to Jesus Christ and Christianity. Let us consider Nigeria as an example. The trouble with Nigeria is that most Nigerians suffer from the inveterate disease which is the desire for unnecessary luxury and for a superfluity of pleasures. Also, most of them are lazy and morally undernourished—hard work and merit as a path to a satisfactory happy life and eminence is unacceptable. What is acceptable is evil/corruption as a means to achieve such things as wealth, power, and fame.

That tendency has become epidemic in Africa. Nigeria is one of the countries of the world where the disease of corrupt practices has almost become endemic. The country seems to have become a natural habitat for that social ailment popularly called corruption, since nothing is being seriously done to check the evil. It is now hereditary—recycling itself from one generation to another. How can a country with such traits, such a social cancer, develop or progress?

Some Nigerians see corruption as being a result of poverty. I emphatically say no to that suggestion. How can that be?! In the country, corruption is more among the rich or those of higher social status with average wealth; most of the victims of the evil are among the poorer citizens. Poverty in a society follows when corruption among those in power and the rich leads the way.

Africans cannot resist the charm of fripperies and transient pleasures, the fleeting vanity of earthly things. If Africans have the courage to own up to their attitude towards life, i.e. to the fact that their social, political, and economic lifestyle is substantially responsible for their lack of progress in reasonable directions, and that to adjust and fall into the right track means shedding off corruption, selfishness, and unreasonable desire for the empty transient luxuries they are much inclined to, and pursue right knowledge and a clean, incorrupt practical lifestyle, then they can make a lot of progress materially, economically, socially, politically, and morally.

Meanwhile, African countries are not ready for a change. They are stuck in the quagmire of corruption and the quest for vainglorious wealth and fame, and are busily pointing the finger at foreign religions and their long-gone colonial masters as obstacles to their development.

The trouble with Africans is that they acknowledge the positive ideas of Christianity but neglect to put them into practice. They do not practise genuine Christianity. Obianyido himself earnestly mentions this situation in Chapter 11 of *Christ or Devil?*, which corresponds to Chapter 14 of *In Defence of Jesus the Christ*. Consequently, corruption and the other evils Christianity eloquently speaks against have become domineering features in the lifestyle of Africans.

Do not say that corruption also exists in developed countries that nevertheless are making material progress, for that I know. It is there, but to a minimal degree, and it is always being seriously, ferociously tackled whenever and wherever it raises its monstrous head.

In their corrupt practices, Africans, Nigerians for the most part, have a culture of showing themselves off as good copycats of Europeans only when it concerns pleasure and the enjoyment of ready-made goods of pleasure: remote-controlled machines, mobile phones, electronics, and expensive cars. At this time, every rich person in Africa is struggling to own a private jet plane. Name any newly invented luxury goods; Nigerians want them—and soon!

In Nigeria, that trait—the endemic pursuit of wealth and luxuries and the enjoyment of pleasures—has been exacerbated since the somewhat superfluous production of mineral oil, which leads to an easy and steady inflow of money into the country's coffers, conspiring with other minor factors to destroy the earlier industry and frugality of the citizens and incline them to abandon themselves to laziness and the influence and tyranny of luxuries and pleasures. The desire for luxuries and pleasures, in turn, feeds the practice of all sorts of evil (1 Timothy 6:10). Nigerians are so immersed in the desire for luxury goods that, as long as exotic luxury goods continue to roll out from the factories of developed countries, that they (and other Africans, of course) will continue to queue up at the end of the production line, waiting to purchase them. How then can one say that poverty is the cause of corruption in Africa, when a situation such as this holds sway? Africans are prepared to scrimp on the essential things of life to be able to own the nonessentials merely for the purpose of showing off and immersing themselves in vain transient enjoyment. Most of those luxury goods are, no doubt, bought with their ill-gotten wealth. That characteristic makes almost every Nigerian a sybarite.

It is, therefore, misdirection for Obianyido to give his readers the impression that Christianity is responsible for the material nonprogress or nondevelopment of backward and underdeveloped countries.

The truth is that Obianyido is maniacally in love with atheism and is vehemently against Christianity. After making contact with his mentor, Tai Solarin, a staunch atheist, he came to hate Christianity, which has remained he case ever since. He has since that time been spraying atheistic venom against Christianity whenever it appears or is mentioned. This is the reason he groundlessly accuses Christianity of one thing or the other in *Christ or Devil?* In that behaviour, he is too blind to see anything good in Christianity. I call that a waste of time and energy as Christianity is indestructible!

OBIANYIDO: Educated and developed countries, excepting my churchgoing country [Nigeria], are successfully waging war against the Christ plague. They are asking, 'Who is this man Jesus Christ that has harassed the human soul for so long?'

REPLY: Obianyido's assertions are scurrilous. They amount to the blatant wrapping of facts in wishful thinking. The contrary is the case about 'waging war against the Christ plague'.

Which countries, in his mind, are waging war against 'the Christ plague'? And what is the nature of this plague? The most educated and developed countries at the time when Obianyido wrote his book were Western Christian countries. I include the Soviet Union, in case he had that in mind. None of those countries could have asked that senseless question, for sure. Even in the Soviet Union, in case he had that in mind, there were and still are Christian countries calling themselves Orthodox Christians. Countries, backward, developing, underdeveloped, developed, educated, or uneducated, all need a moral concept (a religious moral code) to keep the conduct of their citizens in good moral shape while in pursuit of material progress.

In 1994, the British Home Secretary at the time, Mr Pattern, realising the need for strong Christian principles as a means of helping to curb antisocial behaviours, particularly among the young, suggested that strict Christian principles be infused into and practised in all schools in Britain. Teachers were told Christianity must come first. That was the British Home Secretary's opinion.[9] Is Obianyido not aware that Britain is a Christian country and is educated and developed? Perhaps he is not! Yet, he claims to have gone there for further education. Has Britain been asking the question about Christ's harassing the human soul for such a long time or about waging war against the Christ plague? Is it France, Germany, Canada, Switzerland, Italy, the United States? Which country?

Throughout, in educated, developed, developing, or underdeveloped countries, Christianity (even when imperfect) has been making an enormously good moral impact on people's characters and has been spreading like desert sand before a strong wind. The Jehovah's Witnesses organisation has branches all over the world. In the face of such a phenomenon, how can Obianyido's assertion be true? I suppose he perceives illusion for that matter.

Equally illusory is his view that Jesus Christ has been harassing the human soul. The accounts in *In Defence of Jesus the Christ* and in the

---

[9] *Evening Standard*, London edition, 25 January 1994, page 5.

Bible about the mission of Jesus Christ strongly challenge Obianyido's ill-conceived allegations.

The most likely people to feel that human souls are being harassed by Jesus the Christ, and who are likely to ask the question mentioned by Obianyido, are the incorrigible sinners, reprobates, who do not take kindly to the teachings of Jesus urging them to turn to righteousness and away from their sins.

OBIANYIDO: And how far do his [Jesus the Christ's] experience agree with real-life experience and modern reason?

REPLY: I crave my readers' patience for boring them with frequent reference to dictionaries, which I intend to continue summoning when need be; they are neutral and reliable witnesses. Now, I refer to the *New Practical Standard Dictionary* as I once more rely upon it.

According to the dictionary, *Christian* as an adjective means 'humble, civilised, humane'. In the light of that knowledge, Obianyido is of the opinion that such qualities are inharmonious with real-life experience and modern reason. Look at that!

There is no doubt that the teachings of Jesus the Christ are the best of all other teachings by other spiritual teachers, morally and socially speaking, at any given time in the history of humankind. The teachings are invaluable to humanity; they are ageless and flow from the generation alive at time when they were first given up to our modern generation. Essentially, they will continue to be valuable to future generations.

The Ten Commandments, approved with true interpretations by Jesus Christ, make up the cluster of the teachings by Jesus the Christ, and that cluster has compassionate love as its epicentre. Anyone who practises compassionate love can never commit an offence against any of the Ten Commandments or against his or her fellow human beings. As a block teaching, the Ten Commandments is to ensure justice and peace in any society. Justice and peace make up the pillars essential for meaningful development in all aspects of society. A society that falls out of line with Jesus the Christ's teachings on compassionate love is bound to witness social, political, economic, and moral chaos.

Of Christianity, Henry Drummond says, 'Christianity wants nothing so much in the world as sunny people; and the old are hungrier for love than for bread.'[10]

The matter is that Obianyido is characteristically too biased, shy, and cowardly to look at the majestic face of Truth and bow. Otherwise, why is someone like him, who arrogantly claims to be among the elite minority in his community, and who has read the history of Jesus the Christ (or the Bible), asking such an uncalled-for question here? By the practice of compassionate love taught by Jesus the Christ, injustice can be dethroned, and justice enthroned, in all aspects of any society.

William Barclay says, 'Love and justice are the same thing, for justice is love distributed, nothing else.'[11] I am sure the word *love* in the context of Barclay's dictum refers to compassionate love. It is nothing to do with the silly sentimental emotionalism that many people often mistake as love. It is therefore not about erotic love; it chimes in with the idea of the love I have in mind in my discourse.

Since Jesus the Christ preached compassionate love, which gives justice and peace to the world, is that irrelevant and nonessential to real-life experience and modern reason? In our present world, lack of compassionate love is certainly the cause of our social, political, and economic crises, and wars. Therefore, a need for the compassionate love taught by Jesus the Christ exists. The acceptance of the teaching, which means the practice of compassionate love by the modern world, is as essential to the modern world as it was at the time when it was first taught by Jesus the Christ.

---

[10] G. F. Maine, ed., *Great Thoughts Birthday Book*.
[11] William Barclay, *Ethics in Permissive Society*, 73.

Experience dictates that only the practice of compassionate love can make civilisation worthy. 'Civilization is, first and foremost, a moral thing. Without honesty, without respect for law, without the worship of duty, without of one's neighbour—in a word, without virtue—the whole is menaced,' says Henri-Frédéric Amiel.[12]

As if on purpose to answer Obianyido's pointless question, William Barclay, coincidentally, has the following to say: 'The simple fact is that it is impossible to build an industrial community [and, indeed, any form of community] on industrial ethics which is un-Christian [meaning unjust]. Our forefathers did just that, and it is our task to mend the situation, but first, we must understand it.'[13] Barclay continues, 'It is my hope and prayer that these lectures may do something to show that Christian ethic is as relevant today as it was.'[14] It looks as if these beliefs of William Barclay preempted Obianyido's question.

Wisdom has no misgiving about the teachings of Jesus the Christ being priceless to real-life experience and modern reason.

That question by Obianyido will find an expanded and stronger reply in Chapter 16 of *In Defence of Jesus the Christ*, under the subheading 'His Legacies'.

OBIANYIDO: The historical account of Jesus Christ has no supporting evidence. Starting from the birth of Jesus to the so-called ascension to heaven, history has no record.

Modern intelligentsias have searched in vain for facts about Jesus Christ. The authors of the gospels, with their questionable credentials and authenticity, deliberately exaggerated the stories about the birth of Jesus Christ, giving the impression that the birth happened in heaven.

---

[12] G. F. Maine, ed., *Great Thoughts Birthday Book*.
[13] William Barclay, *Ethics in a Persuasive Society*, 100.
[14] Ibid, 11.

When I met a German Jew in Lagos [Nigeria], it took me some mental effort to shake off the silly thought that he was not on trip from heaven. Now, I know that the story about Jesus Christ has to do with world history, if at all it took place.

Many outstanding intelligentsias, the renowned British philosophers, Bertrand Russell, for one, doubted that Jesus ever existed, since there was no historical evidence to that effect. The nearest historical record of Jesus Christ was that of the famous historian born four years after the presumed dates of the birth and crucifixion of Christ, which history failed to confirm the biblical one. Neither in that record nor in the record of the more civilised Romans was there any mention of the mysterious birth of Jesus Christ, the coming and going of angels carrying messages to Mary and shepherds, and the celestial bodies at the birth of Jesus Christ. No writer outside the disciples knew or wrote about these phenomena.

I was conceiving the biblical account of Jesus to be a sort of documentary record taken at the time of the real event. I changed my mind when I heard Bamber Gascoigne confirm on television, as I read in his book, that for the first fifty years of what we now call the Christian era, not a word survived in any document about Christ or his followers. During the next fifty years, the Christians themselves wrote down most of the books that now make up the New Testament.

Philip Graham, with access to the inner recesses of the church, views that no records of the prodigy were preserved by the meticulous historians of the period or hymned by any leftover ghosts from the golden age of Saint Augustine. So, we have to rely on Matthew, Mark, Luke, and John, those four guardians of the bed Christians made and had to lie on—the quarter of the inspired names which now turn out to be mere noms de guerre.

REPLY: It is not unlike Obianyido to entertain silly thoughts! I doubt that he was able to 'to shake off the silly thought' that a German Jew he met in Lagos, Nigeria, was on trip from heaven.

His book *Christ or Devil?* is replete with silly thoughts. He would shake himself to untimely death if he were to attempt to shake off all his silly thoughts in his book!

Challenging Obianyido's doubt that Jesus ever existed on this earth, I find it my pleasure to first introduce to him the Jehovah's Witnesses pamphlet *Awake*. The pamphlet contains the yield of a brilliantly researched project entitled 'Did Jesus Really Exist?' In answer to that important question, the pamphlet mentions both modern and ancient reliable authorities who individually, categorically, demonstrated that Jesus did really exist on our planet. For the modern authorities, it has Michael Grant, a historian and an expert on ancient classical civilisation; Rudolf Bultmann, a professor of New Testament studies; Will Durant, a historian, writer, and philosopher; and Albert Einstein, a German-born Jewish physicist. For the ancient authorities, *Awake* has Tacitus (*c.*56–120 AD). Tacitus is considered to be one of the greatest of the ancient Roman historians. Suetonius (*c.*69–122 AD) was a Roman historian who re-recorded events during the reigns of the first eleven Roman emperors; Pliny the Younger (*c.*61–113 AD) was a Roman author and administrator in Bithynia (modern Turkey); and Flavius Josephus (*c.*37–100 AD) was a Jewish priest and historian.

According to *Awake*, the foregoing collection of facts is from 'Jewish rabbinic writings, the Talmud, dating from the third to the sixth centuries'.[15]

I am very thankful to the Watch Tower Bible and Tract Society for the pamphlet *Awake*.

I hope that Obianyido will find time to diligently study the relevant article in the pamphlet so as to be purged of his negative notion that Jesus never existed on earth.

---

[15] 'Did Jesus Really Exist?,' *Awake*, 5 (2016), 3–6.

I will now calmly challenge Obianyido, from my personal views on the points he raises in doubt that Jesus really existed on earth (without my relying on the facts in the pamphlet *Awake*).

Straight on I go to Obianyido's views that Jesus never existed, that he was not a real historic figure but a mythological personage, that there is no historical evidence of his having existed on earth. I then ask, what is the New Testament about? Is it not historical evidence that proves that Jesus once lived on this earth? Assume that the New Testament has been adulterated here and there, yet it certainly remains a history with Jesus Christ as the chief character. No history is ever given with exactitude, even if inspired. In whatever state, the New Testament has sufficient facts to prove that Jesus Christ did exist in this world. The facts can be extracted therefrom.

Of course, Obianyido refers to the New Testament record of Jesus Christ as historical only when he thinks it favours him or provides him with what looks to be the chance or material for attacking Jesus Christ and Christianity. Thus, he picks and chooses what history is and what it is not from among the facts in the New Testament. 'I now know that everything, including the birth of Christ, happened here and, therefore, must have something to do with world history, if it really did happen,' he writes in his book. The if-clause is his safety valve, which is ineffective. He also relies on the Bible (the New Testament, mainly) to give the history of the Jews and the origin of Christianity (see Chapter 2 of *Christ or Devil?*).

Obianyido looked for his so-called ancient historians among the contemporaries of Jesus Christ and found none, according to him. It is clear he is deceiving himself. There could not have been none; each age has historians. There must have been some. What he could not find was any evidence against the New Testament record of the history of Jesus Christ, because the historians of that time had nothing to say against the biblical record, so they allowed it to stand. Charles Caleb (1880–1832), speaking on a matter of this nature, earns my admiration for saying, 'When you have nothing to say, say nothing.' The so-called ancient historians, the contemporaries of Jesus the Christ, from whom Obianyido expected contradictions in terms of the New Testament's account of the life of Jesus Christ on earth, said nothing. Reason? They had nothing to say against the account in the Bible about the life of Jesus Christ on earth.

Obianyido alleges that intellectuals and historians of recent time, too, have given no account of Jesus Christ as a figure who once existed in this world. Let us pretend nothing is known about the Jehovah's Witnesses pamphlet I spoke about earlier. From where, then, came the knowledge of the historians who told Obianyido—and he believed them—that Jesus escaped crucifixion (see page 45 of *Christ or Devil?*)? He quotes the *Satellite* (a Nigerian newspaper) of 8 November 1982 as publishing an account by Henry Lincoln, Michael Baigent, and Richard Leigh about Jesus the Christ faking his crucifixion and later marrying Mary Magdalene, who later had his child. Obianyido speedily believes this assertion in the book, whose title is *The Holy Blood and the Holy Grail*, wholesale. With greater speed, he completely disbelieves the New Testament account of Jesus the Christ. Yet, each of the two works—the one by Henry Lincoln, Michael Baigent, and Richard Leigh, and the New Testament—supports that a man Jesus Christ once lived on our earth.

In any event, by believing those historians (Henry Lincoln, Michael Baigent, and Richard Leigh), Obianyido inadvertently believes the history to the effect that a man Jesus Christ ever existed on this earth.

Believe me, this man Obianyido does not seem to know his bearings, or else he is totally confused about his points. In one breath he talks as if he believes Jesus Christ never existed on this earth, and in the other, he entertains the notion that there was such a man on our earth.

Let me probe his book further. It says, 'From the very birth to his ascension into heaven, history, which is a record of facts, has been consistent in its refusal to echo the much-dramatised biblical account of the existence of Jesus Christ on earth' (page 35 of *Christ or Devil?*).

Again, the book says, 'The gospel so exaggerated the story about Jesus Christ to look as something that took place in heaven' (page 35 of *Christ or Devil?*). Those statements give the indication that Obianyido obviously believes the historical account that a man Jesus Christ once existed on this earth, according to the Bible, but he quarrels with what he considers an exaggeration in the account. The Bible might have exaggerated, and so might have Obianyido in his perception of the account.

By the way, how can he talk of the exaggeration of a thing if the thing never was in fact, or never existed? Exaggeration means making a thing look more, better, or worse than is the case. Otherwise, what is the exaggeration about?

About whether Jesus the Christ has ever existed in this world, Obianyido's mind is in a whirl.

Further, we consider that Obianyido queries the credibility of the gospel writers. Among his reasons: Gascoigne confirms that no word has survived in any document about Christ or his followers. During the next fifty years (after the supposed death of Christ, I guess), Christians themselves wrote most of the books that now constitute the New Testament. I ask, by the way, if so, then who wrote the other books of the New Testament? Obianyido does not say anything about that.

Let us bear in mind that Obianyido has been babbling and quibbling as to whether Jesus Christ existed on earth or was an image belonging to the realm of fiction or was a phantom. If he does not believe the gospels, then why has he cleverly recognised the gospels as containing facts about Jesus Christ only when it suits his freakish fancy? It is on the gospels he relies to say that Jesus Christ was a racialist Jew, a trickster, a pretender; that he broke away from Judaism to form his own religion, Christianity; that he preyed upon his people, the Jews; and so on. Can one be or do any such things without existing in the first place? Obianyido alleges that Jesus and Peter were crucified upside down (see Chapter 6 of *Christ or Devil?*). He alleges that Jesus was of the same character as the criminals among whom he was crucified (see Chapter 3 of *Christ or Devil?*). There are so many other statements in his book that support the idea that he believes Jesus Christ existed some time ago in this world. Yet, Obianyido shamelessly says that no such human figure as Jesus ever lived in this world. What a pendulum Obianyido is!

In his equivocation, contradiction, and confusion, Obianyido believes Philip Graham, one of his favourite modern historians, who used the description 'tragic results of one man's megalomania' when referring to Jesus Christ. Graham obviously made the reference to someone whose existence in the world, a time ago, he recognised. When discussing the history of Jesus Christ, Obianyido said that to discuss 'the origin of Christianity one, of course, has to start with the Jews and Judaism, the faith from which Christ broke away to form his own religion' (page 34 of *Christ or Devil?*), in so doing making clear the fact of the Jewish history he never doubted, which history contains the life history of Jesus the Christ. Again, Obianyido says, 'It was when Greece and Judah in turn fell under the Roman authority that the man Jesus Christ and his religion were born' (page 20 of *Christ or Devil?*).

What?! There are numerous pages in Obianyido's book where he clearly confesses his belief in the New Testament as the history that shows that Jesus Christ once lived on our planet, pages 21, 25, 27, 33, 34, and 46 being among them. From those pages, there can be no doubt that Obianyido believes a man Jesus the Christ once lived in this world. Yet he wants historians to confirm this, although he has not named any such historians.

Wait! He seems to have found one: Flavius, a famous historian according to Obianyido. Flavius has an account which points to the fact that Jesus Christ lived, some time ago, in our world. Obianyido believes that but says that the account given by the historian fails to tally with that of the gospels. In such a case, how do we know which of the two different accounts is more reliable? Also, it is inconsequential to the argument, which is whether Jesus Christ ever lived in this world. Since the two different accounts agree that a man Jesus Christ once lived in this world, the matter is determined. But is Obianyido's doubting mind put at rest as a result?

At every turn, the ghost of his doubt haunts him. Hear him say, 'But one starts to have doubts when many outstanding intelligentsias, including the renowned British philosopher Bertrand Russell, doubted whether Christ ever existed at all since there was no historical evidence to confirm that.' My view is that the 'one' in this sentence is Obianyido.

Next, he abandons his belief drawn upon the account of a famous historian, Flavius, who told him of the existence of Jesus Christ some time ago in this world. The only reason for him to throw away Flavius's account is that he found that 'many outstanding British intelligentsias' doubted that Jesus Christ ever lived on this planet.

Lest I forget: Obianyido talks about the disciples of Jesus Christ and mentions Peter as one of them. He says that Jesus the Christ and Peter were crucified upside down. How could Jesus the Christ have been not in this world and yet be crucified in this world? Plus, Jesus Christ never lived in this world, yet he had disciples who lived in this world? Obianyido's argument is messy!

He cannot think for himself, and that is his problem. What has become of his original belief that Jesus Christ once lived in this world? What of his belief in Flavius's account that Jesus Christ lived in this world? What of the book *The Holy Blood and the Holy Grail*, by Henry Lincoln, Michael Baigent, and Richard Leigh, that talks about Jesus Christ eloping with Mary Magdalene—he believes that? His belief in that information is proof that he has deserted his capricious mind at the sight of, or in the wake of, the speculations by the British personalities he tagged as 'outstanding intelligentsias'. He becomes doubtful about Jesus Christ as a human figure who once lived in our world.

In the cloudy atmosphere that Obianyido created through his indecision, no one is certain whether the opinions in *Christ or Devil?* are loaned to him by some 'renowned intelligentsias' or his famous historian Flavius or whether they are his. His opinions now look like the droppings of those 'outstanding intelligentsias' he desperately relies upon as a result of his confusion and poverty of knowledge.

That ding-dong shift of his mind trailing every other person's divergent and contradicting opinion, each time, that seems to spark before him does his book no good. The heart of his book does not seem to be tenanted by the spirit of personal thought as he proceeds, unprotected but with caution, among conflicting opinions, namely those of Henry Lincoln, Michael Baigent, and Richard Leigh; of the 'renowned intelligentsias'; of the philosophers; of the academic scholars; and of the famous historian he cites, Flavius. The character of his ever-changing opinions recommends no support for his scathing criticisms against the biblical history of Jesus the Christ.

Isaac Newton, a scientist, and Patrick Henry, an American revolutionary leader, airing their views on the authenticity of the Bible, respectively had this to say: 'No sciences are better attested than the Bible'; 'The Bible is worth all books which have been printed.'

OBIANYIDO: The Virgin Birth of Jesus without the mother's mating is not accepted by me.

REPLY: The matter of the Virgin Birth has been addressed earlier, in Chapter 4 of *In Defence of Jesus the Christ*. It deserves no further treatment, except to say that any temptation to build the idea that Mary conceived Jesus by using the materials gathered from the story of the Holy Ghost should be resisted since such an idea is diametrically opposed to common knowledge as well as to information that appears, here and there, in the Bible. It calls for caution!

OBIANYIDO: The Bible was introduced into Africa as a foreign exchange-earning commodity for Britain and the United States.

REPLY: The notion Obianyido holds, that the Bible was introduced into Africa as a foreign exchange–earning commodity, cannot be substantiated. Obianyido's belief is a clear display of his ignorance. He got his account of international trade woefully very wrong. What a mendacious statement by Obianyido!

At the time the Bible got to Africa, in the early days of colonisation of Africa by Britain and other powers, Britain had tremendous opportunities to freely do what it wanted with the vast, rich resources of Africa. How then could the Bible be its worry about earning foreign exchange? And mind this: how many Africans could read, or had the wherewithal to be able to purchase Bibles in commercial quantities? This is interesting as it totally cancels out the idea of Britain selling Bibles to Africans for foreign exchange earnings. In those early days of British colonisation of Africa, the British and American Christian missionaries, when Africans slowly started to learn to read and write, in order to entice them away from their indigenous religion and to Christianity, and to keep their interest in Christianity, freely distributed Bibles to them.

That idea of encouraging interest in Christianity was behind the free distribution of the Bibles to the students of the college in Liverpool, England, an event narrated by Obianyido in *Christ or Devil?*

Obianyido's allegation that the Bible was introduced into Africa as a foreign exchange–earning commodity for Britain and the United States is therefore trash since it has no scrap of evidence in support.

OBIANYIDO: Nothing is known about the early life of Jesus Christ.

REPLY: That is correct only as far as the popular biblical record goes. Sources other than the popular Bible provide reasonable accounts of the otherwise missing early life history of Jesus the Christ. That means something is known about the early life of Jesus the Christ. I am interested in one of these sources of the history of the early life of Jesus the Christ not accounted for in the popular Bible.

Before I say more about that source, let me ask, what has that gap in the Bible about the early life of Jesus the Christ to do with the teachings the Christ gave to the world and his personality, which Obianyido unnecessarily attacks? My question is, by the way, 'nothing'.

Back to the missing account of the early life of Jesus the Christ. My guesses in respect to its omission in the popular Bible are as follows:

(a) The translators of the original record of the history of Jesus the Christ did not consider that section of his history relevant to the narrative of his mission.

(b) The writers of the New Testament who were Jews living in a Jewish land had no means of knowing what happened to Jesus the Christ because, at the time in question, he was in Asia, beyond the Jewish lands. Any essential information about him during that period must come from the part of Asia where he was.

A brief account of the history of Jesus's early life in Asia is to be given later in Chapter 16. The brief history there forms a bridge over the gap between the history of Jesus the Christ at the time the Bible dropped the issue and again at the time when the Bible picked it up once more.

OBIANYIDO: Jesus, in his typical showmanship and egocentricity, entered Jerusalem, accompanied by his political thugs, in a manner aimed at distinguishing his from other Jewish religious sects.

He entered straight into the temple, breaking up the stalls of the traders who worked in the courtyard. The priest asked him, 'By what authority are you acting like this?' He replied by using his typical dubious parables, insolently rebuking the priests, saying that tax collectors and prostitutes would gain the kingdom before they would. How would modern civilisation see such behaviour? It is like what some wicked landlords pay ruffians and hitmen to do to errant tenants. He could have responded decently and politely to the polite question from the priests. Surely only brutes would walk into a place of commercial activity in a modern city and behave the way that man did. Jesus Christ's impoliteness was the reason the Jews arrested him and silenced him by death, for which the Jews should bear no blame.

REPLY: In Chapter 2 of *In Defence of Jesus the Christ*, which is about Anene Obianyido's introduction to his book *Christ or Devil?*, it is shown that Obianyido alleges that Jesus Christ was punished by the Jews because he broke away from Judaism to form Christianity (something which I have refuted). Now Obianyido wants his readers to accept that the reason for his punishment was his impoliteness to the priests during the incident when Jesus the Christ challenged the traders and robbers in the courtyard of the temple. Of the two reasons which are we to accept? Both? If both, why has Obianyido not presented each as a part of the two? And why did the Jews not present both or any of these reasons against Jesus the Christ during the trial before Pilate?

Obianyido also accuses Jesus the Christ of going about with political thugs. It is enough to learn from the teachings, the words, and the deeds of Jesus the Christ that his mission was spiritual only; it had nothing to do with the politics of the world. I previously mentioned this.

His reply to certain Pharisees and Herodians who wanted to know from him if tribute (tax) should be paid to Caesar—a political question— clearly showed his total lack of interest in politics: 'Render to Caesar the things that are Caesar's and to God, the things that are God's, he told them' (Mark 12:14–17). That answer sharply demonstrates that his mission was not about politics.

Pilate's question to him was another political question: 'Art thou the king of the Jews?' To that he replied unequivocally, 'My kingdom is not of this world.' Thus he divested his spiritual mission from the politics of this world (John 18:33–36). Satisfied, Pilate replied by saying to the Jews who were accusing him of meddling with politics, 'I find no fault in this man.' For Obianyido to accuse Jesus the Christ of political thuggery is therefore a maliciously calculated attack.

Furthermore, it is worthy to note that Obianyido's that Jesus the Christ was moving about with political thugs is nonsense. The teachings of Jesus the Christ are against violence of any kind. For instance, he told Peter, one of his disciples, without mincing words, to put his sword back into its scabbard, for 'he who kills by the sword dies by the sword' (Matthew 26:50–54). Why then did Peter have the sword? The answer is simple and clear: in those days, full-grown men were wont to carry a sword as part of their outfit. No offence was done by so doing. Further, Jesus the Christ taught that one should not seek revenge against one's enemies (Matthew 5:38–48).

I turn next to the incident in and around the temple during Jesus the Christ's triumphal entry into Jerusalem. It is conceded that the tables of the traders and those of the money changers were overthrown and that robbers were flogged and driven out of the temple and its courtyard by Jesus the Christ. But then Jesus the Christ gave his reason for his drastic reaction: he was against the temple of God and its courtyard being irreverently and sacrilegiously used, thus treating God with disrespect (Matthew 21:13). He was against hypocrisy—designating the temple as God's when, at the same time, using it for contrary purposes that were profane and sinful. Is Obianyido of the opinion that the temple for worshipping God ought to be turned into a commercial place and a den of robbers? Perhaps, because he believes not in God. Will 'modern civilisation' (to borrow his fond expression) go along with him in support of defilement of the temple, or the synagogue, or the mosque, or the traditional indigenous religious shrine? No way.

Obianyido's story about Jesus the Christ is mendacious and unreliable because it is distorted. He says that the overthrowing of the tables and whatnot took place in the courtyard without saying what or whose courtyard; he found it hard to qualify the courtyard. Was it not the courtyard of God's temple? Obianyido used the expression 'the traders who worked in the courtyard' in order to deceive his readers; he chooses the word *worked* instead of *traded*. What a mischievous man, joggling words to be able to deceive his readers. He says that the question posed to Jesus the Christ was polite, but he makes no mention of the fact of the indignation of the priests who had asked the question (Matthew 21:15). If the priests were indignant at the answer to their question, could their question have been polite? In all probability the question was intended to have an inflammatory connotation! Why has Obianyido concealed this likelihood?

I need to mention that the question-and-answer incident Obianyido talks about did not take place on the day of the triumphal entry as he cleverly wants his readers to believe. It took place on a different day. Obianyido might have read the Bible, but his mediocrity prevented him from understanding it, or his prejudice against Christianity stood in his way and prohibited him from correctly reporting what the Bible says.

On the very day of the question Obianyido mentions being asked, Jesus the Christ replied to it with his own question, parrying the Pharisees' question with devastating witticism and repartee. He asked, 'The baptism of John, whence was it? From heaven or from men?' The priests and the elders of the Jewish religion who first had asked Jesus the Christ the question was trapped in a dilemma. They replied, 'We do not know.' Jesus the Christ responded, 'Then I won't answer your question either.' There the confrontation ended.

To expose Obianyido's mendacity: For the day of the triumphal entry of Jesus the Christ into Jerusalem and his throwing away of the traders' tables and so forth, see Matthew 21:12–17.

For the day of the question Obianyido talks about, which was on a different day, read Matthew chapters 21–22; Mark chapter 11; and Luke chapters 19 and 20.

Despite that Obianyido goes on to allege that Jesus the Christ answered the question put to him 'in his typical dubious parables, and insolently rebuking the priest, cursing that the tax collectors and prostitutes would gain the kingdom before them', what mendacity Obianyido shows! Or is Obianyido a victim of ignorance? He is worse than the Ethiopian eunuch as far as understanding the Bible is concerned (Acts 8:26–35). The eunuch confessed that he could not understand the section of the Bible he was reading. Then Philip had to help him. Obianyido, in his case, though ignorant of what the sections of the Bible he refers to, arrogantly pretends to know all about the Bible. Or he is crafty and deliberately joggles matter to suit his hopeless desires. Consider his manoeuvring of the facts about the questions and answers between the priests and Jesus the Christ: he slickly omitted the main reply of Jesus the Christ to the priests. Was the reply not in the form of a counterquestion? If that was so (for so it was), then does Obianyido's account of the event not amount to downright journalistic dishonesty, a travesty of facts?

We next go back to Jesus the Christ's reaction to the defilement of the temple of God. On the surface, it seems Jesus the Christ overreacted. Deeply considered, I see it was a righteous reaction, a show of indignation in proportion to the depth of the dishonour those concerned in the defilement of the temple showed to God. In addition, the reaction was to give them a good lesson in their own interests: it taught them to be religious and righteous in the true sense, to shun hypocrisy. That is, they were not to call the building the temple of God and at the same time use it for activities against God's divinity.

Under this present subheading, Obianyido alleges that Jesus the Christ was punished because he the manner in which he answered the Jewish priest's questions 'By what authority are you doing this thing? And who gave you the authority?' was impolite. I do not think Jesus the Christ was impolite to the priests. Even if he had been, his manner of responding was not the priests' headache. The situation was that the Jews had, for a long time, been expecting a political leader who was to rescue them from the tyranny of their political rulers—the Romans—and their hostile neighbours. Some of the Jews, the priests in particular, thought Jesus the Christ was this expected leader, especially, at the time of his triumphal entry into Jerusalem. So those Jews pinned their hopes on him and were jubilant on the occasion. But it turned out that Jesus was a spiritual rather than a political leader. As a result, the priests' hopes were dashed, and they became utterly disappointed. For that reason, among others, they stirred up other Jews into violent indignation against Jesus the Christ. It follows that the major reason for the crucifixion of Jesus was that the Jews were totally disappointed that he was not a political leader.

OBIANYIDO: Christians say that Jesus Christ died to wash away our sins and, at the same time, criticise the Jews and Judas Iscariot, who helped to bring about the washing away of the sins by the crucifixion of Jesus Christ.

Jesus, who knew in advance of his death, ought not to have tried to avoid his death.

If the birth of Jesus Christ among the poor established the virtue of poverty, what does the barbarous death chiefly used in those days for pirates show? The nature of his death, coupled with the characters among whom he was crucified, arouses doubt as to his claim to holiness. The only conclusion is that Jesus shared some common traits with those with whom he died.

REPLY: First, I want to treat Obianyido's opinion that Jesus the Christ bore the same character or traits as those among whom he was crucified and that they all were killed for their criminal activities. 'Criminal activities' is now the third reason given by Obianyido as grounds for the crucifixion of Jesus the Christ. Obianyido's readers must now be wondering which of the three reasons Obianyido holds as the actual grounds for the crucifixion. All three? He should have mentioned each as part of the whole. That is that.

About the crucifixion, the event is incorrectly narrated by Obianyido. The fact is that Jesus and those crucified alongside him were victims of the barbaric acts of those who brought about their deaths. No civilised or modern (if I may use Obianyido's fond expression) society would treat its fellow citizens or any other fellow in that fashion. It is regrettable that Obianyido reaps pleasure from his alleged knowledge that his fellow human beings were brutally, inhumanely tortured and put to death. Does his attitude add up to civilisation? Think about that. Personally, I think not. He is tickled by the brutality because of his iniquitous and sadistic nature, which becomes hyperactive in matters he guesses will be hurtful and harmful to Jesus the Christ and Christianity, and disrespectful to God.

He insinuated that Jesus the Christ was a slave and a criminal because he was crucified among 'pirates and criminals. I want Obianyido to learn that Jesus came to the world on a special spiritual mission. He came to purify himself in his final reincarnation, during which time he was to teach and demonstrate with his life, even unto his death, what a seeker for eternal life should expect to encounter or suffer in the wicked and unrighteous world. He was the greatest spiritual teacher. Campaigners for justice and truth customarily suffer almost in the same manner Jesus did. John the Baptist had his suffering (Matthew 14:1–11). Peter had his (Acts 5:17–18). Paul had his (Acts 19–28). Those stand as some of the ancient examples.

As far as more modern people go, I can think of Martin Luther King Jr. of the United States, Mahatma Ghandi of India, Patrice Lumumba of Congo, and Nelson Mandela of South Africa.

All those martyrs taught with their lives, and some met their deaths in that noble course!

Jesus the Christ knew in advance his death was coming; he knew the consequences of his noble course of action, helping his fellow human beings to gain eternal life. The expected consequences did not deter him from embarking on the campaign and following it to the end.

Even to his disciples and all other aspirants to the kingdom of God, the eternal life, he warned of the consequences of such a course. He told them that they were most likely to be exposed to the knife edge of the wicked world for following the truth. He went on admonishing that they were not to relent in the face of that eventuality when preaching and demonstrating righteousness and truth, because the wicked world could kill the body but not the soul; it is God alone who is able to destroy both the body and the soul (Matthew 10:24–28; 24:19). Jesus was encouraged to hold that view because he knew about the immortality of the soul: a human being does not die but changes form, for a human being has the Spirit of God within him or her.

It was the teaching and the demonstrations of the truth of the kingdom of God that joined with other factors to incur hatred for Jesus the Christ and lead to the consequent death he suffered. *Veritas odium parit* (Truth breeds hatred), says a Roman proverb.

Jesus knew what to expect before he embarked on his mission and, therefore, could not have done anything to avoid the consequence—his eventual crucifixion.

The crucifixion was an obvious miscarriage of justice; Pilate and his dear wife made that clinically clear (Matthew 27:19, 24). Therefore, Obianyido's view that Jesus Christ shared the same traits with the criminals among whom he was crucified is blazingly defamatory and preposterous. We are not to forget that one of the criminals crucified alongside Jesus knew about justice and declared Jesus innocent (Luke 23:39–41). Obianyido seems not to understand this portion of the Bible. Let him take a leaf from the story of the Ethiopian eunuch and ask for help (Acts 8:26–35).

Concerning Judas Iscariot and the Jews who conspired against and killed Jesus, Obianyido is of the opinion that they should be praised for helping to 'wash away our sins' since it has been said that Christ's death washed our sins away. About that, Obianyido talks nonsense—which means he lacks common sense.

Reasons exist why those wicked conspirators who contrived the death of Jesus should be condemned and not praised. Admittedly, according to the biblical prophecy, Jesus was to die in the manner earlier prophesised (remember, the death refers to the physical body, not to the soul), yet the conspirators must stand condemned for the motives behind their acts, before the court of morality and social justice.

We can see that the conspirators acted only to satisfy their selfish, nefarious wishes. The faults found with Judas Iscariot and the Jews involved are well-directed against the reprehensible motives behind the respective parts each of them played in the event. It does not matter that those parts made the said prophecy happen; their acts were grossly immoral and, therefore, distasteful, and ethically reprehensible. Those Jews did what they did for their own selfish interests. That meant doing away with an innocent person who failed to agree with them or be what they expected of him and who stood against their sinful behaviours. Judas Iscariot did his part for his sinful selfish gain. None of the conspirators acted just to make the prophecy come true, for that was not what was assigned to them. Therefore, none of them deserved to escape criticism by moral, reasonable, civilised people. For that, Jesus the Christ said, 'The son of man goes as it is written, but woe unto that man by whom the son of man is betrayed' (Matthew 26:24).

Whatever the case, I conceive that the hostility of those concerned in the persecution of Jesus the Christ was a kind of test which Jesus the Christ faced and won, without which his mission in the world would not have been so enormously glorified.

Another issue: Obianyido alleges that Jesus the Christ did not give himself up, and Obianyido wants to know why, since Jesus was the Son of God, he knew he was destined to die?

Already I have given a partial treatment of this matter. This time I believe the question should not have come up if Obianyido had read the Bible and understood it. Of course, Jesus the Christ gave himself up at the appropriate time (John 17:11; Luke 22:53). He gave himself up after, not before, he made sure his mission on earth was accomplished in fulfilment of the purpose of his final incarnation. Remember this: the Pharisees, the chief priests, and Judas Iscariot were searching for him with torches and lamps. He advanced towards them of his own accord and in his own time and offered himself, telling them that he was the very one they were looking for (John 18:2–8). Remember, too, at the time he knew his mission had been accomplished. He said, 'I have glorified Thee, Father [God] on earth, having accomplished the work which Thou gives me to do. ... And now, I am coming to Thee' (John 17:11). He was not to surrender himself before his mission was over if I may repeat. Remember, too, that he said at the time, to the priests, the officers of the temple, and the elders of the Jewish religion, this: 'When I was with you, day after day, in the temple, you did not lay your hands on me. But this is your hour and the power of darkness' (Luke 22:53).

Jesus the Christ, therefore, gave himself up, without any effort to save his life, as and when he saw fit, not at the time Obianyido thought he would have.

OBIANYIDO: Jesus had spent many years in venomous criticism of those who refused to join his religious sect, threatening them with hellfire. For instance, he said, 'He that believeth shall be saved; but he that believeth not shall be condemned.' He addressed the sinners in language which would be considered obscene in modern time: 'Ye serpent, ye generation of vipers, how can ye escape the damnation of hell?' He cursed the priests of the temple, saying that 'tax-gatherers and prostitutes would enter the kingdom of heaven before them'.

REPLY: For a start, the words *cursed* and *obscene*, used by Obianyido to describe what Jesus the Christ said to the high priests and the sinners, are inappropriate. Jesus the Christ was not cursing his addressees; he was admonishing them, using his words to alert them to the danger if they failed to change from sinfulness to righteousness.

In that sense, the words Obianyido sees as 'cursed' and 'obscene' were a form of admonition—earnest advice aimed at the addressees for their benefit. To heed those strong warnings by Jesus the Christ was to gain them happiness; to disregard them was to incur suffering. Despite that fact, Obianyido makes noises of disparagement that Jesus the Christ was abusive towards those he so addressed for their edification.

OBIANYIDO: The resurrection and ascension of Jesus Christ were hoaxes: the disciples of Jesus Christ deceived the followers that Jesus Christ had gone away.

Reason does not support the account given by the gospels of the resurrection, because the actual resurrection from the tomb is not described, even though it is abundantly illustrated by Renaissance artists. The gospels vary concerning the discovery that the resurrection had occurred. Matthew states that it was Mary Magdalene and Mary the mother of Jesus who came to the sepulchre early in the morning and were informed by an angel that Jesus Christ had risen. Mark states that those two Marys, together with Salome, were first in the tomb and discovered that the great stone that had sealed it was rolled away— 'no doubt with clear marks of somebody's fingerprints.

According to Mark, the three women entered the sepulchre and found that Jesus Christ had risen. In his own account, Luke mentioned the two Marys and several other women. It was John who let the cat out of the bag. He said Mary Magdalene was the first to know what happened and that she told Peter and John that the body of Jesus Christ had been taken away.

Now, there is a growing belief that according to Mary the body was taken away.

According to belief, too, the ascension was a fabrication to support the resurrection hoax, considering Jesus Christ's obsession for self-assertion and his need to convince his enemies of his claimed supernatural power. He would have appeared to the doubting Jewish and Roman public or to the soldiers and not to his close relations.

Why did Christ wait until the soldiers guarding the tomb had fallen asleep? They could not have had enough power to prevent his resurrection if they were awake at the time.

About the ascension, people outside the close relations of Jesus Christ could have seen him in his white flowing robe as he was airborne with arms spread, just as people in my community see a low-flying aeroplane or colourful balloons in the open air. Pregnancy at a certain stage can no longer be concealed.

According to the *Satellite* newspaper, mentioned earlier, Jesus Christ faked his crucifixion and left his native country with Magdalene. He was not the person crucified.

REPLY: About the ascension of Jesus the Christ, Obianyido is boorishly sarcastic. The way he caricatures it makes him a buffoon, a jester!

The events of the resurrection, the appearances, and the ascension were such that ordinary mortals might question them with great inquisitiveness, no doubt. The mysteries surrounding them were embedded in the holy womb of the spiritual realm and did not lend themselves to easy understanding on the surface. Any attempts to understand the mysteries from the surface will end only in sense interpretations, sans reality. The right, the authority, to the real interpretations belongs to the truly righteous, i.e. the holy ones.

When we look at the resurrection according to what the Bible says, we find it says this: 'Jesus suffered physical death but was raised in spirit' (1 Peter 3:18). The spirit of Jesus the Christ took such a physical form that allowed him to be seen only by mortal beings blessed and entitled to behold him in that form (Acts 10:39–41).

The spectacle of the appearance of Jesus the Christ after he rose from the dead was like that which took place during the transfiguration of Jesus the Christ on the mountain. Then Moses and Elijah, long dead, appeared in physical form in order to be visible to particular mortals, Peter, James, John, and Jesus, who were spiritually blessed and entitled to behold them (Matthew 17:1–4).

In *the Aquarian Gospel of Jesus, the Christ*, the matter of the resurrection of Jesus is made clear by Jesus. He says, 'I will lay down my life and will take it up again, that you may know the mysteries of life, of death, and of resurrection of death. I lay me down in flesh, but I will rise in spirit form with power to manifest myself so mortal eyes can see' (*The Aquarian Gospel of Jesus the Christ* 163:38–39; 1 Peter 3:18). His ascension, no doubt, possessed a similarly mysterious quality and process. By that I mean that Jesus became transmuted from his dead human body into a spirit that wore divine flesh. So, the mystery of his physical resurrection, his physical appearances, and his physical ascension was such that sensual eyes (the mortal eyes) covered with the dross of sin could not see, and mortal minds could not comprehend. Only the mortals spiritually qualified could behold the scene. The mystery of such events can never be discovered by logic using human senses because it remains shrouded in mystery.

Obianyido comments that the gospels failed to describe the actual resurrection of Jesus the Christ from the tomb 'even though that is abundantly illustrated by Renaissance artists. My answer to this statement is that, as explained earlier, ordinary mortals could not see or observe the process of the actual resurrection because they were not spiritually qualified or blessed to do so. The Renaissance artists' illustrations were mere projections of their imaginations of the actual process of the rising from the dead, as the physical rising was not able to be witnessed by ordinary mortals and therefore could not be described.

The rising from the dead, making appearances after the rising, and the ascension were all mystical events; only mystics could comprehend them. They were not perceptible by the physical senses of those who were not spiritually qualified. The rising was a mystical process from one state (the physical) to another (the spiritual), and the result was observable only by the spiritually qualified.

The process of the transformation is represented by the word *rise*. The process is not accounted in the Bible because the transformation did not manifest either worldly or physically.

My attention here goes to Obianyido's assertion that the body of Jesus was taken away from the tomb by his disciples so as to fool people that

Jesus had risen from the dead. It is on Mary Magdalene's statement that he relies for his assertion.

Mary Magdalene, being a woman (weaker than a man in feeling), finding the stone that had sealed the sepulchre (tomb) of Jesus removed, became panic-stricken. In that mood, she ran and said to Peter and other disciples, 'They have taken away the Lord out of the sepulchre' (John 20:2). Relying on that statement, Obianyido concludes that the body of Jesus was taken away by his disciples. That is a shoddy and unreliable conclusion.

The word *they* in Magdalene's statement could not have been referring to the disciples of Jesus she was talking to; *they* patently refer to the enemies of Jesus, whom she suspected of having taken Jesus's body. The dimwit Obianyido therefore wrongly interprets the statement by Magdalene.

Let us consider Obianyido's suggestion that somebody's fingerprints were on the stone that sealed the tomb of Jesus that was later rolled away. If that was so, then why were the disciples of Jesus the Christ not arrested or quarried? Why was any person related to Jesus the Christ in any positive way not suspected in the making of an effort to establish whom the fingerprints belonged to?

The soldiers guarding the tomb were asleep at the time of the resurrection, while on duty. Why? The task of the rolling away of the stone that sealed the tomb and the taking away of the body of Jesus could not have been within a nanosecond, making it so that none of the soldiers on duty could get up from sleep at the time in question.

After the whole incident, none of the soldiers were questioned or punished. Roman authorities in those days were known for their strictness and promptness, but they did nothing at the time. Why? The Roman authorities demonstrated their said proclivity and seriousness in their duties when Peter the apostle escaped from prison. Herod, the Roman authority at the time, interrogated those supposed to be guarding Peter in the prison and put them to death on account of Peter's escape (Acts 12:18–19). Why was that procedure not followed in the case of the alleged taking of Jesus's body?

Hang on! It is not funny to return to this subject: Obianyido this time is awake to the fact that Jesus the Christ once bodily lived in this world and was crucified and buried. Obianyido's bellyache this time is that the body of Jesus the Christ was taken away, that he did not rise from dead. Obianyido, again, is awake to the fact the Jesus the Christ did not elope with Mary Magdalene from his native land and allow somebody else to be crucified in his place, according to what the authors of *The Holy Blood and the Holy Grail* told him. Remember that he joyously swallowed the contents of that book.

Below I mention the *Satellite* newspaper and *The Holy Blood and the Holy Grail* once more, but this time with a detailed account of the book's uncertain story. On my part, I hope to tackle the book's account head-on—and in detail too.

Before I do that, I have this comment to make: we are almost at the end of Obianyido's criticisms of the Holy Bible, Jesus the Christ, Christianity, and God, yet he is still twisting and changing his mind on whether or not a man Jesus the Christ actually lived in this world some time ago. *Varium et mutabile semper* Obianyido (Obianyido's mind is fickle and changeable). He has been in utter confusion and has been chasing his own allegations, going in a circle. His readers must feel dizzy following him in his spiral ladder that goes round and round, up and down!

One thing: it is not easy to tell lies and twist facts in order to gain some measure of credence and get away with it. Obianyido has shown he is a raconteur of false stories. His muddled work is clear evidence of his theatrical 'first attempt at writing a book of this nature' (see the introduction of *Christ or Devil?*).

OBIANYIDO: Jesus Christ had a special sexual relationship with Mary Magdalene. I do not think the gospels told us all about Mary Magdalene, a spinster, and Jesus, a celibate. Mary was the first to race to the tomb of Jesus to discover he had risen.

The suspicion about the special relationship between her and Jesus is supported by a book mentioned in an edition of our Nigerian newspaper *Satellite* of 8 November 1982, written by Henry Lincoln, Michael Baigent, and Richard Leigh. The book is *The Holy Blood and the Holy Grail* and is described as secret. According to this book, Jesus Christ married Mary Magdalene, who later had a daughter with him. Jesus faked his crucifixion and fled his native country, to settle in Gani. There his descendants emerged as Clovis I Merovingian, King of Franks. Someone else was crucified in his place.

REPLY: Obianyido is once more on the subject that Jesus the Christ escaped crucifixion and eloped with Mary Magdalene as alleged by the Nigerian newspaper *Satellite* and the book *The Holy Blood and the Holy Grail* written by Henry Lincoln, Michael Baigent, and Richard Leigh. This time the allegation is detailed. I will tackle the allegations in that book hand-on.

In some of the chapters before this, we observe Obianyido doubting that Jesus the Christ ever lived in this world. In this present chapter, his pendulous mind swings again.

Relying on the likely uncertain story in the book *The Holy Blood and the Holy Grail*, he changes his mind and now believes that a man Jesus the Christ once lived in this world. It is interesting to learn why he has had this change of mind. He once changed his mind and believes that the man Jesus the Christ lived some time ago in this world to exploit the negative points in the book directed against Jesus the Christ. Obianyido wants us to believe that a man Jesus the Christ once existed in this world and faked his crucifixion, eloped with Mary Magdalene to a foreign country, and settled there with Magdalene as his wife, who then bore him a daughter. What a clownish joke!

Obianyido with ease accepts the book, imagine the book alleging that Jesus the Christ escaped crucifixion and someone else being crucified in his place. What a questionable Suggestion! Why was no one able to find out at the time material to the arrest, the trial, the torture, the crucifixion, and the burial that it was not Jesus who was undergoing all that ill treatment? How was the swapping between Jesus and whoever took his place carried out without detection? Or was it a case of mistaken identity? If so, did it follow that Judas Iscariot, who betrayed his Master (Jesus the Christ), did not know whom he betrayed and yet killed himself for the stinging act of betraying his Master? None of those deeply involved in the scenario—the high priests; the elders of the Jewish religion; the Pharisees; the Roman authorities; the disciples of Jesus the Christ; Mary Magdalene; Mary the mother of Jesus the Christ, who went to the tomb to look for the body of Jesus; Joseph Arimathea, who took and buried the body in his own tomb; the criminals who were crucified alongside Jesus; et al.—was able to find out that Jesus was not the one arrested, tried, tortured, crucified, and buried? Is this believable?

The discovery of the crucifixion of one who was not Jesus surfaced after the discovery of America, a country from which one or two of the co-authors of the book 'Holy blood, Holy Grail' came. The book seems to have the DNA of a story book 'The Gulliver's Travel'; There rooms for doubting the suggestions it contains: The present Christianity rejects it; the notion of the earlier Christianity is strongly in opposition to the view it portrays.

Paul the apostle, arguing before Agrippa, a Roman king, referred to the scenario—the arrest, the trial, the torture, the crucifixion, the burial, the rising from the dead, the appearances, and the ascension of Jesus—and said, 'This thing was not done in a corner [in secret]' (Acts 26:26). Obianyido does not think so!

Obianyido asserts that Jesus, the Christ had 'Special relationship' with Mary Magdalene—whatever he means by *special*—must connote dirtiness. Such vulgar, raw, blasphemous allegations generally proceed from the dirty minds of perverts. To such people, any form of intimacy or acquaintance between the opposite sexes (male and female) has an automatic sexual or erotic connotation. Must a person, except for the sake of erotic acts, not relate to or show interest in, or like (in a noncanal, platonic way), the opposite sex?

Obianyido reasons that since Jesus the Christ was a celibate and Mary Magdalene was a spinster, combined with the fact that Mary Magdalene was said to be the first to enter the tomb of Jesus, their relationship must have been erotic. What a case of sophism, a daft way of reasoning—absurdity made manifest!

Love between a man and a woman may be consuming yet remain platonic, i.e. just a mere social or spiritual interaction without erotic passion or sexual overture coming into the picture, that is to say, a relationship akin to that between siblings of opposite sexes.

Since the allegations have been circulating and seem to be receiving attention, I am, for the sake of discussion, prepared to confront *The Holy Blood and the Holy Grail*. In particular, I want to challenge the allegation that Jesus the Christ eloped with Mary Magdalene and married her. Assuming, but not conceding, that this happened, I ask, what about it? Would that have been a crime, an abomination, a forbidden act, a sin for them to have married? Were they blood relations so as to colour the marriage with the hue of incest? Obianyido has heaped unnecessary emphasis on the matter and presents it as something despicable that he has unveiled in an attempt to destroy or tarnish the divine personality of Jesus the Christ.

Marriage, after all, is a sacred order of God starting from Adam and Eve. Why has Obianyido so negatively garbled the allegation and taken delight in putting it in such a blazing spotlight when there is not one iota of evidence in support of the story? Since the allegations in the book are yet unproven.

Besides, the marriage issue is not germane to the central point of the issue my book is contesting vis-à-vis Obianyido's book, which matter is about the spiritual character of Jesus the Christ, his divine personality.

Obianyido,s hope of raising hullabaloo that Jesus, the Christ married Mary Magdalene dissolved into a mere worthless dream!.

The authors of *The Holy Blood and the Holy Grail* simply suppose that Jesus the Christ escaped crucifixion, eloped with Mary Magdalene, and married her. That is what Obianyido wants to echo to the Nigerian world, if it were possible for him to do so, with a loudspeaker or an amplifier.

So long as the information in the book remains sheer humdrum speculation without categorical assertions or proof, it remains within the realm of mental construction.

For more than two thousand years after the death of Jesus, historians, philosophers, sociologists, archaeologists and theologians have been searching, combing, and groping for concrete evidence in support of what *The Holy Blood and the Holy Grail* claims about Jesus the Christ and Mary Magdalene. The hope of finding any evidence in the future does not seem to exist expectation—a wild goose chase! All efforts—futile!

I make an allowance: If at any time in future irrefutable evidence is given in support of the view in *The Holy Blood and the Holy Grail*, I will apologise and shamefacedly withdraw my doubt. Let's wait and see!.

OBIANYIDO: The concept of the Trinity is very unacceptable as it is questionable. Why is it that at one end Christ is called the only begotten Son, and at the other, he is said to be God in disguise? He himself boasts that if one sees him, then one has seen his Father, and that a person must go through him if wishing to speak to the Father God.

The concept of God the Father, God the Son, and God the Holy Ghost is based on the mathematical theory of 'things equal to one being are equal to one another'. Father, Son, and Holy Ghost are each equal to one another. Yet, Jesus, when he was dying on the cross, complained of being abandoned by God: 'My God, my God, why has Thou forsaken me?'

There was a theological argument of past times. 'If father begot the son, he that is begotten had a beginning of existence; hence it is clear that there was a time when the son was not.' No. The Son has always been with the Father, not only since time began, but also before all time. For the Father could not have been so named unless he had a Son; and there could be no Son without a Father. The theological argument approaches the proverbial Ibo man's boast that he was begotten a male child before his father.

REPLY: Obianyido quotes an adage: 'If father begot the son, he that is begotten had a beginning of existence; hence it is clear that there was a time when the son was not.' That adage Obianyido calls a 'theological argument of past times. In my modest view, he has christened that argument with the wrong terminology (a wrong name). The argument is not theological; it is an epistemological argument because it deals with just the theory of knowledge, i.e. the method and validity of knowledge, the fact. Theology, on the other hand, is about theistic religion—the nature of God, of God's influence on people, and of religion and religious beliefs.

Obianyido may take note of that assessment while we move on to his other questions. The subject of Jesus the Christ and his relationship with God, which Obianyido questions, has been sufficiently treated in Chapter 4. It is, however, to be faintly retouched upon here where it relates to the concept of the Holy Trinity. I am to address the concept next. Obianyido does not accept the Holy Trinity concept and ridicules it.

The Holy Trinity is among the many concepts strongly believed in by Christians today. Although that is the situation, the concept is a mystery and troubles the minds of some Christians who privately feel uncomfortable about it. Some such Christians openly question it; others privately do the same.

The Holy Trinity is a mystery of the Christian religion. There are other mysteries about the religion. One thinks of the Virgin Birth, the resurrection, the appearances after the resurrection, and the ascension to heaven of Jesus the Christ. Of all those mysteries, the Holy Trinity is, in a sense, the only one that is unique. All are specifically mentioned or named except the Holy Trinity. By that I mean that the Holy Trinity in the Holy Bible is not named as a unit or given a block name or description. What we know is that the Bible makes mention of the Father, the Son, and the Holy Ghost as separate entities, not as a block name— Holy Trinity. And the names occur independently of one another and on different occasions in the Holy Bible. Putting the seeming separate identities (names) together in a block name (Holy Trinity) looks to be a contrivance by present-day Christians, and some readers might find the block name strange and not easy to accept. The nearest thing to the block name in the Bible is in Matthew 28:19, which reads, 'Go ye, therefore and teach all nations, baptising them all in the name of the Father, and the Son, and the Holy Ghost.' Can that be a block name? Does that refer to an entity? Debatable! It gives the impression that there are three Gods. The fact that the article *the* immediately precedes each of the three Gods named is taken into consideration.

That condition leaves us in a quagmire, an embarrassing situation in which we find it difficult to understand and explain the concept. St Augustine, in his attempt to define the concept, found himself in difficulty and behaved like a person in a labyrinth. He went round and round without finding a definite way out. Describing the Holy Trinity, he reasoned, 'Yet when it is asked what the three are, human utterance is weighed down by deep poverty of speech. All the same, we say *three persons*, not that we wish to say it, but that we may not be reduced to silence.'

When we look into the complexity of the concept of a three-in-one God and consider the fact of the perplexity the concept has caused, it becomes easy to forgive Obianyido, who has a very poor knowledge of the Christian religion, for deprecating and questioning the concept.

Personally, I was hesitant before I came to accept the concept of the Holy Trinity. It was after I had gained some knowledge about the mystical code of numbers that I saw some truth in the concept of the Holy Trinity. For purposes of our discussion, the number three is decoded as perfection, i.e. spiritually completion. I now sense the concept of the Holy Trinity as a block name.

At this juncture, I want to mention a few numbers known to have links with certain matters or events. The Bible has *one* relating to monotheism (of one God); *seven* relating to the seven sons of Sceva; and the Twelve relating to the twelve disciples of Jesus the Christ. No wonder the number twelve was maintained, kept constant. After Judas Iscariot betrayed Jesus and was gone, no more than one disciple was chosen to replace him, keeping the number at twelve. That one was Matthias. Why must it be so?

For our matter now, let me leave out other numbers and necessarily discuss only the relevant number, three, which relates to the Holy Trinity.

The number three, as I have already said, has spiritual/mystical significance. *Ome trinum est perfectum* (Everything in three means perfection) is a Roman saying. Jesus was visited by the Three Wise Men at his birth and was given three gifts by them. He was tempted three times by Satan. He predicted the temple would be destroyed and rebuilt in three days. He took with him only three of his disciples—Peter, James, and John—to witness his transfiguration on the mountain. Those disciples suggested that three tents be set up for three persons—Jesus, Moses, and Elijah. Jesus gave the parable of the Good Samaritan involving three classes of people—the priest, the Levite, and the Good Samaritan. He rose from death on the third day—and so on, in the New Testament.

Further, in the Old Testament, Jonah was in the belly of the fish for three days and three nights; the Lord God asked Abraham for a heifer, a goat, and a ram (three creatures), each three years old. There are other matters in the Bible involving three—a mystical number.

In other religions besides Christianity, but including mystic circles that indulge in numerology, the number three is of great significance and features in their symbols for rituals, for example the triangle (a figure with three sides, three angles, and three points, signifying perfection), whatever the triangle is being used for.

Everyman's Encyclopaedia has a lot of interesting information to offer on the number three. The encyclopaedia uses the word *triad* in place of *three*. It goes on to say, 'In religion and mythology there is a notion of group of three related deities.' In Brahmanism, the Hindu triad denotes the three leading gods (Brahma, Vishnu, and Siva). The Sumerians had a triad of gods (Anna, Enlil, and Enki). Babylon's triad consisted of Anu, lord of the heavens; Bel, lord of the earth; and Ea, lord of the abyss. In Egyptian religion, the triad in any district consists of a goddess, a god, and their son. The Greeks had Zeus, Poseidon, and Hades. In Chinese religions, there are three holy ones. In the Scandinavian religion are Thor, Odin, and Loki. In Wales, the triad is an arrangement of similar events in series of three.

It may surprise Obianyido to learn that even in indigenous African religion (say, in his Igbo community), there are three features in making up their religious gods. The religion recognises three gods represented as father, mother, and child (son) in carved images or some other form.

So goes the list of religions of different races, nations, and tribes, each having three gods as a religious concept.

It is astonishing and delightful to observe that each of the different religions of different races, nations, and so on, of its own accord, mystically captured the concept of three gods. The observation arouses this question: why is the concept of three gods in religion universal, without any prior arrangement or agreement among the different races, nations, and tribes of the world? This is a difficult question. There must be something mysterious about the universality of the concept since it did not come by way of agreement among the various religions.

I wish to humbly suggest an answer to that question. My belief is that humankind is a religious animal (or being, if you prefer), and in humankind is planted at Creation the Spirit of the Creator, God. For that reason, in a person's spiritual (religious) journey towards his or her Creator, he or she gropes instinctively or by nature through the concept of the Trinity, perceived within his or her inner spiritual self. Otherwise, why would this universal concept be known to the different religions of different races, nations, and tribes of the world without preagreement or arrangement among them? That much I can say.

Outside religion, the mystical significance of the triad exists, for example red, yellow, and blue, the three cardinal substances of colour. We find that *triad* is the name given to those major elements in chemistry which can directly unite with, or replace, three atoms of hydrogen, chlorine, or some other monatomic element. In music, *trian* (three) denotes a certain chord or harmony formed of three radical sounds—a fundamental note, its third, and its fifth. We talk of three cheers and such.

I believe humankind's concept of a three-in-one God is instinctive. It is planted in humankind at Creation and is made manifest through divine illumination, which Christ within humankind gives (without the person relying upon his or her senses or rational processes). In other words, humankind must accept the concept of the Trinity by faith.

J. L. Goodall, a lecturer in divinity, in his book entitled *An Introduction to Philosophy of Religion*, mentions in passing a thought about St Augustine. St Augustine's definition or description of the Holy Trinity has earlier been quoted; it need not be repeated here. His description of the Holy Trinity leaves us to conclude that St Augustine admitted the perplexity of concept of the Holy Trinity. St Augustine's suggestion, to me, is another way of attributing the notion of the Holy Trinity to instinct, with a natural action or behaviour independent of reasoning or intellect; it arises unintendedly within the actor.

We read in William Shakespeare's play *The Merry Wives of Windsor*: 'There is divinity in odd numbers.' Coincidentally, our number three is an odd number. No doubt, therefore, there is divinity in the Holy Trinity.

With the knowledge we gained from the foregoing discourse, we must accept the Christian concept of the Holy Trinity by faith.

My next concern is this: How do we see the status of each of the three identities that make up the Holy Trinity? And what does the Trinity itself stand for?

The popular Christian Bible has not done enough to answer our two questions. All the Bible has for us is the bare skeleton of the Holy Trinity. We are left to find the flesh of the skeleton. For that I approach the book entitled *The Aquarian Gospel of Jesus the Christ*, translated from the Akashic records by Levi H. Dowling, for help. The book has details about the Holy Trinity as follows:

An Indian sage, Vidy Apati, wrote: 'Eternal Thought is one; in essence it is two—intelligence and force; and when they breathe a child is born; this child is love.' And thus, the Triune (three in one) God stands forth, when called Father–Mother–Child (*The Aquarian Gospel of Jesus the Christ* 58:18–20).

Jesus the Christ, in the same book, gives his analysis (it is like that of the Indian sage) of the Holy Trinity to Peter, James, and John. He said,

> 'The Spirit of eternity is one unmanifest; and this is God the Father, God the Mother, God the Son in One.

> 'In life of manifests the One became the three and God the Father is the God of might; and God the Mother is Omniscient God, and God the Son is Love.

> 'And God the Father is power of heaven and earth; and God the Mother is the Holy Breath, the thought of heaven and earth; and God the Son, the only Son,

is Christ, and Christ is Love.' (*The Aquarian Gospel of Jesus the Christ* 163:28–33)

The necessary flesh to cover the bare skeleton of the Holy Trinity has been supplied then.

I have come to the end of my discourse on the Holy Trinity. However, I wish to top up the discourse with emphasis on two vital issues generally misunderstood. The concept of three Gods in one is the first; the second is about the crucifixion. Each of these issues wants explanation.

About the three Gods in one: When we talk about the three Gods in one (the Holy Trinity), we are unwarily inclined to conceive three Gods making up One God in the Holy Trinity. This is spiritually a very doubtful concept. The Holy Trinity is not about Gods distinct from one another; it is not about gods. It is about one God seen or perceived as having three distinct aspects or functions.

No one can scientifically, metaphysically, or philosophically describe God, except by the effects of his functions made manifest, which we observe as his cardinal aspects—his character as Father, his character as Mother (the Holy Ghost), and his character as Son (Love). Therefore, we are to say no to the concept of three Gods in one and say yes to the concept of one God to whom we attach three aspects or functions.

By way of analogy: I was in London, England, for a very long time, during which period my family remained in Nigeria. I was impressed and very excited to learn how my dear wife was coping with the children. Satisfied with her brilliant performance, I wrote to her, saying thankfully, 'You are my wife, my mother, my daughter, my friend.' By that, I was referring to the aspects of her personality, her character, her quality as a wife. I was not talking about four persons or four wives, but about one person, my dear wife.

If the concept of the Holy Trinity is viewed from a similar perspective, then the perplexing nature of the concept will dissolve and disappear, leaving behind the hard core of monotheism (one God) in the concept of the Holy Trinity. Otherwise, viewing the Holy Trinity as three Gods in one will, without circumspection, take us to polytheism, which, to the Christian religion and some other religions, is unacceptable for being spiritually unreal.

About the common saying or notion that the Christ was crucified: I contest that. I hold that the Christ was never and can never be crucified. Jesus (the flesh and blood that encased the Christ) was what was crucified.

I have, throughout *In Defence of Jesus the Christ*, been making an effort to distinguish Jesus (the human being, flesh and blood, the son of Joseph and Mary) from the Christ (the aspect of God, the love of God that manifested through Jesus, making him the Christ, Son of God, by faith). The Christ is beyond destruction, beyond crucifixion!

Approaching my view from another angle: God, as I said earlier, is not made up of separate or distinct entities (three Gods). It is not possible for God to be composed in that sense (three Gods in one) and still qualify as a necessary existence independent of anything else. That is to say, he would not in such a state be a prime mover, the Source of all things. A body whose parts depend on one another to exist, metaphysically, cannot be a prime mover, self-dependent. Therefore, to accept the concept of the Holy Trinity, one must think away the idea of the three Gods in one and take on the idea of one God with three manifest aspects that represent three cardinal functions of the one God. So, the three-Gods-in-one idea must be jettisoned in order to arrive at the *reality* that God is *one*.

We need to be cautious how we conceive of the Holy Trinity. If not, we will stray blindly into tritheism (three Gods).

According to Maimonides, 'If a thing is the composition of two items, and that composition is the indispensable cause of its existence as it is, then it is not of necessary existence in its essence, since its existence depends upon their being put together.'[16]

---

[16] Moses Maimonides, *The Guide of the Perplexed*, Book 11, 89.

Relying upon that truism by Maimonides, I contend that Christ as an aspect of God was not crucified and can never be crucified. I repeat: it was the body (Jesus) that housed the Christ that suffered the crucifixion and died. If the Christ, an aspect of God, were to have died, and since it takes three aspects of the Holy Trinity for God to function as God, then God would not be a necessary existence, since God could not be without the complete set of functions that make him God at the very time of the death of the Christ, an aspect of his function.

The Holy Trinity, I conclude, is about one God—not fewer, but more—to 'qualify as a necessary existence independent of anything' other than itself, 'a prime mover, a source of all things'.

Let's move on to another issue raised by Obianyido. According to him, 'Jesus Christ is called God's only begotten Son; at the other end he is said to be God in disguise. And he himself boasts that if one sees him, then one has seen his Father, and that one must go through him to God the Father. Yet when he was dying on the cross, he complained of being abandoned by God: "My God, my God, why has Thou forsaken me?" 'Who then has forsaken whom?' Obianyido wants to know.

For my reply to Obianyido's question, I need to first call back the explanation I previously gave concerning how Jesus became the special Son of God by faith. Then I explained how Jesus, a human being (flesh and blood), by his righteous conduct, rejected worldliness—the lusts and pleasures of the worldly person, the selfhood of the lower self— and totally embraced the heavenly spiritual things of the higher self that please God, to become the Christ, the special Son of God by faith. Basing my choice on that mystic transformation, I will go on to address the circumstances that concern Jesus as the only begotten Son of God and the matters of 'If one sees me, then one has seen his Father,' 'One must go through me to the Father,' and 'My God, my God, why has Thou forsaken me?' All those statements were made by Jesus the Christ.

Now, the circumstance that made Jesus the only Son, the special Son, of God by faith has earlier been explained. By the explanation, we realised that Jesus became the Christ, an aspect of God, in the likeness of God. Since by the explanation Jesus became an aspect of God, the likeness of God, one who sees him has seen the Father, and one must go through him, who is an aspect of God made manifest in the world, to communicate with God the Father.

Obianyido, relying on the Christian notion of the Holy Trinity as a form of three Gods—God the Father, God the Son, and God the Holy Ghost, 'each equal to one another'—wants to know why Jesus the Christ, as one of the Gods, when he was dying on the cross, complained of being abandoned by God—'My God, my God, why has thou forsaken me?'

First of all, let me reiterate that the Holy Trinity is not made up of three Gods; it is one God with three aspects (attributes, if you choose). Therefore, the idea of 'each equal to one another', as Obianyido has put it, does not arise. There is no other God besides that one God.

My readers may want to be reminded of my attempts in previous chapters to distinguish Jesus (as human) from the Christ (the Spirit of God, the aspect of God, or the special Son of God in a sense). I refer to Matthew. In Matthew, as well as in other gospels of the New Testament, all that Jesus said and did was most of the time said and done under his status as the Christ. In Matthew 26:41–42 we read, 'The spirit indeed is willing, but flesh is weak. Oh, my Father, if this cup may not pass away from me, except I drink it, thy will be done.' 'The spirit' in this context refers to the Christ in Jesus, the flesh, the body, within which the Spirit was encased. A human being, by nature, is dual—the flesh and the spirit. Given that arrangement, when Jesus said, 'My God, my God, why has Thou forsaken me?' it was Jesus, the weak flesh, the human being aspect of Jesus the Christ, who was complaining; the complaint was not by the Christ, the aspect of God, the Son of God, but by the human side of Jesus the Christ. When Jesus (the weak, the flesh) surrendered, asking that God's will be done in the circumstance, God's will was done.

I have, I hope, done enough to convince Obianyido and others who may be inclined to share his doubts.

CHRIST'S TEACHINGS

(CHAPTER 4, *CHRIST OR DEVIL?*)

OBIANYIDO: Nobody is sure what Jesus Christ taught. The accounts of his teachings given by his disciples upon which one is to rely are from a hearsay oral tradition. In many areas they vary and were designed to satisfy the community in such a way as it suited the writers.

Father Raymond E. Brown, a professor of theology, had this to say concerning Christ's teaching: 'The gospels offer only limited means for reconstructing the historical Jesus.'

REPLY: Anene Obianyido incorrectly assesses the gospels and maliciously rates the inspired writing of the gospels as 'hearsay oral tradition'. If the writers were the disciples of Jesus the Christ (and they were) who followed him about, then how could Obianyido grade their writings about their Master, Jesus the Christ, as hearsay? The writers, being the disciples, heard from the horse's mouth the things they later wrote down. Given such a circumstance, their writings are direct evidence and not hearsay. Obianyido is to take note.

There are no grounds for doubting that the teachings in the gospels were by Jesus the Christ. A meticulous study of the gospels reveals that this is so.

The teachings are unique and bear common characteristics that point to one person as their author. They stand tall, towering, in quality, above all other teachings in the Bible, in their scriptural and spiritual wisdom. They could not have preceded from the disciples of Jesus the Christ or from anyone else. The divine wisdom in them transcends the bounds of ordinary mortals; they bear the stamp of a fully enlightened spiritual master. Who else could be the source if not Jesus the Christ? Consider the allegories, the metaphors, the analogies, the aphorisms, the maxims, the dicta, and the parables in the gospels. They relate to one another, like siblings to each other, in style and quality. Observe that in all those teachings, compassionate love stands out as the linchpin that holds the lessons in the teachings together. No other name in the New Testament could lay claim to such teachings except the divine name of Jesus the Christ.

As if to air his view on the subject, the prolific and brilliant writer A. N. Wilson, a newspaper columnist, whose courtesy I hereby plead, writes in his book entitled *Jesus*, 'The words attributed to Jesus by the gospels are so remarkable that they deserve to be studied and memorised, whoever said them. Nor is complete scepticism about their authenticity entirely well placed. Taken as a whole, the teachings of Jesus, both in synoptic gospels and even, on occasion, in fourth gospel, have a distinctive manner which it is difficult to believe was concocted by the four evangelists—each of whom wrote for different times and place.'[17]

Wilson's opinion supports all I am struggling to say about the teachings in the gospels being those of Jesus the Christ. Even if Wilson's view is taken alone, it completely and successfully challenges Obianyido's negative view about what the four gospels present as the teachings of Jesus the Christ.

---

[17] A. N. Wilson, *Jesus*, 135.

Take this striking opinion, from Wilson once more: 'Taken as a whole the teachings of Jesus, both in synoptic gospels and even, on occasion, in fourth gospel, have a distinctive manner which it is difficult to believe was concocted by the four evangelists—each of who wrote for different times and place.' Obianyido disagrees. To him it is easy to believe or see that the teachings were concocted by the four evangelists who wrote the gospels. Obianyido thinks himself a polymath. You see!

Being a polymath, Obianyido feels he knows of all criticism of the gospels of the New Testament. He says, 'Nobody is sure of what Jesus actually taught.' To support his claim, he quotes Father Raymond E. Brown, thus calling him as a witness. Brown remarks, 'The gospels offer only limited means for reconstructing the historical Jesus.'

Unfortunately for Obianyido, he called a hostile witness. Father Raymond E. Brown's comment about the gospels' stories concerning Jesus the Christ is not in support of what Obianyido claims; in no way does Professor Brown's comment support Obianyido's assertion that 'nobody is sure what Jesus actually taught' and that 'his teachings given by his disciples upon which one is to rely are from hearsay oral tradition'. Brown's comment quoted by Obianyido recognises the teachings in the gospels as those of Jesus the Christ. Brown does not doubt the authenticity of the writers of the gospels. All that is meant by the professor's comment is that the information in the gospels about the historical Jesus is limited. It is not detailed or simple enough to make the history and the teachings of Jesus easily understood and interpreted in full. That being the professor's view, it follows then that Obianyido and the professor are not saying the same thing. They are not even talking about the same issue.

As to the professor's opinion, I am reluctant to go along with it in full. I believe that the information offered by the gospels about Jesus contains reasonable means for 'reconstructing the historical Jesus' though the information be not perspicuous. Yet with patience and perspicacity, one can capture the core meaning of the teaching. It is completely limited to certain people—hardcore, stubborn sinners. According to the Bible,

'Even if our gospel is veiled [i.e. limited], it is only to those who are perishing. In their case the god of this world has blinded them from seeing the light of the gospel of the glory of Christ, who is the likeness of God' (2 Corinthians 4:3–5).

Obianyido's view is that the gospels 'in many areas vary'. I agree. I believe that Obianyido worries about this issue because he has scanty knowledge of the gospels and very poor knowledge of human nature. If the gospels vary, that is not unexpected. The writers were separate individuals, and each, though inspired, wrote in his own peculiar fashion. No two (or more) reporters present the same event with the same detail and in the same fashion. Therefore, the gospels may differ slightly in style and substance. These are expected nuances. Yet the four gospel writers' stories are substantially the same in terms of content.

In summary, Obianyido's doubts as to what Jesus actually taught and the authenticity of the gospel writers, and his opinion that the gospels vary, cannot hold their places in the context of his larger argument.

OBIANYIDO: Jesus Christ was obsessed with hellfire and had unbridled passion for vengeance upon the unbelievers and sinners.

At various times he made the following statements:

(a) 'Ye serpent, ye generation of vipers, how can you escape the damnation of hell' (Matthew 23:33).
(b) 'Go ye into the world and preach the gospels to every creature. He that believeth and is baptised shall be saved; but he that believeth not shall be damned' (Mark 16:14–16).
(c) 'And whosoever shall speak a word against the son of man, it shall have forgiven him; but unto him that blasphemed against the Holy Ghost it shall not be forgiven' (Luke 12:10).
(d) 'If a man abides not in me, he is cast forth as a branch, and is withered; and men gather them into fire and they burned' (John 15:5–6).
(e) 'The wages of sin is death' (Romans 6:23).

(f) 'The son of man shall send forth his angels, and they shall gather out of his kingdom all things that offend and they which do iniquity, and shall cast them into a furnace of fire; and there shall be wailing and gnashing of teeth' (Matthew 24:50–51).

(g) 'Love thy neighbour as thyself' (Luke 10:27–28).

(h) 'Blessed are poor in spirit; for theirs is the Kingdom of Heaven' (Matthew 5:3–45).

(i) 'To those who have, more is given, and those who have not, even the ones they have will be taken from them' (Matthew 25:29–30).

(j) 'For you have the poor with you always. Do them good' (John 12:4–8).

By those sayings, Jesus Christ put cruelty in the world.

REPLY: Jesus the Christ was the greatest spiritual Master and teacher (and remains so today) who has ever lived. He was dynamic, lively, and unique in his style of teaching his gospel; he showed indomitable spirit in spreading the laws of God. Bravely, without mincing words, he taught the laws that govern the lives we live, no matter whom he was addressing. For this, he was viciously and intensely opposed by some leaders of the Jewish religion. Yet he did not flinch in his pursuit.

In order to lay emphasis on his points, he most of the time used the power of figures of speech—parables, similes, metaphors, allegories—to convey his spiritual messages. In very important and serious cases, his teachings were coated with hyperbole and strong words so as to make the teachings memorable and effective. By proceeding in that fashion, he meant no offence (*absit invi dia*). His only aim was to convince his addressees of the truth in his speech so as to get the audience to repent and follow the righteous path for their own spiritual benefit. So, though his language was sometimes strong, it was a true friend's admonition and reprimand. That fact notwithstanding, some of his addressees, the incorrigible wrongdoers, might have felt hurt.

As a prologue to my comments on Obianyido's complaints against the type of language employed by Jesus the Christ while he was talking to his addressees, I hereby quote two proverbs from the Holy Bible:

(a) 'Open rebuke is better than secret love' (Proverbs 27:5).
That was Jesus the Christ's attitude each time he reproached and counselled those he spoke to.

(b) 'Faithful are the wounds of friends; but the kisses of an enemy are deceitful' (Proverbs 27:6).
This means that open truth that hurts is better than hypocrisy, i.e. love on the surface but enmity beneath.

The wisdom in these two proverbs agrees with the manner taken by Jesus the Christ whenever he addressed wrongdoers.

I have, below, arranged the statements Obianyido ascribes to Jesus the Christ and complains about in alphabetical order. To each I have attached the relevant sections of the Bible for easy reference. Each of the statements is to be explained as briefly as possible. That will make them easy to understand.

My comments on the statements follow:

(a) *Serpents* and *vipers*
Each of these words stands for 'deceitful' and 'poisonous'. In the statement, *serpents* and *vipers* mean those who are deceitful, not straightforward in conduct, and not reliable, but wicked and dangerous.

(b) 'He that believeth' means that he (or she) who accepts and practises the truth given by Jesus the Christ 'shall be damned', meaning 'shall be blamed and punished'.

(c) 'The Son of Man' refers to Jesus as a human being (flesh and blood). 'The Holy Ghost' refers to an aspect of God (one of the three aspects of the Holy Trinity).

(d) 'Abides not in me'
The 'me' is the Christ, an aspect of God that manifested through Jesus. 'Abides not in me', then, means he who submits not to the Christ in Jesus, the still small whispering voice of the Christ, that teaches through Jesus by accepting the teachings and practising them.

'Cast forth as branch' means jettisoned from among the acceptable righteous lot for heaven so that one shall suffer severely.

(a) This was not by Jesus the Christ, anyway: 'The wages of sin is death.' *Death*, in this context, refers not to the death of the body (the flesh and blood), for everyone must die after all, but to the death of the soul, which God alone can make happen, for nonrepentant sinners.

(b) 'A furnace of fire' symbolises the enormity and intensity of the punishment against nonrepentant sinners.
The 'wailing and gnashing of teeth' symbolises the enormity of the punishment the nonrepentant sinners are to receive.

(c) The statement here teaches that God is in all human beings, and all human beings should be loved as the God we can see loves us. This shows that loving our fellow human beings is as good as loving God, whom we do not see.

(d) 'Poor in spirit' refers to those who are humble (not to those who suffer material poverty) and submissive to God in recognition of the fact that he alone has power and control over our fate. This means those who are not inclined towards self-pride, egotism, and vanity, but rely on God as the only Source of their needs.

(e) 'Those who have means those who receive the words of God and practise them, and benefit from them.'

The former group is industrious, making good use of the words, and as a result they benefit. The latter group receives not the words of God or else receives little but makes no good use of the words, therefore gaining no benefit.

In that situation, it would be wasteful to let the latter group keep what they make no use of. The much they have is better taken from the group and given to the former group, who are industrious and who can benefit from that which is gained.

With the parable of the talents, the 'Those who have means those who receive the words of God and practise them, and benefit from them' (Matthew 25:14–30) is clearly illustrated.

(f) The statement showing disapproval of those who do nothing to help the poor and desolate, who are with them always, but who pretend to have compassion for the poor.

I have diligently examined and explained the statements which Obianyido ascribes to and holds against Jesus the Christ. He reckons that by those statements, Jesus the Christ put cruelty into the world.

It is impossible, after we have assessed the explanations of the statements, to see how the statements could have put cruelty into the world. Jesus the Christ, by uttering these statements, was attempting to persuade the wrongdoers and the evildoers to abandon their evil ways and turn over a new leaf. That underpins his suggestion to the inveterate sinners that if they do not change from their sins to righteousness, if they take no care, then prostitutes and tax collectors (professional sinners) would transform from their sinful ways and enter the kingdom of God before them (Matthew 21:28–32)—because those classes of sinners were more ready to change to righteousness than Jesus's addressees were. In support of this fact, I give two instances from the Bible: Rahab the harlot (James 2:25) and Zacchaeus the tax collector (Luke 19:1–9), both of whom changed!

The book of Proverbs says, 'He that refuseth instruction despiseth his soul: but he that hears reproof getteth understanding' (Proverbs 15:32).

Obianyido conceives that those addressed with such hard language felt hurt and were annoyed. That, of course, is not unexpected from the foolish ones among them. 'It is a strange paradox that people are not at all vexed at having committed a fault, but very angry at being reproved for it,'[18] says A. C. Grayling.

Obianyido should think again given that remark!

OBIANYIDO: The church relies on the teachings of Jesus Christ to say that the poor should be satisfied with their poverty in the world in expectation of reward in heaven.

REPLY: Obianyido fails to mention what in the teachings of Jesus the Christ he considers the church to rely on when saying that 'the poor should be satisfied with their poverty in the world in expectation of reward in heaven'.

I have scanned the whole New Testament for the teachings of Jesus the Christ and have come up with the most likely teachings Obianyido had in mind when making his remark. They are as follows:

(a) Jesus the Christ's teachings on the beatitudes—'Blessed are the poor in spirit: for theirs is the kingdom of heaven' (Matthew 5:3).

(b) Jesus the Christ's parable of the rich man and Lazarus (the poor man)
On earth, Lazarus was a righteous but poor beggar who went to the rich man for help, but the rich man rejected him. Both died after all. The rich man went to hell, and the poor man, Lazarus, went to heaven.

---

[18] A. C. Grayling, *The Good Book* 15:15–16 (2011).

(c) Jesus the Christ's encounter with the rich young man who kept all the commandments of God but refused to obey Jesus the Christ's suggestion to sell all he had and give his gain to the poor so as to follow Jesus the Christ to gain entrance to the kingdom of heaven. Following the rich young man's refusal to sell his property and give the proceeds to the poor, Jesus the Christ made a comment, before his disciples: 'It is easier for a camel to go through the eye of a needle than for a rich man to enter into the kingdom of God' (Matthew 19:16–24).

(d) What Jesus the Christ said to a scribe, one of the teachers of religious law, who vowed to follow him: 'The foxes have holes, and the birds of air have nests; but the son of man [Jesus Christ] hath nowhere to lay his head' (Matthew 8:19–20). He wanted the scribe to know in advance the cost of following him—namely lack of material wealth.

Obianyido is too worldly and does not understand the teachings of the Holy Bible, which are spiritual. As a result, he misinterprets the teachings of Jesus the Christ offered by the Bible.

As I get on in my discussion, I hope to explore the ideas in each of the portions of the New Testament I have selected as (a), (b), (c), and (d), in an effort to give the subjects I am discussing the right interpretations.

When Jesus the Christ said, 'Blessed are the poor in spirit for theirs is the kingdom of heaven,' he was not referring to material poverty. To be poor in spirit means to be humble and nonegotistic in character, recognising that as an ordinary mortal, a human being, one has no authority over oneself or one's affairs. The only true and reliable Source of all in life is God. One, therefore, must be humble before God.

Obianyido views that the saying of Jesus the Christ means that material poverty is a means to heaven. By innuendo, his gossip suggests that Jesus the Christ encouraged laziness, which leads to poverty, as a means of gaining the kingdom of heaven. What a diabolical reconstruction of the reasonable teachings of Jesus the Christ by a confused, dirty mind! Jesus the Christ in no way taught what Obianyido implies, and no genuine Christian church, to my knowledge, teaches that.

At the same time, it is important to remark that, concerning worldly possessions, God is no respecter of persons in any form but treats the poor and the rich alike in accord with one's moral conduct.

Yes, it is true that Jesus the Christ gave the parable of the rich man and the poor man (Lazarus), where the poor man (Lazarus) went to heaven and the rich man went to hell (Luke 16:19–31). But then that was to illustrate the result of the type of moral life each—the poor man and the rich man—led on earth before dying. It shows the need for the rich to help the poor, one's fellow beings in want, while on earth (but not a fellow in want as a result of laziness). The parable was a lesson on moral conduct.

It is also true that on another occasion Jesus the Christ made a statement that appeared to condemn riches. After his encounter with a rich young man who refused to sell his possessions and give the proceeds to the poor before following him as he suggested, Jesus to his disciples, 'It is easier for a came to go through the eye of a needle than for a rich man to enter the kingdom of God.'

In the two preceding parables, the moral conduct of each of the actors concerned was the peg upon which Jesus the Christ hung his conclusion—his praise or reproach. Poverty and wealth have nothing to do with the determination of who goes to hell or who goes to heaven. 'One reaps what one sows,' says Paul in Galatians 6:7.

There is another teaching of Jesus the Christ, this on the periphery of richness (wealth) and poverty. When a scribe, a teacher of religious law, vowed to follow Jesus the Christ about, Jesus the Christ warned him, 'But the son of man has nowhere to lay his head.' In other words, he told him the cost of following him: to follow him, he had to be like him, focusing attention on the teaching and spreading of the gospel, having no divided attention between acquisition of riches and the spreading of the gospel at the same time. It is a matter not for wealth and not for poverty; it is simply making the spread of the spiritual gospel a focal point.

I have intently explored the main teachings of Jesus the Christ which Obianyido has messed about with. Imagine his assertion that some of the teachings of Jesus the Christ were to the effect that poverty gains one heaven. Has Obianyido got that right?

Whenever I consider Obianyido's interpretations of any portion of the Holy Bible, particularly where they concern the teachings of Jesus the Christ, the following questions line up at the end: Is Obianyido, by the way, intentionally twisting facts or innocently doing his very level best when he always gets his interpretations wrong? Or has his deep-rooted hatred for Jesus the Christ robbed him of his common sense? Otherwise, he should read and understand the simple teachings of Jesus the Christ. The saying 'Blessed are the poor in spirit for theirs is the kingdom of heaven' he translated to mean 'Blessed are the poor in *material wealth* for theirs is the kingdom of heaven.' You see that!

I consider that Obianyido sometimes thinks he is mad (or he pretends to be so), but I am certain he is not mad; he knows what he is doing. He deliberately circumvents facts and twists matters so as to get at a falsehood upon which to stand and accuse Jesus the Christ and Christianity. That is his stock-in-trade whenever he comments on Jesus the Christ and/or Christianity. That is outrageous!

I reiterate that the 'poor in spirit' in the context of the saying or teaching of Jesus the Christ refers not to material possession, worldly wealth, but to humility in one's conduct before God. At the same time, God is no respecter of persons or possessions; God treats the rich and the poor alike, in accord with one's moral conduct. And that is what Jesus the Christ taught. The contrary view, that Jesus the Christ taught that poverty is favoured and wealth is condemned by God, which Obianyido seeks to sell, is utter nonsense!

Christianity in no manner teaches or condones self-creation of poverty. Though it sympathises with the poor, it does not support poverty brought about by laziness (Matthew 25:1–30). Paul, one of the apostles of Jesus the Christ, was of that opinion when he said, 'He should not eat that does not work' (2 Thessalonians 3:10). That shows that Jesus the Christ, his Master, did not suggest that poverty was a licence for, or ticket to, heaven. When one is poor, heaven falls into his palm like a ripe fruit, and if one is rich, he is consigned to hell.

Heaven can be earned only through righteousness and God's grace. Hell is for the unrighteous. From where Obianyido tapped his blatant waffle baffles me!

This is remarkable: a good study of the teachings of Jesus the Christ yields the idea that he did not recommend postponement of material enjoyment until one is in heaven. What his teachings imply is that material wealth, or any worldly possession, should not be acquired by corruption or at the expense of justice or righteousness. Therefore, one, while on earth, is entitled to material possessions and enjoyment of them so long as those things are justly acquired and reasonably, piously, and morally shared with the less fortunate among one's fellows.

According to a book entitled *Is Revolution Change?*, Jesus Christ did not teach that expectation of future bliss must not give Christians permission to ignore present misery. He taught his followers about the life hereafter, where there will be no sin and the Father's will, will be done, but he also taught them to pray to the Father: 'Your will be done on earth as it is in heaven.' He preached to them of the bread of life which never perishes, but he would not dream of sending the crowd away when they were hungry until they had been fed with ordinary perishable earthly bread. He preached life eternal, but he also restored life on earth to the widow's son, to the centurion's daughter, and to Mary and Martha's brother, Lazarus.[19]

It is common knowledge that wealth, wine, fame, and power each intoxicates its possessor and propels the possessor to all sorts of

---

[19] Brian Griffiths, ed., *Is Revolution Change?*, 34.

unrighteous behaviour. Paul the apostle says, 'For the love of money is the root of all evil' (1 Timothy 6:10).

Because of the evil side of money (wealth, fame, power, and other worldly lusts), Jesus the Christ warned those deep in material trappings of the world against the temptations generally associated with possession or pursuit of such things. He demonstrated his caution in matters of worldly lust when, during his famous period of temptation, he rejected them (Matthew 4:1–11).

The parable of the prodigal son is about a son who took a wrong decision just for his love for wealth (Luke 15:11–24).

The parable of the rich man and the poor man, Lazarus, is about a rich man who, for love of money, denied help to a poor man (Luke 16:19–31).

Then there is the story about the rich man who, for love of wealth, declined the invitation of Jesus the Christ to follow him in spreading the gospel of the kingdom of God (Matthew 19:16–24).

Judas Iscariot, for love of money, betrayed his Master, an innocent man (Matthew 26:14–16). Ananias and his wife, Sapphira, committed fraud as a result of love of money (Acts 5:1–10).

The foregoing Bible stories show how the lust for or possession of wealth, fame, and/or power can incline one's conduct to evil. Jesus the Christ's warning against going after wealth without caution is, therefore, in order and makes moral sense. It does in no way indicate support for poverty.

Where one righteously and justly acquires wealth or power and treads the path of righteousness and justice in the use of said wealth or power, of course, the kingdom of God is within one's grasp by the grace of God. That is precisely the teaching of Jesus the Christ. And that means that Christianity never considers reliance on laziness or poverty as a form of insurance against hell, or as an assurance of heaven, nor does Christianity see mere possession of wealth with no unrighteousness associated with it as assurance of hell. Whatever one's social or economic status, what matters in terms of going to hell or heaven is one's moral conduct supported by God's grace.

As the Holy Bible witnesses, Jesus the Christ associated with the poor who were interested in his teachings. He also had good rapport with the rich who were good and struggled to become righteous, for example Joseph Arimathea (Matthew 27:57–60) and Nicodemus (John 3:1–21).

At this time, I want to look into Obianyido's fictitious story about his so-called porter, R. B.

The story has it that the porter stated that when he dies, he will go to heaven and sit in the royal chair of God for being poor, while the rich will be in hell. I have, to a large extent, already discussed the subject of the rich man and the poor man as regards heaven and hell. I need not add to that.

For making up the story, Obianyido is simply impish. He carelessly makes a derisive joke of the teachings of Jesus the Christ. No doubt, he invented the story as a bit of mordant humour to ridicule Christianity. Neither openly nor by implication do Christian teachings contain the childish information in Obianyido's fabricated story.

The fantasy of the story deserves no more than the brief time and the tiny space I have allowed it. The story is a gag that is better reserved for fools and simpletons to gobble.

CHRISTIANS

(CHAPTER 5, *CHRIST OR DEVIL?*)

OBIANYIDO: By 'Christians', I suppose one is referring to all those who follow the teachings of Christ and Christianity in its wide variety of interpretations and who believe that he is the Son of God. They range from the first group of converts, to the modern groups of organised Christianity, to minor denominations of the same faith, including those whom Kenneth Woodward referred to as 'Jesus freaks—the curious religious sect of children of drug culture'.

REPLY: The heading of this chapter of *In Defence of Jesus the Christ* is 'Christians'. That is also the heading of Chapter 5 of Anene Obianyido's book *Christ or Devil?*

Obianyido opens the chapter with his definition of Christians, which definition is an obvious instance of journalistic obscurantism. It is a mixed bag designed to misdirect people as to the true meaning of the word *Christians*. He deliberately improperly defines the word to serve as a basis for his attacks against Jesus the Christ, Christianity, and God. In other words, he has a hidden agenda by providing this definition.

By his definition, he turned Christians into all sorts of characters—good and bad. His definition has no particular content, no exactitude that makes it a reality. In his treacherous manner, he intends to blindfold his readers and lead them into a labyrinth where they can find no other way than to follow his misguided criticism of Christianity.

The correct definition of *Christians* is very fundamental in the contest between his book *Christ or Devil?* and mine, *In Defence of Jesus the Christ*. If the definition goes wrong, then the whole contest will become useless. Therefore, the definition must be seen to be, as far as possible, correct. For that reason, I intend to give a reasonable measure of time and space to finding the right definition.

I trust my readers, by exercise of patience and tolerance, will grant me permission to take them along on what is likely to be a long, boring journey in my effort to arrive at the correct definition of *Christians*.

I begin the journey with questions: Is the word *Christians* elusive to definition? Does it defy definition to nudge Obianyido into the use of the expression 'I suppose' in his definition of Christians? My immediate answer to both questions is 'Not at all'. I therefore reiterate the point I earlier made: the features of Obianyido's definition point vividly to a mischievous lexical adventure calculated to misdirect attention from knowledge or fact. The fact is that a thing cannot be what it is not by insertion of the phrase 'I suppose' into its definition. Under pretence of ignorance, Obianyido attempts to give the word *Christians* a new meaning, an extended dimension that is odd and bizarre as compared to the real meaning. He smuggles strange characters into the definition of *Christians*. No knowledgeable and reasonable person, I am sure, is prepared to accept that his dubious 'neologism' with nonsensical meaning is referring to the word *Christians*.

As is observable in his definition, Obianyido uses the phrase 'I suppose' and invokes the view of Kenneth Woodward where Woodward describes 'Jesus freaks' as including 'the curious religious sect of children of drug culture' as a supplement to Obianyido's definition. I pause and ask, does

Obianyido understand what Woodward was talking about when he used the words *freaks* (meaning unusual, odd) and *curious* (meaning strange) in his statement? He seems not to understand. What an ignoramus!

The *Collins Cobuild Dictionary of the English Language* defines a freak as 'someone who is considered unusual, because of their behaviour or attitude, used showing disapproval'. The *Penguin A–Z Thesaurus Dictionary* gives the meaning of *freak* as 'abnormality, oddity, malformation, deformity'. The two dictionaries see the word *freak* to mean 'at odds with reality'.

Woodward's expression, therefore, is not about Jesus in fact (or Christians in fact). So, there is no meeting of minds between Obianyido and Woodward on the subject of 'Jesus freaks—the curious religious sect of children of drug culture'. Woodward's expression means that 'Jesus freaks—the curious religious sect of children of drug culture' are not true Christians. Obianyido's expression says they are. You see that!

Yet, Obianyido hijacked Woodward's expression 'Jesus freaks—the curious religious sects of children of drug culture' and maliciously, under pretence of ignorance, smuggled it into his personal definition of *Christians*. Having done that, he wants his readers to accept that Christians are the children of drug culture. With his claim to knowledge, he misunderstands Woodward, or he is simply daft. His ignorance has kept the actual meaning of the words *freak* and *curious* away from him. He has put the word *Christians* in a wrong mould. That is an absurd etymology, an intentional abuse of the word *Christians*, a grumpy, cynical ploy done *malo animo* (with evil intent). What a lexical dud of a definition!

Again, I humbly request my readers to bear with me; I am not yet ready to let go my stranglehold on Obianyido on the very matter of the right definition of *Christians*. All through this chapter and beyond, where need be, the correct meaning of the word *Christians* will be shown or highlighted. The contest must continue between Obianyido's 'inclusiveness' and my 'exclusiveness' on the matter of the definition of *Christians*.

How 'inclusiveness'? Because Obianyido seeks to include all evildoers masquerading as Christians in the definition of *Christian*. Exclusiveness? Because I contend that such evildoers who pass themselves off as Christians are to be excluded from the definition of *Christians* since they possess not the prerequisite character or qualities to make them Christians.

By including any rubbish characters in his definition of Christians, Obianyido can find something about Christianity or Jesus the Christ to attack. That is his lexical game, a frolic, a personal lexicographic adventure created on purpose to gain an advantage over genuine Christianity. To cover up his bias and prejudice against Jesus the Christ and Christianity, he employs the expression 'I suppose', i.e. 'I guess,' 'I'm not sure.' What bad faith!

Take the other arm of his definition of *Christians*; he uses the expression 'wide variety of interpretations'. He says, 'By "Christians", I suppose one is referring to all those who follow the teachings of Christ and Christianity in its wide variety of interpretations.' That idea gives his definition a wide-open door that is to admit characters of all sorts of behaviour as Christians. I liken it to making a jacket that fits all sizes and shapes—no discrimination between good and bad.

Once a thing has 'a wide variety of interpretations', it ceases to have a specific meaning; it acquires as many meanings and uses as there are interpretations derivable therefrom. The correct meaning of a word is determinable only within the context and amid the circumstance in which the word occurs. The word must have one meaning if it is to make the required sense. I ask, in the religious context, what is the particular meaning of the word *Christians*?

For the correct meaning of *Christians*, we put that question to any English-language dictionary of words and phrases. The *English Oxford Dictionary of Words* is at this juncture consulted. It defines a Christian as 'a person believing in, or professing, or belonging to religion of Christ and following his teachings'. The same question is put to *Doctor Ogilvie's English Dictionary*, which says of a Christian, 'one who professes the religion and doctrine taught by Jesus Christ and his church, and who adheres to the code of conduct enjoined by them'. The *New Practical Standard Dictionary of English Language* defines a Christian as 'manifesting the spirit of Christ or his teachings'. As an adjective, *Christian* stands for 'humble, civilised, charitable, humane'. Those dictionaries all say the same thing, but in diverse ways. It then emerges that the dictionaries' correct definition of *Christians* sharply contrasts with Obianyido's definition.

From one of his lectures, it is evident that Professor W. Barclay agrees with the meaning of the word *Christian* provided in the dictionaries I consulted. The professor says, 'For a man cannot be a Christian and flatly contradict the teaching of Jesus Christ.'[20]

If we accept the meaning of *Christian* as furnished above by the dictionaries and the professor (of course we have to), then it follows that all those evil characters—'the curious religious sect of children of drug culture' Obianyido squeezed into the meaning of *Christians*—must be flushed out in order to get to the correct meaning of the word *Christians*, since those characters contradict Christ's teaching.

It may be a carefree practice that has gained currency to refer to all who falsely and wrongly pass themselves off as Christians as such as 'Christians in fact'. But that is as far as a word or name goes. It makes sense that Woodward used the word *freak* to distinguish fake Christians from genuine ones.

A thing is what it is by its essence, quality, or attributes and the characteristics that the thing possesses, not by the word or name the thing calls itself, nor by that given it by someone else. As if bearing that in mind, William Shakespeare wrote, 'What is in a name? That which we call a rose by any other name would smell as sweet.'

---

[20] William Barclay, *Persuasive Society* (1971), 208.

There must be a clear distinction (discrimination) between something freakish (fake, counterfeit, spurious, strange), on the one hand, and something real, genuine, on the other. Otherwise, the use of the same word or name for both is nothing but making a mockery of fact. Ponder this view: 'Discrimination is a prerequisite on the path of spirituality. It distinguishes between truth and untruth. ... It is a quality by which one can realise the nature of a thing correctly. It produces detachment.'[21]

This juncture is appropriate for the use of one of Aristotle's principles with regard to philosophical logic—a simple one:

First premise. A Christian is one who accepts the teachings of Jesus the Christ and practises them.

Second premise. William A. Barclay accepts the teachings of Jesus the Christ but does not practise them.

Conclusion: William A. Barclay is not a Christian.

Third premise. William A. Barclay accepts the teachings of Jesus the Christ and practises them.

I therefore hold that any person (or group of persons) who believes in Jesus the Christ and accepts his teachings but fails to put them in practice should not rightly be called a Christian. If one is a regular churchgoer, then call him or her a churchgoer. Simple. The practice of the accepted Christian teachings is the last and most important piece of the jigsaw puzzle of who is a Christian.

These days the word *Christian* is so commonly and rapidly used that it has become a cliché. Every churchgoer is called a Christian. Yet, when the true meaning of the word *Christian* is in question, as in our present argument, the dross around the word must be beaten off so as to get to the very core meaning. If that reasonable technique is applied in our search of the correct definition of the word *Christians*, then it will

---

[21] Huzur Maharaj Sawan J, *Philosophy of the Masters* (1964), 243.

certainly follow that Obianyido's definition of *Christians* is incontestably wrong.

OBIANYIDO: The Roman Catholic Church, the Methodist Church, the Presbyterian Church, and so on, each has its own interpretation of the teaching of Jesus Christ, and claims superiority over the other.

REPLY: Different churches or denominations claiming to be Christian churches may be at one another's throats, but so what?

First and foremost, we need to find out whether, by the correct definition of *Christian*, they (or any of them) are rightly called Christian churches. Do they (or any of them) possess what it takes to be a true Christian church? That is the pertinent question. Those that go by the name of a Christian church but lack the quality of genuine Christianity are fake Christians—they are not Christian churches, strictly speaking. They are Christian churches in name only. Therefore, whatever wrongs they commit have nothing to do with Jesus the Christ or true Christianity. 'By their fruits you shall know them' (Matthew 7:15–23). For that matter, Jesus the Christ warned, 'Beware of false prophets which come to you in sheep's clothing, but inwardly they are wolves' (Matthew 7:15); 'False teachers will arise and say here is Christ, there is Christ, do not listen to them, they deceive' (Matthew 24:23–26).

In the same vein, even if sectarianism, differences in denomination, acrimony, and schism exist among present-day Christian churches, this does not cancel out the fact of the proficiency of true Christianity in promoting moral and social values taught by Jesus the Christ concerning the kingdom of God.

OBIANYIDO: Faith healing is one of those techniques now enjoying a boom in my area. There are examples of such faith healings, among whom is a middle-aged woman, a local farmer's wife, in my community.

She cures the sick and, as a result, pulls a multitude of people sick of various diseases.

Jesus's healing technique is not different from that of the woman. Jesus relied on faith healing and the magic he performed among a backward peasant community. And these are what Christians call miracles. Healing by magic, he feigned to be a superhuman with mastery over natural forces and objects—a display of witchery!

REPLY: There is no denying that some people attempt to heal the sick by means of magic and witchery. But then, in the end, that sort of healing turns out to be illusory, a sham healing. On some occasions, one witnesses resemblance of healings after a pretentious healing performance by such so-called healers, i.e. the healing happens to be an incident waiting to happen, a chance event that has nothing to do with the theatrical display by the so-called healer. Such a healing is a mere coincidence which I like to call a fortuitous healing. It is Nature that heals without any external help when she repairs damaged parts of the human body.

In some cases, some semblance of healing occurs when smart quacks manipulate the sick, induce mental gymnastics in them, or overpower them with hypnotism to stimulate their minds and give them a false feeling of having been healed. Sooner or later, that feeling dies away and the person is reduced, once more, to his or her former unhealthy condition. The healings by Jesus the Christ were unlike the hypnotic healings by fake healers. The healings by Jesus the Christ were real, instant, certain, and permanent because they, unlike the hypnotic ones, had their source in God, the Beginning and the End of all things.

Obianyido accuses Jesus the Christ of healing by the power of magic and witchcraft. What a sacrilegious view, a defamation of the divine personality of Jesus the Christ. That is nothing less than blatant blasphemy! Jesus the Christ healed by the power of God, and he proved that beyond any doubt. The Holy Bible has that fact. For example, during Jesus's encounter with the Pharisees and the priests of the Jewish religion, they asked him by what power he performed his healings and other miracles, suggesting it was by the power of Beelzebub, the prince of demons, just as Obianyido is today accusing Jesus of. Jesus the Christ replied, 'Every kingdom divided against itself is laid to waste' and 'No city or house divided against itself will stand; if Satan casts out Satan, he is divided against itself, how then can the Kingdom stand?' (Matthew 12:22–29). On another occasion, the chief priests and the elders of the Jewish religion asked Jesus by what authority he was doing his deeds. He asked them from where John the Baptist had gotten his authority to baptise, from human beings or from heaven? They replied that they did not know. The reason they did not answer that question in the affirmative is that they well recognised John the Baptist as a prophet from heaven, and in turn John the Baptist recognised Jesus the Christ as higher than him spiritually (Matthew 12:23–29).

The two foregoing instances show that Jesus the Christ healed by the power of God, not by magic, witchcraft, or the power of Satan. So Obianyido is daft.

All through his ministry, Jesus the Christ made no secret of his strong opposition to evil powers of Satan and witchery. During his forty days and forty nights of fasting and enduring temptations in the wilderness, he demonstrated his total hatred for and rejection of Satan (Matthew 4:10). The two, Satan and Jesus the Christ, are like darkness and light, respectively. They do not agree; the enmity between them is well defined.

A member of a satanic cult, Sean Setter, who killed his mother and his stepfather, recognised the deep divide between Christianity and satanism and, realising he was in the wrong camp when he committed his offences, pleaded that he would renounce Satan to become a born-again Christian.[22] That further highlights the unlimited difference between Satan and Jesus the Christ—whatever Obianyido takes Satan to mean.

---

[22] *Murder Casebook*, no. 60 (1990).

OBIANYIDO: Faith-healing technique is not the exclusive preserve of Christ; improved education has now shown that faith healing is not a miracle. Modern science or psychology has now shown that healing power is in the mind. Christ exploited that power. Given absolute faith and the right psychological technique, the law of suggestion can trigger the type of physical reaction that can result in a cure. It is all in the mind.

REPLY: Obianyido speaks of faith healing as if it is his discovery or invention, then he uses it to reduce the healings by Jesus the Christ to simple, common acts. If faith healing is not a miracle, then what is?

Faith could be an ingredient in healing, of course, but just an ingredient. Everyone who has read the Holy Bible (the New Testament) should know that. 'What is obvious needs no proof,' say those white wigs in the hall of contention. No one, therefore, wants Obianyido's lecture on faith healing.

The Holy Bible contains many instances of healings that had to do with faith. Let me refresh Obianyido's memory: 'And when Jesus saw their faith, he said, "My son your sins are forgiven. ... Arise, and take up thy bed, and walk." ... And immediately he arose, took up his bed and went' (Mark 2:5–12). That was a faith healing. In Matthew, Jesus the Christ says to the woman suffering from haemorrhage, 'Take heart, daughter, your faith has made you well' (Matthew 9:20–21). That involved faith. That faith as an ingredient of healing goes on and on, the Holy Bible reports.

The crucial question that arises and lingers on, after all, concerning faith healing is one that may be asked by logicians and philosophers: 'Faith in what?' Jesus the Christ healed by faith in God. That was very lucidly proved at the time of Jesus the Christ's encounter with the priests and Pharisees.

With the measure of education Obianyido claims to have, together with his claim to be knowledgeable in healing techniques, he is unable to tell his readers why he cannot heal at all. Or is he an ostrich, a bird with beautiful feathered wings that cannot fly?

In his community (which he is fond of mentioning without naming it) particularly, in his immediate family, there must be people very close and dear to him who, before the time he wrote his book and thereafter, have been writhing with trauma in the face of the ravages of disease and sickness, some of which are chronic, yet he cannot boast of being able to give them their most desired quest, that is good health, through the faith-healing technique he claims to have knowledge of. He claims proficiency in healing and can recite faith-healing and mind-power techniques but cannot go farther to put them into practice or use. 'Faith-healing technique is not the exclusive preserve of Jesus Christ,' he garbles. Is he excluded from healing by using that technique? Or does he simply know the 'chemistry' of the techniques of faith healing and of the healing power of the mind, not knowing how to make these things work? Or does he lack 'improved education'? According to him, with improved education, one can heal. Or is he able to make the healing techniques work but, wickedly, does not want to do so? Most unlikely. He is hereby reminded that any faith-healing technique that does not work is dead (James 2:17, 20). Also, 'Action is the proper fruit of knowledge.' Obianyido is unable to put his knowledge of healing techniques into practice, yet his vanity, his full-blown pride in the knowledge of healing techniques, does not allow him the civility and humility to give due credit to Jesus the Christ for being able to make faith work.

About his knowledge of healing by the power of the mind, Obianyido says, 'Modern science or psychology has now shown us the enormity of power in the mind' and 'The so-called miracle on which Christ built both his reputation and church resulted from natural exploitation of the power of human mind' (page 57 of *Christ or Devil?*). What a hypothesis by an empty bag that cannot stand! What knowledge Obianyido claims to have, he is unable to put into use.

By the way, lest I forget, he derogatorily refers to Jesus the Christ and his disciples as lacking in civility. This time he tells us, 'Modern science and technology have now shown that healing power is in the mind.' It follows that modern civilisation is, of late, awaking to the knowledge Jesus the Christ and his disciples, whom Obianyido considers uncivilised, had and practised more than two thousand years ago. Strange, the logic in this reasoning! See page 67 of *Christ or Devil?*, where Obianyido balloons his pride and ego out of all proportion: 'When I was part of the ignorant majority.' That means he is now part of the educated, knowledgeable minority among his community; he is now Mr Know-all, a charlatan. Yet his book *Christ or Devil?* exposes him as an armchair reciter of acquired knowledge who, like a tape recorder, simply repeats what is given him by the books of science and psychology on quack healing techniques, like a parrot that repeats what is given it by the owner. Does Obianyido not sound, at best, as if he is using his master's voice? Disgusting.

After his claim to have knowledge of healing techniques, he remains inept, unable to put the knowledge into practical use. The dictum of Francis Bacon is spot on here: 'Knowledge is to be put into action. It is not a couch or tower, but as a rich storehouse for the glory of the Creator, and for the relief of man's estate.'

'What determines a worthy and gallant personality is one's ability to put into practice what one claims to possess knowledge of' is a saying of the Igbo tribe of Nigeria. In Igbo, it reads as follows: 'Ife ekwu na onu emelu naka, kaeji ama dike.' You'll find this is a favourite of Oliver De Coque, on one of his albums, *The Tenth Anniversary of the People's Club, Nigeria.*

Allow this repetition, please: no sick or ill person, particularly in Obianyido's family, is interested in his recitation of healing techniques when he cannot perform healings. All that the sick or ill want from him is his ability to deliver the goods, i.e. to be healed by him with his so-called healing techniques, so they can break away from the festering traumatic condition of their health. They want application of his knowledge, not an abstract notion of it. Therefore, he should act with dispatch to that end or forever hold his peace and break his pen.

Obianyido prattles on about healing by faith and the 'healing power in the mind' without understanding it himself. Consider just a few of his empty viewpoints about the healing power of Jesus the Christ. According to him, 'Jesus the Christ relied on faith healing and magic performed among a backward peasant community. And these are what the Christians call miracles.' Earlier we saw that Jesus the Christ did not rely on magic or any power other than God's for whatever he did, including healings (Matthew 12:22–29, 21:23–27; Mark 11:27–33; Luke 11:14–24).

Obianyido claims to know what *miracle* means, but he is not able to define it. He knows only what a miracle is not. It therefore seems to me that he knows more than his head can contain.

From time to time in *Christ or Devil?*, he makes up stories. This time he has faked a story that a middle-aged woman, a local farmer's wife in his community, was performing a faith healing and pulling a crowd. Yet, he fails to give the name of his community, the name of the woman (the healer), or the name of the woman's husband, and he fails to let his reader know what sicknesses the woman heals or has healed, because his story is faked. It was made up to deceive and convince his readers!

He talks about faith healing and about the healing power in the mind, but we are not told which party possesses the faith, either the healed or the healer. What of when Jesus the Christ raised the dead? Whose faith made the rising from the dead happen, the corpse's or Jesus's? Similar questions can be asked in the case of the healing power of the mind. Whose mind, that of the one who is healed, or the healer's?

I think Obianyido should shut up, keep away from things he knows nothing about, and make do with the little knowledge he has. Dabbling in faith healing and in healing by the power of the mind, Obianyido overreaches for sure!

By comparing the healing by the local farmer's wife and the healing by Jesus the Christ, Obianyido messes himself up. The foregoing analysis of the fake healings by healers such as the local farmer's wife shows that the healing by the woman does not compare with that by Jesus the Christ. Jesus Christ's healings are beyond compare—they were from God!

OBIANYIDO: Following the profile of the Christian religion, starting from Christ and Paul, the followers of Jesus Christ were most despised and hated of all religions. The reasons were their usual secrecy, their aggressive attitude to both Roman authority and other cults, their lack of civilisation, their foreign outlook, and their low social status.

REPLY: Obianyido's view is that the followers of Jesus the Christ were the most despised and hated of the followers of any other religion, but he fails to mention any of those religions. So, he deprives his readers the opportunity of determining the credibility of his opinion. His conclusion is therefore nonsensical. In my view, Jesus the Christ and his followers were the most loved in the past, during their era, and are the most loved in the present generation. And I can safely predict that they will be the most loved of generations to come.

The fact that a multitude of people followed them and thronged them in their day remains as clear and irrefutable evidence of the people's love for them. In the gospel of Matthew (as well as in other gospels), we read of the gathering of the crowd around them to be healed by, and listen to, Jesus the Christ so as to receive the benefits of his teachings and his healing (Matthew 9:36–38). Could such beneficiaries have hated them? The gospel of Mark has it that the multitude so happily gathered around Jesus the Christ and his disciples that they had no chance to have their meal (Mark 3:9). The scene of the triumphal entry of Jesus the Christ into Jerusalem was remarkable. It saw all types of people teeming, laying branches of trees, and some their garments, on the path taken by Jesus the Christ and his disciples into Jerusalem. Though some went to be healed, and some went to listen to his wise teachings, and some thought him to be a ruler come to liberate them (the Jews) from the Roman authority and defend them against their aggressive neighbours, it was love for Jesus the Christ that attracted most of the crowd (Matthew 21:8–11). Children even took part in the festive moment, singing Hosanna to

Jesus the Christ and his disciples (Mark 18:2; 19:13–15). When the chief priest and the Pharisees sought to arrest him (Jesus the Christ), they feared the multitude, because the multitude held Jesus the Christ to be a prophet (Matthew 21:45–46).

The scribes and the chief priests took counsel to determine how to seize Jesus the Christ and kill him, but considered, 'Not at the festival in order that no uproar may arise among the people [who love him]' (Matthew 26:3–5). 'When Jesus the Christ got back, the crowd received him kindly, for they were all expecting him' (Luke 8:40). Here weighs the adverb *kindly*. Is this a sign that Jesus the Christ and his disciples 'were the most despised and hated'? Let Obianyido answer that question.

All the instances I have just given concerning the issue that the followers of Jesus Christ were the most despised and most hated of all religions, according to Obianyido, demonstrate the deep and profound love the people of Jesus Christ's era had for him, his disciples, and their religion.

Of course, the love was not by any means 100 per cent; it could not have been so. A very insignificant number of people, unreasonable though influential, disliked them: some of the Pharisees, some scribes, and those among the Jewish priests and elders who initially thought Jesus the Christ was a political leader but discovered that he was a spiritual leader instead, who was asking them to repent of their sins. In that circumstance, they became bitterly disappointed at his goal.

We have now established, beyond all reasonable doubt, that only a negligible portion of the people in the time of Jesus the Christ hated him, his disciples, and their religion. Inquisitively, I ask, besides the disappointment of those who initially believed that Jesus the Christ would be a political leader, what other possible reason could anyone have had for hating him?

The reasons are not far-fetched. They can easily be extracted from the biblical history of the life of Jesus the Christ. They vary, but combine to produce hatred. The reasons are as follows:

(a) Ignorance

The people who hated Jesus the Christ were those who were unable to understand the benefit of his teachings. For example, Paul (formerly known as Saul of Tarsus) persecuted Jesus the Christ out of ignorance. Later, when he came to understand the benefits of the mission of Jesus the Christ, he converted and joined him (Acts 9:3–18; Romans 10:2; 1 Timothy 1:12–13).

(b) Envy

As a result of the popularity of Jesus the Christ among the common people of his time, his persecutors were looked down upon. They became unhappy and said, 'The world has gone after him' (John 12:19).

The multitude following the apostles of Jesus the Christ around roused the envy of the Jews, who got involved in hating Christianity (Acts 13:45–50).

(c) The truth

The truth which Jesus the Christ taught was diametrically against the wrong and ungodly traditions, teachings, and practices of some Jews. That gave rise to the hatred these Jews had for Jesus the Christ, his disciples, and their religion. A Roman proverb goes, 'Varitas odium parit' (Truth breeds hatred).

Despite this hatred, the love that the overwhelming majority of the people of that era had for Jesus the Christ, his disciples, and Christianity prevailed and paced on.

Strikingly, that love marched on, fast and steadily, from that generation to our present one. Today, those who despise and hate Jesus the Christ and Christianity are only confused atheists, among whom are Obianyido and his atheist friends. Their numbers are very negligible and are therefore inconsequential as far as Christianity is concerned. However, efforts are being made to convert these atheists as Paul the apostle was converted.

How hard it is today to find any part of the world where the name of Jesus the Christ is not a byword for spiritual and moral matters; the name has become a household one, a loving and admiring echo of a long-gone age. I surmise, of those who love Jesus the Christ, that the enormity and intensity of their love prompted Obianyido's question in his book, 'Who is this man, Jesus Christ, who has harassed the human soul for so long?'

This is my guess: the human souls being harassed are only those of the sinners who are very deep in wrongdoing and want a change but find it hard to change course.

These days we (Obianyido included) are witnessing an explosion in the number of those professing Christianity, be the Christian churches perfect or weak. The fact remains that almost all those after Christianity sincerely believe in it. Though some may find the practice difficult, they constantly struggle to improve their moral conduct along the lines laid down by Jesus the Christ.

Christian churches sprout up here and there in the world. In Nigeria, the country from which Obianyido hails, the towns and villages are swarming with people who have an interest in Christianity. Is this a sign of hatred for Jesus the Christ, his disciples, and their religion?

Let me make allowance for the fact that some of those who found Christian churches these days are after personal wealth, as this is undeniable, and not unexpected in our evil world. Still, most of the followers of these churches are concerned with their personal interest in Christianity and their love for Jesus the Christ.

After making his thoughtless assertion that 'Jesus Christ, his disciples, and their religion were most despised and hated of all religions', Obianyido gives five grounds upon which he relies for the assertion. The grounds are (a) the usual secrecy of Jesus and his disciples, (b) their aggressive attitude, (c) their lack of civilisation, (d) their foreign outlook, and (e) their low social status.

Let us consider those grounds one after the other, following the order in which I have set them out:

(a) The usual secrecy of Jesus and his disciples

Obianyido should have given at least one example of what he means. Throughout his ministry, Jesus the Christ did not teach secrecy, nor did he suggest the practice of it. He taught that 'one could not light a candle and put it under the table, but on it, so that all could make use of the light' (Luke 8:16–17). That idea opposes secrecy. He taught, 'What I told you in dark, utter in the light, what you hear whispered, proclaim upon the house top' (Matthew 10:27).

Are such instructions those of people who engage in their 'usual secrecy'?

(b) Their aggressive attitude

(c) Again, Obianyido fails to specify the aggressive attitude towards both Roman authority and cults. What does that mean? When and how were Jesus and his disciples aggressive towards Roman authorities? We are not told. And what does he mean by 'other cults'? Could he not have named them so as to be specific? My guess is that he is referring to the Pharisees, the chief priests, and the elders among the Jews. The aggressive attitude Obianyido mentions refers to the reaction of Jesus the Christ to the traders, robbers, and money changers he challenged in and around the temple during his triumphal entry into Jerusalem.

In that case, the group of people Obianyido sees as victims of aggression by Jesus the Christ, besides being insignificant, was made up of sinners, wrongdoers. Jesus the Christ, being a bespoke teacher, gave them a befitting dressing-down. That was, of course, to correct their wrongs in their own interest. The overwhelming majority of the people addressed at the time of the incident were unaffected and enjoyed the truth and the benefits which Jesus the Christ offered them.

(d) Their lack of civilisation

Let us not forget Obianyido's view mentioned earlier, that 'modern science and psychology have now shown that healing power is in the mind'. This is about what Jesus the Christ and his disciples demonstrated more than two thousand years earlier, well ahead of modern science and psychology, if we're talking of civilisation. Yet Obianyido describes Jesus the Christ and his disciples as lacking in civility.

Also, I refer to the dictionary description of Christians as 'civilised'. This has previously been discussed and needs no further treatment here.

Well, it depends on what Obianyido means by his expression 'lack of civilisation'. Admittedly, Jesus the Christ and his disciples did not invent anything scientific or technological, if that is what civilisation means to Obianyido. Yet, their teachings and their social behaviour were patterned on the highest moral conduct. And right moral conduct is the highest and most important aspect of the hallmark of civilisation. The past generation (that of Jesus the Christ's era) needed that, and the present generation needs that. Until the evils in the world end, the need for right moral conduct, which Jesus the Christ and his disciples taught, will not end. Therefore, Jesus the Christ and his disciples built a model civilisation that is to last until the end of time.

Scientific and technological advancements were outside the scope of the mission of Jesus the Christ and his disciples. Therefore, they offered nothing directly in way of those fields. They were on a spiritual campaign of incorporating right moral conduct for eternal life, not after transient material things of the world.

It would be tragic for a society if the aspiration of civilisation were to concentrate on science and technology to the neglect of the most important social matter, which is right moral conduct as taught by Jesus the Christ.

Earlier, I mentioned in passing that Christians are described as civilised by an English dictionary. This time I want to be detailed. Lexicons, in qualifying Christians, use such words as *civilised, charitable, humble, kind,* and *gentile.*[23] Obianyido uses similar descriptive words when referring to the Christians who handled his manuscript with civility. He praises the civilised behaviour of his typist and says of him, 'He is a gentle character—so devoted a Christian.' To the rest (the members of his family, including his wife), who are all Christians and had the chance to denounce his profane manuscript but treated it kindly, as Christians are supposed to do, he said, 'I am thankful to every one of them' (see the acknowledgements section of *Christ or Devil?,* and Chapter 2 of *In Defence of Jesus the Christ*).

The ingredients of right moral conduct inherent in Christian teaching give civilisation its hue and worth. Civilisation, says Amiel, 'is first and foremost, a moral thing. Without honesty, without respect for law, without the love for one's neighbour, in a word, without virtues, the whole is menaced'.[24]

William Penn Patrick's writing *Resistance* is in the same camp as my claim when he refers to Jesus the Christ as 'the greatest of all men'. The superior intelligence and unequalled wisdom of Jesus the Christ baffled his contemporaries. There is no parallel in recent times to his knowledge and integrity; there is little or no hope of finding one in future. I am of the opinion that this is an alternative reason Obianyido poses the question in his book, 'Who is this man Jesus Christ who has harassed the human soul for so long?'(page 34 of *Christ or Devil?*). That shows Jesus the Christ's spiritual strength. The unprecedented quality of his personality is up to date, amazing the so-called civilisation of today.

We, the so-called civilisation of today, draw endlessly upon the rich storehouse of the wisdom of Jesus the Christ and that of his disciples and apostles in our effort to solve the problems of our socially ill generation. From time to time, we propagate peace and love, which Jesus the Christ and his disciples and apostles taught, whenever social problems arise.

---

[23] 'Civilised', *New Practical Standard Dictionary of English Language.*
[24] G. F. Maine, ed., *Great Thoughts Birthday Book.*

In the circumstances outlined above, if Jesus the Christ and his disciples and apostles fail to qualify as civilised, then one wonders who will succeed.

(e) Their foreign outlook

That phrase 'foreign outlook' is too vague to make any sense in this context; it prevents one from determining what Obianyido specifically means. Be that as it may, we must guess, and get on with the subject.

So, we plunge into the subject and take it from what we think he has in mind. From the history presented in the Holy Bible, we learn that Jesus the Christ and his disciples carried out their mission among their people and their neighbours. If they were 'despised and hated' because of 'their foreign outlook', that means those who despised and hated them disliked having foreigners in their midst. Such people were chauvinistic nationalists to the core, to the point of being xenophobic—starkly racist. That discriminatory attitude falls short of civilisation.

One can rightly compare Obianyido to the people who hated foreigners in their midst when one considers that Obianyido hates the white Christian missionaries in his country, Nigeria, because of their foreignness and race.

(f) Their low social status

This description is also vague. It is very problematic to have no exact meaning and no example or illustration. It is again anybody's guess what the meaning is.

I like to guess that it means that Jesus the Christ and his disciples led a simple, humble, modest, meek, honest, civilised lifestyle—down to earth.

Well, they were itinerant preachers moving from place to place most of the time, with no permanent address. They entertained no lust for luxury, worldly pleasures, or enjoyment at the expense of fairness and justice, while their fellow human beings suffered in painful poverty.

Jesus the Christ himself said that the Son of Man (i.e. he, himself) had nowhere to lay his head—meaning he had no property or wealth to call his own (Matthew 8:20). It had to be so: he and his disciples were not after mundane, transient things, but after spiritual, heavenly matters, which are for fairness and justice, and eternal life.

They were not like the Pharisees and adherents of other Jewish religious sects who went about in 'flamboyant robes and loved to sit on high tables in public places, passing themselves off as people of high social status' (Mark 12:38–39).

Paradoxically, Jesus the Christ and his disciples, whom Obianyido describes as of 'low social status', were admired, loved, and cherished by those of high social status who swarmed round them like bees from a hive. Take for example the Roman officer (a centurion) whose servant was sick who went humbly to ask Jesus the Christ to heal his servant. Jesus the Christ healed the servant (Matthew 8:5–13). The ruler of the synagogue, Jairus, whose daughter was sick, did the same: humbled himself before Jesus the Christ so that his daughter could be cured. She indeed was cured (Luke 8:41–42). Nicodemus, a Pharisee, ruler of the Jews, approached Jesus the Christ several times, asking for spiritual knowledge (John 3:1–3). Zacchaeus, chief among the publicans, a rich man, a tax collector, had to climb a tree, because he was a short man, to see Jesus the Christ in the crowd. Eventually, he invited Jesus the Christ to his house (Luke 19:1–9). Joseph Arimathea, an honourable counsellor of the Jews, was friendly with Jesus the Christ. He was the one who took the body of Jesus the Christ, after his crucifixion, and buried it in the tomb Jesus had prepared for himself (Mark 15:42–46). The list goes on!

The list shows that Jesus the Christ and his disciples were loved and were held in high esteem in their era. Yet, Obianyido shamelessly describes them as of 'low social status'.

None of the five reasons Obianyido makes up and relies on to allege that the followers of Jesus the Christ and his disciples, with their religion, were the most despised and hated of all religions in their time is tenable.

In fact, Jesus the Christ and his disciples and followers were of the highest social status in their day. Morally, they were the paragons of uprightness, peace, and civilisation.

OBIANYIDO: The Christians in their general behaviours—their prayers, songs (hymn books), and so on—display a slave mentality when they use such expressions as 'Lord, have mercy on us miserable offenders', 'We thy slaves', 'We thy unworthy servants', and so on. Such behaviours only suit slave–master relationships.

In developed countries, prime ministers (or presidents) are easily told off by ordinary citizens and receive no songs of praise. The said behaviours of Christians towards God derive from ancient oriental despotism. I do not agree that a Father of supernatural goodness would want his children to reduce themselves to the status of slave and employ the best of language of royalty in his praise in order to win his favour.

REPLY: Obianyido equates human beings—the prime ministers (or presidents) of our earthly nations—with God. That tells it all! It shows his misguided reasoning based on the shallowness of his spiritual knowledge; it is a descent to the point of blasphemy! See how far down he has gone when suggesting that God should be compared to a prime minister or a president and sometimes be told off? Insanity!

The things he says about reducing Christians to slave mentality before they can expect to earn God's favour do not have the meanings he assigns to them. Christians use the expressions metaphorically; Obianyido, in his ignorance, gives them literal interpretations that carry unintended meanings. What an ignoramus, a nitwit!

Another matter is that Obianyido opines that it is wrong for a sinner (a wrongdoer) to be repentant, show remorse for the wrong he or she has done, and ask for forgiveness. According to Obianyido, the one who has done wrong (the sinner) should even tell God off. No rational person, religious or nonreligious, would be prepared to trek that disgusting, execrable, profane, sacrilegious, uncivilised road with him. It is unethical, churlish, vulgar, and uncouth. May his 'sermon' be acceptable to his atheist friends only.

God has good relationships with his children. Jesus the Christ taught about the relationship between humankind and God. He said, 'If a son shall ask bread of you that is earthly father, will you give him a stone?' (Luke 11:11–13). 'If ye then being evil, know how to give good gifts unto your children, how much more shall your heavenly Father give the Holy Spirit [or any good thing] to them that ask Him' (Luke 11:9–13; Matthew 7:7–10).

That means Christians who are obedient to God receive from God their requests; those who are disobedient, the sinners, need to repent and become good in order to receive their requests from God the Father.

OBIANYIDO: The God I want is the God who wants his children to hold their heads up and look the world in the face; who judges his children according to their individual contribution towards human development; who is too magnanimous and modest to entertain flattery and praise-singing; and who communicates directly with his children, not through self-appointed agents or a superson.

REPLY: Unfortunately for Obianyido, he has no God at all to relate to in the first place. His conclusion of the TV debate between his atheist friend and a Christian on whether or not God exists was that his friend had won the debate and proved the nonexistence of God, which shows Obianyido does not believe in the existence of God (see Chapter 3 of *In Defence of Jesus the Christ*). That at this point he returns to God and wants 'the God whose children hold their heads up and look the world in the face' is astonishing. Having turned around, he wants his imaginary God's children's moral and social behaviour to be of no issue. That the children may be wrongdoers, disrespectful to their Father, God, is of no consequence to Obianyido. Put another way, it is not necessary for a child laden with the guilt of his or her sins and wrongs to tilt his or her head symbolically, under the heavy weight of guilt, as a show of regret or remorse for his or her actions when approaching the Father, whom he or she has offended, for favour. That is disgusting! It is a grossly impolite attitude. The parable of the prodigal son has no lesson for Obianyido (Luke 15:11–32). It is very odd and awkward for one to conceive that a son who has done wrong should not show remorse, but 'hold his head up before the world' in pride for the wrong done. Obianyido has characteristically gotten his moral philosophy in a complete muddle. His manner is well pronounced here as uncivil and bad.

To hold one's head up and look the world in the face is a privilege for the upright in the name of civilisation. Wrongdoers, sinners, are not entitled to such a privilege in a civilised society.

Next, what does Obianyido mean by 'the one God who judges his children according to their individual contribution towards human development'? Is he talking about moral conduct or material development? Obianyido is fond of inexplicit statements. The answer to the question is anybody's guess. From his personality and way of thinking, gathered from his book, I sense he means material development. For him to think of development in terms of moral conduct would be unlikely because that would take him to religion, and he is averse to religion.

My view is that God wants, first and foremost, for one to develop in terms of moral conduct, coming to care for human beings and other creatures. Moral development is an essential ingredient to general development in the social, scientific, technological, economic, and political spheres.

The centrepiece of moral development is compassionate love—compassionate love for one's fellow creatures. Without that, all worldly material developments are of no use to humankind.

If God were to judge his children based on their individual contributions to human development (materially), as Obianyido suggests, the inevitable result would be very unfair and catastrophic. Those who were too unintelligent or too unfortunate to fail to contribute materially, through no fault of their own, would be condemned by Obianyido's imaginary God. And in a situation like that, more than 80 per cent of the world population would be trapped in the bracket of unfair and inequitable for their condemnation and God's denial of favour. The developing and underdeveloped countries of the world would have the greatest percentages of people in that hapless situation.

Another subject: Obianyido wants 'the one God that is so magnanimous and modest that He does not entertain flattery or praise-singing'. Obianyido was created by God. He does not believe in that God. He wants his own God with attributes specified by him, a God who 'does not entertain flattery or praise-singing'. Let him create such a God by himself, for himself!

Flattery, which he has mentioned, in my humble understanding of the word, is excessive, insincere praise. Jesus the Christ rejected flattery when he was called 'good', and said, 'Call me not good. There is none good but God' (Matthew 10:17–18). That shows that flattery is opposed to Christian principles. The Christian goes for genuine and deserved thanks or praise, not for fake gratitude or praise that translates into flattery, which is hypocrisy. Jesus the Christ, throughout his teachings, condemned hypocrisy and insincerity (Matthew 15:7–9). He approved gratitude and appreciation when they were genuine and shown at the right moment. He approved the gratitude of one of the ten lepers he healed, who showed his appreciation to him for healing him; he damned the other nine of the ten lepers, who had failed to say 'thank you' to him (Luke 7:12–19).

Christianity is therefore in favour of sincere appreciation and genuine praise for the benefits one receives. Appreciation, thanks, or praise is genuine when it comes after the benefit received; it is not genuine if it comes before, because then it is a cousin to currying favour (a form of flattery) and lacks in sincerity, unless it is well founded upon faith, real faith. Why? Because of the nature of faith, the essence of which is: that which is asked for honestly, genuinely (by faith), is as good as already received before it becomes manifest (Hebrews 11:1).

If Obianyido is averse to any show of appreciation for any benefits received from God, and aspires to the attitude of ingrates, that is entirely his choice. No civilised person, I believe, would settle for that. There is civility, virtue, and fulfilment in the show of appreciation and praise-singing for any good received. That, precisely, is all that Christians show when they relate to God.

Again, Obianyido wants the God who communicates directly with his children. Jesus the Christ taught direct communication with our Father, God. He demonstrated this when he taught, 'Ask and it shall be given you' (Matthew 7:7–11). He taught, 'When you pray, say, "Our Father who is in heaven"' (Matthew 6:7–13). Do not be confused about his saying, 'I am the way, the life, no one comes to the Father except through me.' The 'me' is the Word of God made manifest through Jesus, the aspect of God that is the Christ. In this circumstance, to communicate through the Christ, which Jesus became, is to be in direct communication with God.

Concerning the matter of a 'superson' and 'self-appointed agent', as Obianyido puts it, he is unable to understand what 'superson' (special Son of God) stands for: it means that God the Father is well pleased with Jesus as he became the Christ, i.e. an aspect of God functioning through him (Matthew 3:17). How? Jesus pleased God when he recognised the Christ (if you like, the aspect of God in him, which of course is in every other human being) within him and surrendered himself (the flesh-and-blood human being) to it so that the Christ took over Jesus's life, functioning through him; 'God in me is working, not I Jesus.' For that, Jesus the Christ said, 'If I bear witness of myself [Jesus, the flesh-and-blood ordinary human being], my witness is not true.' That is to say if I Jesus, a human being, claim that my functioning is by me, I am not saying the truth; it is the Christ, the aspect of God in me I surrendered to and became, that functions (John 5:19–36). That mystical transformation demonstrated that Jesus, as the Christ, was not self-appointed, but was sent by God the Father.

The subject of the transformation from Jesus to the Christ (or to Jesus Christ, for short) has been treated in Chapter 4 of *In Defence of Jesus the Christ*.

If, in addition to all I have been saying about Jesus becoming the Christ, we study the gospel of John (and some portions of other gospels)—John 7:27–29; 8:42; and 17:3—and some other sections of the New Testament, we will be propelled safely into the conclusion that the Christ which Jesus mystically transformed into was not self-appointed; being an aspect of God, Jesus the Christ was, and still is, fulfilling God's will.

As for the other issue raised by Obianyido, on the matter of self-appointed agents or the superson, we have addressed the question of the self-appointed superson and proved that Jesus the Christ was not 'self-appointed' but acted on God's fiat. I come now to the other part of that issue, self-appointed agents.

If by 'agents' Obianyido refers to or means the priests of the Christian church (he is not specific as to what meaning he attaches to the word *agents*), then I will make bold to inform him that the same agency arrangement occurs in other religions besides Christianity. Islam, Hinduism, and each indigenous African religion has agents. Obianyido knows this but chooses to bury facts and supplant them with falsehoods.

He glibly talks about indigenous African religion and culture and portrays himself as one of the cognoscente on the subject of African religious matters. Yet he pretends not to know that indigenous African religion (and culture) has an agency system as a way of dealing with God. He should know that Africans worship the Almighty God through the agency of their subsidiary gods as representatives of God on earth, with their priests (human being) as the caretakers of the subsidiary gods.

In passing, let me mention this: Obianyido talks of more than one God, for example 'the white man God' (Chapter 4 of *Christ or Devil?*), and says, 'the one God I want'. He fails to understand that there is one God only for all creatures. Each religion may have its peculiar way and manner of worshipping that one God. Whatever the case may be, there remains one God for all religions.

Whatever the religion, what matters in the end is the teaching of the right laws of the one God and the putting of those laws into practice for the good of humanity and to the glory of the *one God*.

SPREAD OF CHRISTIANITY

(CHAPTER 6, *CHRIST OR DEVIL?*)

OBIANYIDO: The followers of original religions, like Christianity, Muhammadanism [Islam], and Buddhism, are fed with only such information designed by the leaders of their faiths in order to keep their loyalty.

The designed or misleading information about Christianity was responsible for my dedicated Christian aunt's feeling surprised to learn that Bethlehem is not in heaven but in this world.

REPLY: One point of correction: none of those religions mentioned by Anene Obianyido is original religion. They may be, in today's circumstance, among the first conventional religions that came later, but paganism (heathenism) is the original religion. That is that.

Now, on to Obianyido's headache. If his aunt, a dedicated Christian, according to him, mistook Bethlehem to be a place in heaven, the leaders of the Christian religion never taught her so. Certainly, her misjudgement resulted from her paucity of education and abject scriptural ignorance. Jesus the Christ, whom Obianyido fiercely attacks, is not to bear the blame for that. It was a mistake waiting to happen when an uneducated mind faced what was beyond her intellectual and scriptural grasp.

The fact that the mistake took place strengthens Earl Ludwin's reason for asking, 'How can the untutored African conceive God?' He, of course, was thinking of the European manner of worshipping God. Remember that it was Ludwin's opinion that caused Obianyido to stir, kick, and almost fall into a fit (see Chapter 4 of *Christ or Devil?*). Remember, too, that earlier Obianyido himself confessed that he once imagined that the story about Jesus the Christ was something that took place in heaven and not on this planet. Again, who was to blame for his lack of knowledge or his overheated imagination? Answer: the stage of education he was at and the social circumstance he was in.

OBIANYIDO: When I was part of the ignorant majority, I figured Peter as the only link between the church in heaven and that on earth. Those in heavenly churches found their way to earth when Christ, nay, God himself, handed the big key to Peter, both to unlock the earthly church door to humanity and to guard the gate to heaven against unbelievers.

REPLY: Feeling self-satisfied and self-intoxicated, not to mention being egomaniacal, Obianyido affects superiority over most of his community (in Igboland, Nigeria). Granted, later in his life he became part of the educated and knowledgeable minority in his community. Let not his claim to charlatanism stand in our way in this discussion. So, now we can go straight to the matter of the 'big key' he foolishly ridicules. That relates to the section of the New Testament where Jesus the Christ told Peter he would hand over the key of heaven to him (Matthew 16:17–19). I am very shocked by the triviality and levity with which Obianyido talks about this matter. He addresses it like one with a scattered brain. What a gag! What a facetious character! He is derisive, sagacious, and totally lacking in any form of seriousness. Imagine his fine-toothed-comb criticism churlishly garbed and festooned with exaggeration. What reason has anyone not to take him as an ignoramus who cannot understand simple figurative or metaphoric expression?

The giving of the key to Peter symbolised the handing over of authority to Peter so that he may continue the gospel, that is the teachings of Jesus the Christ.

OBIANYIDO: Christianity—the Pope and his Roman Catholic Church in particular—spread the gospel by force and violence, causing destruction and imposing their religion on people. The white Christian God was imposed on Africa by the white colonial masters.

REPLY: For a start, let me repeat what I said previously: there is only one God for all nations, races, and religions, though there are many and various ways of worshipping that God in terms of practice and procedure. Obianyido's concept of 'the white God' is tinged with phobia against the white Christian missionary who brought Christianity to Africa.

About the presence of Christianity in Africa: I suspect that Africans converted to Christianity because they saw in it a better social life; they found their indigenous religion weaker and more negative concerning human dignity than Christianity. They realised the evils in their indigenous religion and so succumbed to the influence of Christianity, which speaks against such evils.

That reason for their conversion was made certain and easy by the fact that Africans were in those days of early Christian missions porous in character. In any case, I am prepared to admit that Africa's colonial masters must have exerted some measure of influence on Africans to persuade them to embrace Christianity. Yet, I believe that no force or violence was employed in their entire campaign.

The mission of Jesus the Christ through Christianity was to correct the wrongs, the sins of individuals and religions of that time. Jesus the Christ campaigned not for change of religion but for a change in the conduct of individuals and religions in such a way that led them to serve humanity justly and please God. So, in that case, Africans reserved the right to make all necessary moral changes in their service to God without necessarily abandoning their indigenous religion completely.

I did mention the Papau New Guinea tribe's-people earlier, who refused to throw away everything about their indigenous religion and culture but accepted the Christian teachings in the areas they saw necessary for pleasing God. Their colonial masters—France, Britain, et al.—tried each in their turn, but none could persuade them against their choice, nor could any apply force to make them swallow intact the form of Christianity given them. They did not embrace Christianity as offered them. So Obianyido's assertion that Christian missionaries applied force and violence and imposed Christianity on Africa is highly questionable.

If Christianity ever used force as a means of converting people to the faith, then it happened a very, very long time ago in Europe, during the age of the Roman Empire under the Christian bishop in Rome—the papal authority of the early age. Africa had no sniff of that mode of conversion.

Whatever the case, Jesus the Christ and his disciples and apostles neither practised nor suggested the practice of violence or force as a means of gaining converts. Their mission was peaceful and friendly. Jesus the Christ enjoined his disciples to spread his gospel in a friendly manner. I refer to Matthew 10:5–16 in this case. In particular, I quote verses 14 and 16: 'And whosoever shall not receive you, nor hear your words, when you depart out of the house or city, shake off the dust of your feet' [i.e. treat the person with contempt]. ... Behold I send you forth as sheep in the midst of wolves: Be you, therefore, wise as doves.'

By no means do these instructions suggest force or violence.

This book of mine is written in defence of Jesus the Christ. Whatever is done by anyone or any organisation that falls outside the ambit of the teachings of Jesus the Christ, therefore, may receive no support, no defence, in my book.

Obianyido goes on and on, relentlessly prospecting for any faults to hang upon Jesus the Christ and Christianity. This time he struggles to attach any wrong committed by the papacy or other so-called Christian organisations of later times to Jesus the Christ and Christianity. I imagine that the Pope and the Roman Catholic Church which Obianyido talks about as spreading the gospel by force and violence was that of second-century Europe, if I may reiterate. Religious historians coined a word, *Christendom*, to achieve status for the so-called Christianity of that period. I hope to explain what I understand the word *Christendom* to mean, and how it came about, in a later chapter. Suffice it for now to say that it describes a period when Christianity was made the common religion of the Roman Empire, at which time the Roman authority (Emperor Constantine, I think) changed the original Christian principles of the apostles of old to a system accommodating some of the principles of the heathenism that was omnipresent across Europe at that time. A religious historian, Vance Ferrell, among others, in his writing has the information we are looking for.

OBIANYIDO: Jesus and Peter were crucified upside down for their deeds.

REPLY: What deeds? If any, they seem to be known only to Obianyido, who has failed to mention them.

Even if they were crucified upside down for whatever their deeds, what important point does the nature of the crucifixion add to the fact that they were crucified and/or add to the contest between *In Defence of Jesus the Christ* and Obianyido's book *Christ or Devil?* The one thing that the nature of the procedure followed in the crucifixion suggests is that those responsible for it, as well as those who, like Obianyido, later recount the story 'with hilarity and fondness', should hang their heads in shame for such a horrible barbaric, inhumane attitude towards the sad event. By rejoicing at the nature of the crucifixion, Obianyido clearly displays his malice and sadism towards anything about Jesus the Christ and Christianity. His claim to education and civilisation is in doubt!

In civilised countries such as Britain, it is a serious criminal offence to torture animals, even those for food before they are legally killed for food. Mind you, our case in question is about human beings. Despicable, that manner of crucifixion!

How Obianyido is satisfied and happy at the story of the savage conduct, which is diametrically opposed to civilised behaviour, is perplexing. Visualise how his pleasure feeds on his fellow human beings' misfortune! Does that not show the depth of his iniquitous mind? He seems to hug and embrace the story of the shameful event. For that, is he not wretchedly callous? What a miserable sadist!

To end this chapter, it may be necessary to remind my readers that Obianyido, throughout the previous chapters, has been shown to both believe and disbelieve that the man Jesus the Christ ever lived on this earth. Characteristically, he has changed his mind and believes Jesus the Christ once lived on this planet. Why again? Because he does not want to miss the alleged story that Jesus the Christ and Peter were crucified upside down. His frequent change of mind on the same subject has become a boring circuit!

CHALLENGES TO CHRISTIANITY

(Chapter 7, *Christ, or Devil?*)

Obianyido: Christianity, particularly in the early centuries of the Middle Ages, did a lot to suppress the spread of knowledge.

Owing to the negative activities of the church in those early times, civilisations made no progress. The period was therefore described in history as the Dark Ages.

I still remember that about thirty-five years ago, in the midfifties, the ordinary members of the Roman Catholic Church in my village were not allowed to touch the Bible, let alone read it.

Reply: Briefly speaking, Jesus the Christ preached openly, intensively, and extensively to all nations and all classes of people. In his efforts to spread knowledge, he instructed his disciples thus: 'You are the light of the world. A city that is set on the hill cannot be hid. Neither do men light a candle, and put it under a bushel, but on a candle stick; and it giveth light unto all that are in the house' (Matthew 5:14–15). In Mark's gospel he says, 'For there is nothing hid which shall not be manifest; neither was anything kept secret but that it should come abroad' (Mark 4:22). I previously made references to similar instructions by Jesus the

Christ to his disciples. The instructions were not those of a character who sought to suppress or back the suppression of knowledge.

However, Anene Obianyido, in his criticism, particularly mentions the Christians of the early centuries, the Middle Ages—the Roman Catholic Church. Already I have referred to the Christianity of that era. Obianyido is concerned with Christendom and promised to say what a book by a religious historian has about Christendom later. So, I leave the matter here for now.

Although the purpose of my book is not to defend Christendom or the Roman Catholic Church of that era, or indeed of any other era, I plead to stray into a neutral position, that is to put myself in a good stead for making impartial judgements as I consider the accusations by Obianyido against the Roman Catholic Church of that era.

About the matter Obianyido is concerned with, my humble guess is that the Roman Catholic Church of that period might have acted the way it did in order to prevent the possibility of anyone going against what the church conceived (wrongly or rightly) to be the correct interpretations of the Bible teachings. The church might have thought it better to let the interpretations of the biblical scriptures come from one source, their priests, for who were trained in Bible interpretation. The effect of this would be an avoidance of variations and confusion about the church's teachings on the Bible. The incident with the Ethiopian eunuch might have influenced the church's behaviour (Acts 8:26–35). About the incident: Philip was sent by an angel of the Lord to explain to the eunuch a portion of the biblical scriptures he was messing about in.

Probably, the event concerning the Ethiopian eunuch and the Holy Bible made the church in Africa (better, in Obianyido's village in Nigeria) take precautions and prohibited Africans, especially in the early years of the introduction of Christianity to Africa, from being sufficiently educated to comprehend the Christian teachings without the trained priests of the church guiding them through. Let us put the whole matter in this context: in the early years of Christian instruction in Africa (better, in Obianyido's village), Christian teaching of the Holy Bible was to Africans unchartered territory, so to speak. In that circumstance it was better that they were instructed not to study the Holy Bible but to learn the contents of the Bible from the trained priests. That is my humble guess.

That notwithstanding, I am of the opinion that keeping knowledge from anyone in need of it is against the teaching of Jesus the Christ and, therefore, Christianity is against such a practice. Earlier I quoted the teachings given by Jesus the Christ to that effect.

Finally, forget not that Obianyido has alleged in *Christ or Devil?* that in the early days, Britain and the United States had the Bible in Africa as a foreign exchange–earning commodity. He writes, 'The ordinary members of the Roman Catholic Church in my village were not allowed to touch the Bible, let alone read it.' How then could the earning of foreign earning work? To whom were the Bibles being sold to earn the foreign exchange? Are his ideas not muddled up? Such confusion in ideas can only come from nincompoops!

CORRUPTION IN THE VATICAN

(CHAPTER 8, *CHRIST OR DEVIL?*)

OBIANYIDO: The church would want us to believe that God called the Pope to take over from the historical Peter of the Bible. Yet, the Pope, the medieval popes, have been turning religious institutions into brothels; monasteries into hotbeds, of homosexuality; and convents into homes of perversion, lesbianism, abortion, the murdering of children, and the breeding of bastards. The Pope lived an extravagant life and indulged in corruption.

REPLY: I have no means of knowing the details of all that Anene Obianyido accuses the Pope (the Vatican) of, except that I read, a very, very long time ago, in my teens, a book entitled *Awful Disclosures of Maria Monk* telling of such evils as mentioned by Obianyido. I had a mixed belief then about the truth of the contents of the book—could be fact, could be fiction. My guess is that Obianyido extracted the information in his book from that book, *Awful Disclosures of Maria Monk*, and perhaps from other books similar to it.

The most I know about the Roman Catholic Church of this generation concerns the frequent abuse, by some of its priests, of children—male and female—which matters have burst out into open in recent times. The Roman Catholic Church does not deny that; the church, on several occasions, publicly, solemnly apologised for such atrocious, monstrous, abominable, and un-Christian behaviour.

Depending upon the incident, the atrocities committed (or being committed) by clergy of the Roman Catholic Church (and on a few occasions by priests of other Christian denominations) within my lifetime, and relying on the logic 'from the known to the unknown', I am inclined to consider the accusations levelled by Obianyido against the Roman Catholic Church as true. To the Christian, all immoral conduct is despicable and uncivilised and, therefore, un-Christian. Genuine Christianity is clearly against all sexual immorality, for example homosexuality and lesbianism (see Romans 1:26–29; 1 Thessalonians 4:3).

Christians of the era of the apostles never behaved in that fashion, as far as history goes. My belief is that such un-Christian conduct found its way into later Christianity at the birth of Christendom—the Christianity of the Roman emperor Constantine, Bishop Sylvester of Rome, and Bishop Eusebius of Caesarea, which came to life following the promulgation of the National Sunday Law in the Middle Ages, about AD 202.

I earlier deferred on giving my understanding of the term *Christendom*. At this stage of my discourse, I am prepared to say what little I know about the word *Christendom* as it relates to religion. My knowledge about this topic is gathered from four books: *The Story of Civilization*, iii, *Caesar and Christ*—both written by Will Durant, a historian— *The Crucible of Christianity: Judaism, Hellenism, and the Historical Background to the Christian Faith*, by Harry A. Wolfson of Harvard University, and *The Fabulous First Centuries of Christianity*, by Vance Ferrell.

According to Vance Ferrell's account, the Christianity set up by the early apostles suffered frequent and tremendous persecution at the hands of the heathen Roman emperors. This was in the second century, about AD 202.

Events rolled on in that situation, and a stage arrived when Emperor Constantine, who had a soft heart for Christianity, became the sole emperor of the Roman Empire, with his capital at Rome. He then earned the title of Pontifex Maximus (the supreme priest of the pagan religion of the empire), i.e. the head of the Roman Empire, as well as the head of the religion of the empire.

At that period, Bishop Sylvester of Rome, as the head of the Roman Christian church at the time, with his counsellor, Eusebius, the bishop of Caesarea, desired that the Sunday worship, a pagan religious day for worshipping their sun god (Mithra), be chosen for both Christians and pagans as a day of worship. That was a strategy devised by Bishop Sylvester for expanding the status and members of his local church at Rome. Emperor Constantine agreed. Then, working in concert with the head bishop, Sylvester, and his counsellor, the bishop of Caesarea, Eusebius, the emperor, Constantine promulgated the National Sunday Law. According to the law, the Christians were to join the pagan Sunday worship. (By the way, that explains how Sunday worship supplanted Christian Saturday worship, i.e. the Sabbath.)

So, the two distinct religions—Christianity on the one hand, and paganism on the other—were fused into one under the name Christianity. The fusion was termed by historians 'Catholic' or 'Christendom', the latter of which means universal, that is uniting all Christians in the whole known world—for everyone.

In that fusion, the true Christian principles and concepts were mercilessly compromised to accommodate the pagans' so to attract the pagans to and keep them in Christianity. Emperor Constantine, who at the time was still a heathen (pagan), continued to be the head of the Roman Empire and became the head of neo-Christianity as well—the Christianity that has survived as the Roman Catholic Church of today. Not until Emperor Constantine was about to die did he become baptised as a Christian.

Before then, he moved his capital from Rome to Byzantium (Istanbul), leaving the entire western half of the empire under the control of the head of the Christian church, Bishop Sylvester of Rome. That situation placed the bishop in a position where he was able to enjoy the state left vacant by Emperor Constantine's departure. The bishop thus became both the political and the spiritual head of the state and called himself 'Pontifex Maximus', which was the title for the Roman emperor at the time of Jesus the Christ.

Leaning on the foregoing account, I am set to address the two major issues mentioned by Obianyido against the Roman Catholic Church. The first is that Christians say that 'God called the Pope to take over from the historical Peter of the Bible.' I ask, is that correct?

We have already seen that Emperor Constantine, by promulgation of the National Sunday Law, after making changes to Christianity—introducing pagan concepts and principles like the use of candles, incense, and bells, and the title Pontifex Maximus, when worshipping God, so as to accommodate the pagans within Christianity—became the head of the new Christian religion that emerged, as well as the political head of the Roman Empire. That earned him the title Pontifex Maximus. Still he was a heathen to the core, never mind his baptism later as he was dying.

We have also seen that the head of the Roman Catholic Church in Rome at the time, Bishop Sylvester, by dint of historical chance, took over from the Roman emperor Constantine, a heathen, and later became the head of the church as well as the head of the Roman Empire.

In the circumstance surrounding the events just narrated, the line of leadership of Christianity from the biblical Peter to the person who was to become the next leader snapped at the very time Emperor Constantine, a heathen then, made the said ruinous changes to Christianity and, at the same time, became the spiritual head of neo-Christianity. Therefore, Bishop Sylvester took over before the first pope.

In that sequence, the mantle of leadership of the Christian church of Peter's time did not continue beyond Peter's era, the sequence having been interrupted by Emperor Constantine and Bishop Sylvester, with the mantle of Christianity leadership going to Emperor Constantine and his neo-Christianity. Therefore, I conclude, God did not call the Pope to take over from Peter.

The second matter has to do with the accusations made by Obianyido against the Vatican—the Pope and the priests of the Roman Catholic Church. The accusations are about the evils in the Vatican. He named many of the evils, so we are aware of those named.

Already we have determined that our present-day Christianity is not the same as the Christianity of Peter's era. There was a great change in the original Christianity at the time of Emperor Constantine. Present-day Christianity has its roots in the deformed Christianity set up by the promulgation of the National Sunday Law about AD 202. In this case, it can safely be viewed that the papacy-based (Vatican-led) Christianity of Rome, and all other Christian denominations that later stemmed (including those that will in future stem) from it, bear a strong relationship to the Christianity of Emperor Constantine.

Since the Christianity of the Pope (Vatican) has been shown to be different from that of Peter's era, whatever wrongs the Vatican committed or is committing have nothing to do with the original Christianity of Jesus the Christ and his apostles. The wrongdoings of those practising a spurious Christianity—the type of Christianity that came after that of the apostles of old, as in the Acts of the New Testament—tend to supply ammunition to the atheists for use in attacking the genuine Christianity of Jesus the Christ.

In the Christianity of Jesus, the Christ, it is taught, 'You must be perfect to be a teacher of the gospel' (1 Peter 5:2–3). From the practical teaching of Jesus the Christ when he overturned the tables of the traders and money changers in the temple in Jerusalem during his triumphal entry into the city, we could say for certain what would have been his reaction if he were to have witnessed in person the corruptions Obianyido has mentioned against the Vatican. He would have dealt with the offenders harshly.

The imperfect character of most of the teachers of the present Christianity are so obvious and widely known that the need to recount it here is unnecessary. Suffice it to say that while the early Christianity of the historical Jesus the Christ (with his disciples and apostles) was after spiritual matters and eternal life, the Christianity of this later time craves for worldly gains and pleasures. The present Christianity seems to forget that serving God requires the sacrifice of the flesh and seeks the pleasure of the spirit, which leads to eternal life.

The Aquarian Gospel of Jesus the Christ, in talking about the priests in the time of Jesus the Christ, says, 'They show their gaudy robes and broad phylacteries and smile, when people call them reverend. They strut about and show pride when people call them Father so-and-so' (*The Aquarian Gospel of Jesus the Christ* 155:40–41).

That means the pagan priests of the era of Emperor Constantine distinguished themselves by their special robes, their empty titles (e.g. Reverend Father), their pride, and their corrupt practices. Those characteristics were passed on to Christianity after the promulgation of the National Sunday Law, because of which the characteristics entered Vatican Christianity and later found themselves in almost all Christian denominations, including Protestantism, which rose subsequently.

Jesus the Christ and his disciples and apostles had no such distinguishing characteristics. Jesus the Christ was simple and wore common clothing as did his disciples and the common people of his time, and he assumed no special title, so he did not show off. Remember what Jesus the Christ said to one who called him 'Good Master': 'Why call thou me good? There is none good but one, that is God' (Matthew 19:16–17).

Refer to the quotation from *The Aquarian Gospel of Jesus the Christ* 155:40–41, above. What does the word *father* in that context stand for? Let me reframe the question: what was Jesus Christ's teaching on calling a priest or other religious teacher 'father'? He recognised only two kinds of fathers to my knowledge—the earthly (biological) father and the spiritual (heavenly) Father, God. He referred to both when he said, 'Or, what man [referring to an earthly biological father] is there of you, whom if his son ask bread, will be give him a stone? ... How much more shall your Father [referring to the spiritual Father, God] which is in Heaven give good things to them that ask of Him?' (Matthew 7:7–11). In that context, there are only two kinds of fathers, the earthly biological father, and the spiritual heavenly Father. Again, Jesus gave us a model prayer: 'Our Father which is in heaven' (Matthew 6:1–18). In this, he recognised the earthly father and made sure that this was distinguished from the other Father, the spiritual, when he described God as heavenly. Yet again, another time he said to the scribes and the Pharisees, 'For God commanded, saying, Honour they father and your mother: and he that curseth father or mother, let him die the death' (Matthew 15:4–6). *Father* in this context refers to the earthly biological father.

On another occasion, Jesus the Christ went on to warn, 'And call no man your father upon the earth: for one is your Father, which is in heaven' (Matthew 23:9). So, there is no other spiritual Father than God in heaven.

Against that obvious scriptural and spiritual instruction, the Vatican says that their priests should be called reverend fathers.

Jesus the Christ condemned the attitude of the scribes and the Pharisees for their disregard of the commandments of God and for following their own traditions. In support, he quoted the prophecy of Isaiah which called them hypocrites (Matthew 15:4–9). On one occasion, Jesus the Christ said, 'He who is not with Me is against Me, and he who does not gather with me scatter abroad' (Matthew 12:30).

The question facing all who profess Christianity is in this matter, as well as in similar matters, for example when God himself said, 'Remember the Sabbath day and keep it holy' (Exodus 20:8, 11; Deuteronomy 5:12)— the fourth of the Ten Commandments, which is older than the other commandments, being contemporaneous with Creation, is whether the replacement of Sunday for the Sabbath Day, a day for human beings to worship God, was OK to do by the men of the Vatican (the Roman Catholic Church). Whom are we to obey, Jesus the Christ and God, or a human being from the Vatican?

Concerning such matters, hear Peter and John: 'Whether it is right in the sight of God to listen to you more than to God, you judge' (Acts 4:19). Hear Peter and other apostles: 'We ought to obey God rather than men' (Acts 5:29). Consider Paul's view on such matters: 'Know ye not, that to whom ye yield yourselves servants to obey, his servants ye are to whom ye obey?' (Romans 6:16).

As for me, I have chosen to obey Jesus the Christ and God. The choice is yours, my reader.

This is very important: take a closer look at the services provided by present-day Christian priests to the people. As we look at this issue, it becomes apparent that the primary objective of their service to people is material gain. Thus, most of the time they serve mammon instead of God. The teaching of Jesus the Christ, 'You cannot serve God and mammon,' is for the most part disregarded (Matthew 6:24). For conducting Mass, weddings, baptisms, funeral services, and so on, the church is after material gain. Thus, it tends to make service to God and service to mammon blur into each other. Almost all Christian churches of today indulge in the pagan practice of serving mammon. That is one of the reasons I conceive that the Christianity of this generation has lost its spiritual bearings as a result of the dysfunctional pagan compass that has been guiding it from the time the National Sunday Law was put in place by Emperor Constantine of the Roman Empire in the second century.

Spiritual, not material, salvation should always be the slogan of true/ genuine Christianity.

Yes, I have to some degree joined Obianyido in his criticisms of later Christianity. Intact remains my profound respect for the original

Christianity that rose at the time of Jesus the Christ and his apostles—
the Christianity of the Bible.

I base my criticisms on my personal observations and the knowledge I
procured from the sources I herein mentioned before, which sources I
regard as reliable.

Though in shambles, present-day Christianity is 'like a toad ugly
and venomous that wears yet a precious jewel in its head' (William
Shakespeare, *As You Like It*), for its ability, to some degree, to improve
the moral conduct of its followers.

It could do better. I hope it improves in serving God through serving
humanity.

Jesus the Christ's teaching is apposite here: 'For I say unto you, that
except your righteousness shall exceed the righteousness of the scribes
and the Pharisees, ye shall in no case enter into the kingdom of heaven'
(Matthew 5:20).

THE MODERN WORLD
AND ITS CHURCH

(CHAPTER 9, *CHRIST OR DEVIL?*)

OBIANYIDO: 'Man proposes, and God disposes' goes the common saying. But it is the other way around in terms of the role of the church in human evolution. God rather proposes well for humankind by providing them with an innate dynamism for self-development. If it were not for the influence of religions—Judaism, Christianity, Islam—blocking the way to knowledge, humankind's progress would have been higher.

Religion, Christianity, for that matter, tucked away knowledge for its own private use, keeping humankind in profound ignorance. Great scholars such as Galileo Galilei, Leonardo Da Vinci, Michelangelo, Titian, and Raphael, who sought to improve humanity through promotion of knowledge, had either themselves or their works destroyed by the church. But God, or whatever you chose to call the benevolent force behind Creation, must have his way. The fall of the Christian city of Constantinople in 1453 liberated knowledge from the clutches of humankind in general.

In Russia, Karl Mark, Friedrich Engels, and Vladimir Lenin inspired the downtrodden masses to smash the oppressive tsar and the powerful church who were oppressing the working class. China with its home-grown religion never tolerated the tyranny of the church.

The radical humanist Tai Solarin rejected everything about deity as a result of his visit to Europe.

REPLY: Before going into the matter of Tai Solarin as 'the radical humanist', I ask, what does it mean to be a humanist? The *Oxford Dictionary* defines *humanism* as a 'system of thought concerned with human rather than divine or supernatural matters; an outlook emphasising common human need—the welfare and happiness of human beings.

What business is it of Anene Obianyido's to describe Tai Solarin, a veteran atheist, as a radical humanist, except to say that atheism and humanism are interchangeable concepts, that the words are synonymous, and, more important to him, that the practice of humanism is better than the practice of Christianity in matters pertaining to human welfare, namely human happiness and fulfilment? But if we compare the two concepts (Christianity and humanism) diligently, we are bound to find Obianyido's conclusion wrong and misleading.

Christianity has within it some defined universal laws (a ready-made code of conduct). The laws have one Source—the Self, the Almighty Being that is the Creator of all other beings, manifest and unmanifest. To the creatures (human beings, for our discussion) are apportioned rewards or punishments following their moral conduct, i.e. the individual's obedience, or disobedience, to the said laws. The laws are what Christianity teaches.

In this respect, the human being is offered the opportunity to individually work out his or her welfare, his or her happiness, his or her fulfilment, and his or her eternal life. Where one fails, one earns perishable life.

The features of humanism are partially different. The concept has no defined universal code of conduct for the practitioners. Every individual humanist determines, of his or her own accord, what conduct, or behaviours fit into his or her personal definition of humanism. Humanism prescribes no rewards and no punishments for the practitioners and has no definite goal.

Since what humanism is, is a matter individually determined by humanists, the concept has more than one source. It therefore makes room for discrimination, partiality, and injustice. In which case it offers a very poor vision for humankind's happiness and fulfilment in life. This makes the practice inferior to the practice of Christianity.

Obianyido's joyful presentation of Tai Solarin as a radical humanist ends as an empty show! Tai Solarin's practice of humanism was only meretricious!

Obianyido's description of Tai Solarin as a radical humanist is over and done with. I will next turn to other matters raised by him.

I am surprised to read Obianyido's statement 'but God, or whatever you chose to call the benevolent force behind Creation'. On this note, we cannot afford to forget the euphoria he displayed when he biasedly concluded that his atheist friend proved that God does not exist during a televised debate with a Christian. That showed he does not believe in God. Throughout his book, there is no clear indication that he has changed his mind on that matter. Here, he seems to have made a mistake in acknowledging the existence of God. Realising which, he quickly and tactfully retracted to use the expression 'benevolent force behind Creation' to avoid the word *God* and not be seen to believe in God, a concept in opposition to atheism. One can easily see that Obianyido's idea about God is in shambles. He does not even know whether he believes in the existence of God. He has used the word *God* and wanting to escape from the impression the word would give about his belief, he used the expression 'that benevolent force behind Creation' to supplant the word *God*. By so doing, he was trying to give the impression that he does not accept that God exists. Thus, he engages himself in a fight against his own word and later wants to escape.

Shamefully, he is unable to make good his escape: His use of the expression 'that benevolent force behind Creation' caught him and put him back into the belief in the existence of God, for God truly is the benevolent force behind Creation.

Even then, what a capricious mind Obianyido's is! A man with more than one face cannot be reliable. He is a confused hypocrite.

As a means of introducing his opinion that Christians suppress knowledge, Obianyido quotes the saying 'Man proposes, God disposes', but by no means is he to be taken as one who seriously believes in the existence of God. He believes in God only when it suits him.

His allegation that Christians suppress or tuck away knowledge has been dealt with in Chapter 10. There, I showed that Jesus the Christ and his disciples and apostles never suppressed or hid knowledge. This time I must consider that Obianyido's accusation is against the later Christianity of the Middle Ages—the second century—rather than against the Christianity of the era of Jesus the Christ. Obianyido names in his book some of the victims of such suppression of knowledge. Going by history, I am prepared to agree with him only to the extent that the victimisation was done by so-called Christians of the later times, not by Jesus the Christ or the original Christianity. It seems to me that the suppression of knowledge was not the direct aim of Christianity in those times. The suppression, I guess, could be a side effect of Christianity's misconceived conduct based on wrong knowledge or profound ignorance.

In any case, the said side effect was disruptive of the progress of knowledge at the time. This was unacceptable in terms of civilisation and the principle of the true Christianity of earlier times.

To my knowledge, the Christian church has long regretted the misjudgement and has apologised. Why is Obianyido harping on the matter at this time?

From that criticism of suppression of knowledge by early Christians, Obianyido jumps to another matter, invariably looking for any fault in the Christian principles. He views that in Russia, Karl Marx and Vladimir Lenin inspired the downtrodden masses to smash the oppressive tsar and the powerful church. He goes on to say that 'China with its home-grown religion never tolerated the tyranny of the church.'

I do not intend to go far into the aspects of Russia's social and political history, except to ask, what happened after the so-called 'tyranny of the church' was smashed?

Does China tolerate its 'home-grown religion'? Obianyido is mute about that. My answer is that some Chinese people do not.

Some Chinese citizens are, up to this day, howling like Irish dogs at the moon, asking the outside world for help in concerning the religion of Dalai Lama.

The reason Obianyido takes us to Russia and China is to suggest that those countries, where, according to him, religion (Christianity) became less pronounced after each respective revolution, provided a better life for their citizens—that the revolutionaries fought for and gained the liberation of the oppressed—and then to allege that in Christian countries, citizens are being oppressed.

For the sake of comparison and knowledge, we need to examine the attitude of Christianity towards the same class of people—the oppressed, the downtrodden, the poor, orphans, and widows—in Christian countries who also exist in Russia and China. For that it becomes necessary to search the Bible for what it has to say on such a matter. Jesus the Christ with his disciples and apostles was always on the side of the victims of injustice and the poor. He taught Christian principles for dealing with injustice against the poor and the underprivileged.

He asked his disciples to go and preach love, justice, and freedom to all nations, all races, and all classes of people. His teachings in the Bible are with us to this day. His Sermon on the Mount (Matthew 5) is about being good to the poor; his parable of the Good Samaritan (Luke 10:30–37) is about helping anyone in trouble; his parable of the rich man and the poor man, Lazarus, is about being good to the poor (Luke 16:19–31); his golden rule (Matthew 7:12) is about loving one's neighbour; his lesson on selling one's possessions is about helping the poor (Matthew 19:19); and his teaching on helping the hungry, the sick, the naked, et al. is clear in Matthew 25:35–40.

Check the following references in the Holy Bible for further Christian teachings on the need to help the poor, the oppressed, and the helpless: Ezekiel 43:9; Jeremiah 5:27–28; Isaiah 1:23; Amos 5:7–15; Micah 6:10–12; Habakkuk 1:3–4; Isaiah 10:1–2; Ezekiel 45:9; and James 5:1–4.

We have, by taking a reasonable path, arrived at the conclusion that, in fact, Christianity, of all organisations, cares most for the poor, the destitute, and the oppressed—in short, for all in need—by way of its teachings and actions. No wonder the *New Practical Standard Dictionary* tells us that as an adjective, *Christian* stands for 'charitable, humane, civilised'.

In the light of that correct definition of a Christian, a Christian church that oppresses the poor and the downtrodden is a Christian church in name only; it is not a Christian church in fact.

We have another matter. Obianyido informs us that Tai Solarin visited Europe and, as a result, rejected everything related to deity. It is common knowledge that Tai Solarin was neither the first Nigerian to visit Europe nor the last. Many Nigerians visited Europe before him, and many more have visited Europe after him. Why he is the only one to have contracted the atheistic virus is not known. He must have neglected the scripture that says, 'Only fools say in their hearts there is no God' (Psalm 14:1). Such people deceive themselves and should not be believed. Paul warned, 'Beware lest any man spoil you through philosophy and vain deceit, after the tradition of men, after the rudiments of the world, and not after Christ' (Colossians 2:8). Tai Solarin failed to heed that warning! His negligence might have left him vulnerable to atheistic virus attack, so to speak. He became a sufferer of chronic atheistic mania. That is unfortunate!

Also unfortunate is the fact that Obianyido's information about Tai Solarin's visit to Europe is shoddy. He fails to disclose the country or countries in Europe Tai Solarin visited. His account of the visit suggests that everyone in all European countries at the time of the visit disbelieved in God. That is a dubious way to narrate an event. Europe is a vast continent made up of many countries. It is true that almost all, if not all, the countries in Europe believe in a deity. I do not mean the Christian God specifically, but a deity of any kind at the time material to the visit. Even now, it remains true that all the countries in Europe believe in a form of deity.

For the sake of discussion, let's say that if Tai Solarin visited any country in Europe that happened to be atheistic, a country that did not believe in any deity, that country could not have been 100 per cent made up of atheists. And was it the case that he had to blindly follow those in the country who did not believe in God, like a shadow does a moving object? Had he no mind of his own? The reason for Tai Solarin's rejection of everything about the Deity is not given by Obianyido. Why? All Obianyido has for us is that Tai Solarin visited Europe and 'as a result rejected all about deity'. What vague information!

In this circumstance, I see Tai Solarin as a fickle-minded simpleton, weak and easy prey for new ideology, in this case atheism. He could not act as the master of his fate.

After just one visit to Europe, Solarin became infested with atheism, falling deeply in love with the concept. The next thing he did was to go back to his country, Nigeria, and found a school called Mayflower as a mechanism to spread the concept of atheism. What a brazen proselytiser seeking to turn his country, Nigeria, upside down, spiritually and socially!

Funnily enough, Obianyido in his copycatism went to Europe later (Britain in his case) and went back to his country, Nigeria (the same country as his mentor Tai Solarin)—and since then he has been following his mentor's attitude by spreading atheism. But he is spineless and not bold enough to declare his faith in atheism openly; he talks about it in a muffled voice— 'my new faith'. What is the faith? Tai Solarin, his master, openly calls himself an atheist (see Chapter 1 of *In Defence of Jesus the Christ*).

Being an atheist, Tai Solarin lacks spiritual light and walks in darkness. Yet, Obianyido follows him about. Their cooperation smacks of the blind leading the blind (Matthew 15:14).

OBIANYIDO: Europeans hardly go to church, except for certain events like weddings and baptisms of babies. Churches are in decline, many have closed, and some have had their buildings sold.

There was this experience I had while in Liverpool, in Great Britain. For my first church attendance there, I chose Liverpool Cathedral. Not because it was the nearest church to my residence, but for the fact that it was the biggest church in the area. I wanted to start from the top. I wore a colourful agbada dress and took a back seat at the church, early. By the time the service took off, I discovered there was a wide gap between my seat and the rest of the congregation, who sat right in the front. The church was almost empty.

In Britain, churches were being closed or used for mundane purposes.

REPLY: Obianyido's narrative of his comical first church attendance in Britain, except for being as entertaining as a melodramatic scenario, is substantially fruitless and uncalled for in the contest I am having with him on the personality of Jesus. His story of his church attendance is an overdramatisation of a trivial event. But since he decided to put it forward as important, I am prepared to face it and deal with it in detail.

Obianyido chose Liverpool Cathedral because, according to him, it is the biggest church in the area. Mind you, not because the God he was to worship could not be found in the smaller church buildings nearer to his residence, but because he 'wanted to start from the top'. Does that make sense? To get directly to my point, his wanting to start from the top portrays him as an ostentatious person, a person of ordinary social class trying to show himself off as one of high social status. Or did he think that the biggest church building (a cathedral) would get him to, or nearer to, heaven? He totally failed to understand what a true Christian is all about: humility, simplicity, modesty, and like virtues. He behaved like the Pharisees who 'take high seats in public places' (Matthew 23:5–9). A big church (cathedral) has nothing to do with worshipping God or serving God correctly.

Little did Obianyido know that to achieve sound success, one must start from the bottom—a humble beginning. His idea of wanting to start from the top is an awkward though humorous comedy because of his misguided notion of Christianity.

In his voluminous agbada dress, he went on foot, clumsily, from his residence, past all nearby churches with small buildings, to the biggest church (a cathedral), miles away from his residence perhaps. Imagine a neophyte, sort of, in the circumstance of his first church attendance in Britain. There lies Obianyido's problem—showbiz and empty pomposity!

At the time of his attendance, Obianyido dressed foppishly; he wrapped himself up like a woodlouse in his special colourful agbada—a flowing Yoruba (a tribe in Nigeria) gown that is like an exaggerated or magnified woman's gown in appearance.

It takes a great deal of fabric (some of it in gaudy colours) to make such a dress. The volume permits the dress to be easily expanded and contracted sideways at will with one's hands, as if one is playing the accordion. The dress is not without its charm, though. It is generally beautifully and brilliantly embroidered with skilful designs. But what has that got to do with worshipping God? Nothing!

Wrapped up in his agbada, Obianyido must have looked a frump in his bloated appearance. He walked on his way to the biggest church, sauntering, posing, and posturing in his strange attire, I guess with the intent to give the impression that he was a chief or the son of a royal family in Africa—a false impression.

The spectacle which he might have orchestrated at the time is better conjectured than described. To borrow from G. T. Basdon, 'Those who wear this costume may more suitably be imagined than described. ... The picturesque dress .... Abundance material is a prominent feature of its make-up, and the long flowing shirt and surplice-like sleeves constantly trail along the ground as the man walks.'[25]

So Obianyido wanted to create a public spectacle with his strange appearance, in his strange dress, in a strange country. I guess he succeeded. All eyes might have turned to him, with only the blind keeping their attention from him. Those who could see might have abandoned their engagements temporarily to give full attention to the strange scene created by his outlandish dress and his strutting gait. The pairs of eyes that might have been peeping through windows, and the number of people flocking to their balconies upstairs to witness the strange spectacle, can easily be guessed. His intention?

All that he did was done in the vainglorious hope of attracting attention and reverence to himself. He went to the church seeking to earn the admiration of the congregation of the biggest church, a cathedral, in his area of residence.

Can anyone believe that in the circumstance described, Obianyido truly set out from his residence for the church to worship God? Far from that! It is safer to presume that he went not to worship but to be worshipped.

---

[25] G. T. Basdon, *Among the Ibos of Nigeria* (1966).

One definite fact sticks out more than others in his pictorial narrative. Before he left his country, Nigeria, for Great Britain, and in fact thereafter, when he returned to his country, he did not understand the true essence of genuine Christianity. Flamboyant dress, showy behaviour, and pride are not what worshipping God is all about. Worshipping God is about humility, simplicity, love for one's fellow beings, and other moral virtues.

Like the Pharisees and the scribes of the Bible, Obianyido is a blazing hypocrite, professing one thing and doing the other. And he loves worldly praise. Here ends my response to his comical story, the pantomime of his first attendance of a church in Britain.

We now have time to turn to what Obianyido thinks about church attendance in Europe, England. As usual, he is very wrong in his calculation of the number of churchgoers or those who believe in God in Europe. He reckons that the Christian church is in decline and that church buildings are being sold. I am certain he has based his calculations only on the prominent Christian churches that were once in the forefront, such as the Roman Catholic Church and the Protestant Anglican Church, particularly the Roman Catholic cathedral he visited. There is no denying that some of such churches are having a hard time trying to keep their membership numbers high and stable. But that is a concern for only a few of them. The reasons for the downward turn of the membership of such churches are understandable. Three possible factors may be mentioned as being responsible:

(a) Movement of the population
Certain areas in Britain, like Liverpool, are experiencing an economic downturn. As a result, people in search of a better life have moved from Liverpool to other towns, thereby reducing the number of churchgoers there.

(b) Emergence of charismatic Christian churches
With their mesmeric and festive style of service, charismatic churches entice and seduce churchgoers, mostly youth, so that ageing churchgoers are left behind in the conventional churches.

Then the conventional churches suffer greater reduction in membership as their ageing members die off.

(c) Morning, midday, and evening services
Some of the conventional churches, especially the Roman Catholic Church, have kept to offering three services on Sundays. Such churches are to be excused for not expecting a full church at the time of each of the three services.

Obianyido attended one of the three services on a Sunday at the biggest church in Liverpool where, on purpose, he took a seat far behind the congregation so as to be easily noticed and admired by everyone in the church, and he expected a full church. That was his error!

Do not forget that his calculation of the membership of this church was based on his first and only attendance at the church; he did not have any idea of what the population was before the day of his attendance. How then could he say that the population was on the decline? 'Nothing is big or little, otherwise, by comparison.'

In this way, his notion of the number of worshippers in attendance on the day and time of his attendance is skewed. Yet, he relied on his miscalculation to generalise that the membership of all Christian churches was dropping. That is immature calculus!

All he wanted to communicate to his readers was his wishful thinking that the number of people who believed in God and attended church services was dropping. That is false. He should learn that all over the world, including Britain, different groups or sects professing Christianity are on the increase, sprouting up fast like mushrooms, and their membership is increasing by leaps and bounds. Europe, Asia, the United States, Russia, and Africa are each having their fair share of the proliferating number of Christians with a multiplying number of church buildings.

Church buildings are in great demand in many parts of the world today. Obianyido cannot deny the fact of this trend. In Nigeria, his country, the number of Christian churches increases in the manner of the multiplication table. Whatever the ambition of their founders, the members of these churches are attracted and are after serving God for the spiritual benefits that go along with such service. The new churches buy up no-longer-wanted halls or buildings, which they convert into church buildings; they sometimes purchase land and build makeshift temporary churches before later setting up permanent church buildings.

By the way, why does Obianyido make noise and mockingly declare that church buildings and the number of people in attendance are on the decline? Church buildings and churchgoers do not determine the population of those who profess Christianity, nor do they affect the spiritual truth which Jesus the Christ taught and asked his followers to continue teaching. It is impossible to capture mathematically the correct census of people professing Christianity in the world just by computing the number of those in attendance at the largest Roman Catholic church—the cathedral—in Liverpool, in a matter of one attendance.

Obianyido wants to be reminded that the question 'Who is this man Jesus Christ who has harassed the human soul for so long?' might have been asked because of the astronomical number of people following Christianity from the time of Jesus the Christ to the present day.

His headache about the number of church buildings in decline and the number of people who every Sunday are present in them is a mark of his having nothing serious to say against Christianity. Christianity itself is not concerned with those things. What Christianity wants, after all, is that people should know about the teachings of Jesus the Christ and practise them to please God. Jesus the Christ did not work for an increase in the number of church buildings, nor for an increase in the number of those in attendance at these churches. Such material things are the quest of worldly people like Obianyido and his atheist friends. While on earth, Jesus the Christ, after teaching, healing, and converting those who came to him, told them to go and sin no more (John 8:11; Mark 2:5, 5:19). It was not part of his culture to gather converts into a building called a church for a Christian census. The only times he wanted any people to follow him were when he needed them to join him in the spreading of his gospel. In fact, increasing the number of people for heaven was his sole aim, rather than multiplying the number of church buildings and the number of churchgoers.

De-emphasising worshipping God in tangible places, Jesus the Christ suggested to the Samaritan woman he met at Jacob's well that God should be worshipped in spirit and in truth, not necessarily on a mountain or at the temple in Jerusalem (John 4:21–24). In a similar vein, he told a lawyer to learn the lesson of the parable of the Good Samaritan and go and put it into practice (Luke 10:25–37). These illustrations are about the priority of conduct of believers who seek the kingdom of God. That is to say, Jesus the Christ relegated mere churchgoing to a place far, far down on his priority list.

Finally, I add that in the book of Acts in the New Testament, one reads, 'God, who made the world and everything therein, is the Lord of Heaven and earth and does not live in temples built by hand' (Acts 17:24). This scripture goes far in answering Obianyido's concern about church buildings and churchgoers. Remember: 'Many are called, few are chosen.'

OBIANYIDO: The story of Adam and Eve as the first two human beings on earth no longer makes sense as the concept of creation. It bears a similarity to the question 'Who made us?' which children ask, instead of 'How did humankind come about?' The former question presupposes a physical existence of making.

REPLY: Obianyido witlessly, irrelevantly, splits hairs. The two questions 'Who made us?' and 'How did humankind come about?' have the same meaning as both expect the same answer. We know that the way things come about is by their being made (created). So, Obianyido's reconstruction of the question is an annoyance. He messes himself up in his interpretation of the English language.

The *Collins Cobuild English Language Dictionary* says, 'If you make something, you create or produce it.' The same dictionary has this: 'the making of the universe, earth, and creatures by God as described in the Bible'. Going by Obianyido's reasoning, the dictionary's definitions are wrong. Obianyido, by himself, earlier said, 'But God, or that benevolent force behind Creation [making], must have His way.' Remember that the dictionary just consulted shows that to create is to make. So, what is Obianyido up to? Why is he fumbling for what is not the case?

The word *makes* (past tense *made*) has several meanings. It is versatile, variable, and homonymous; its meaning very much depends on the context in which it is being used. There is nothing wrong, grammatically, with the use of the word in the question which Obianyido criticises: 'Who made us?' He is an Igbo man. His problem here is that the English language is not his mother tongue; it is foreign to him. He studied it later in his youth to learn as much as he knows of it. He approached his interpretation of the sentence 'Who made us?' from the perspective of an Igbo native with certain phraseology. He conceived in his mind what the word *made* means in the Igbo language, and he transferred the meaning onto he English word *made*. With that, he translated the question 'Who made us?' I call that 'Engligbo'—a mixture of English and Igbo, when it comes to the meaning of the word *made*. That was how he came up with the idea of 'a physical existence of making'. Wrong!

If I say, for example, 'I make John laugh,' does that mean 'a physical existence of my making' is what causes John to laugh? I refer to the Authorised King James Version of the Holy Bible, which says, 'Ye should turn from these vanities unto the living God, which made heaven and earth' (Acts 14:15). I wonder what Obianyido has to say about the import of the word *made* in this context.

If in his understanding the first question, 'Who made us?', presupposes 'a physical existence of making', then what does the second question, 'How did humankind come about?', which he constructed, mean? Criticising 'Who made us?' he substituted his own construction, 'How did humankind come about?' His aim was to sweep away the word *made* or *create* because that would take him to God as the Maker or Creator of humankind. In his mind, he was conceiving of the theory of evolution or the Big Bang as the way humankind came about, the theory which some shallow-thinking philosophers and scientists peddle. In other words, Obianyido wants God out of the picture and prefers the theory of evolution or the Big Bang to explain how the universe and humankind came into existence. What a dimwit he is!

I am reluctant to stray into the blind theory of evolution or the Big Bang, which he hides behind in his reconstruction of the question 'Who made us?' I can only recommend for him the *Evangelical Times* article 'Teaching Controversy—the Creation vs. Evolution Debate' (January 2003), and the article 'How Did Life Begin?' published in the Jehovah's Witnesses magazine *Awake* (January 2015), pages 3–7. The rationale given in the article for belief in God as the Maker of the universe and all in it will drill Obianyido and convince him of the existence of God as the Creator of all things. That will, no doubt, convince him to disbelieve in the said theories, unless he chooses to be a pig-headed bigot.

The root of the word *made* (present tense, *make*) is a discipline for philologists. But I am not one of them. The discipline therefore deserves no further treatment here.

Enough has been said about the word *made*. I propose to return to our main subject, Adam, and Eve, next.

To Obianyido, the Holy Bible's 'story of Adam and Eve no longer makes sense as the concept of creation'. I have already guessed that what now makes sense to him as the concept of creation is the theory of evolution or the Big Bang theory. About that I have said enough. I still hold onto the information in the Holy Bible as the best and most reliable of anything offered to humankind as to how the universe and all therein came into existence.

I was perplexed by the nature of the story in the Holy Bible telling us about the creation by God. The story does not expose itself to easy understanding; it is not friendly to the imagination. At one point I became curious about the biblical meaning of the story of Creation and meditated to find tangible knowledge of what the story conveys to humankind. Diligently, I listened to the still small voice of God within me—my inner self. From that divine voice, I believe I captured what Moses meant to impart, what his presentation to humankind as to the history of Creation was about. In summary, Moses informed us that God created the universe and all therein, Adam and Eve as the first two human beings included Adam and Eve were put by God in the Garden of Eden—Paradise on earth. They lived there happily, enjoying to the full all the pleasant things therein.

It is necessary to mention that after their creation, God commanded them to eat all the fruits of the garden except the fruit of the tree in the middle of the garden, and warned that they would suffer and die, consequently, if they disobeyed his commandment. Adam and Eve did disobey God's commandment. Therefore, God flung them out of the garden and punished them.

Humankind, being the descendants of Adam and Eve, inherited the disobedient nature (characteristic) of their forebears Adam and Eve. Now humankind has been struggling to get back to the Garden of Eden, to Paradise, by way of repentance, penance, and obedience to God.

As I mentioned earlier, I desired to gain some knowledge from Moses's story about the creation of the world. I went into meditation and listened diligently to what I believed to be the divine still small voice of my inner self. I came up with a hypothesis: that this fact about the Creation might have been given to Moses by God in divine language (Genesis 1–2). Human beings could not understand the reality of creation in the words by which it was revealed to Moses because it was too mystical or too divine a concept for comprehension by worldly human beings. Moses himself could not speak the divine language, though he might have spiritually understood it (without the help of reason).

It was a mystical phenomenon. But then Moses was to convey the notion to humankind. So, he had to decode and demystify the divine language of the revelation and convey the revelation in a simile that was worldly though somewhat cryptic. That turned out to be the story of Creation given us in the Old Testament.

In this case, we cannot but accept, by faith, the story and make do with the lessons the story has handed out:

(a) God is the Creator, the Maker of the universe and all in it.

(b) In creating the universe, God set out the laws to govern his creation, that is creatures. For example, he commanded Adam and Eve, the first two human beings on earth, to enjoy everything in the Garden of Eden (Paradise on earth), except the fruit of the tree in the middle of the garden.

(c) He prescribed suffering and death to be the consequence for disobeying his commandment.

(d) Adam and Eve disobeyed God.

(e) They suffered the consequence of their disregard for the law given them by God, namely suffering and death.

What of this, the acts and/or omissions of each of the culprits involved in the matter? My humble opinion is as follows:

By nature, Satan (the Serpent) was an enemy of righteousness and was an outsider to the partnership set up by God between Adam and Eve.

While an interloper (busybody), the Serpent exercised control over Eve and got her to eat the forbidden fruit.

By creation, Eve was Adam's wife, therefore Adam's subordinate. She ate the forbidden fruit and wrongly exercised control over Adam, her husband, persuading him to eat the forbidden fruit.

So, the Serpent was punished for interloping in a matter that concerned God, Adam, and Eve only (Genesis 3:14).

Eve was punished for listening to the Serpent, instead of subjecting herself to Adam, her husband (Genesis 3:13, 16).

Adam was punished and could not get away with his disobedience by telling God that the woman he had given him was the cause, when he listened to her (obeyed her) instead of keeping her under his control (Genesis 3:12, 17).

NB: Prudence suggests that a husband must consider his wife's opinions but is to have the final say in matters concerning them both.

For any inquisitive readers of this book who may want to know what I think of the commandment of God to Adam and Eve that says, 'Of every tree of the Garden thou mayest freely eat: But of the tree of knowledge good and evil, thou shalt not eat of it: for the day that thou eateth thereof thou shalt surely die' (Genesis 2:16–17), I guess that with matured sense it is easy to see the story about Adam, Eve, the Serpent, and the fruit of the tree in the middle of the Garden of Eden as a figure of speech (which I classify as an allegory). My next concern is to find out what the allegory translates to, literally, i.e. in real life.

That question does not seem hard to figure out. Consider that the tree in the middle of the garden is a sexual organ (which is in the middle of the human figure); Adam and Eve were created naked and knew not good and evil, and were not ashamed. They ate the fruit and possessed the knowledge of good and evil, i.e. discovered their nakedness. They were punished. From the fact of their discovery of their nakedness, I conclude that the allegory relates to a sexual act. Literally, therefore, God commanded Adam and Eve to enjoy everything in life except the sex act.

Enquiringly, I ask, why then did God create Adam and Eve with the necessary sexual tools—the male sex organ for Adam, the female sex organ for Eve—for the possibility of performing the sex act and putting the two together?

Additionally, why did God later command humankind to increase and multiply but earlier punished Adam and Eve for their act that would have made the increase and multiplication possible? These are questions no one can answer. Only God himself knows! Humankind can only make empty guesses.

My guess is that the Creator, our Father, God, has his own agenda and priorities and wants things to happen according to his chosen divine order. His ways are not our ways.

Therefore, though Adam and Eve each had the necessary sex organs, given them by God at the time he created them, they did not have the necessary Creator's command or authority to put those tools into use; they had been specifically told by their Creator, God, not to use the tools. They disobeyed. Their act was, I think, premature as they cared not to wait for God's command! They committed a sin, therefore.

Consider this: Eve, after having first tasted the forbidden fruit, might have given Adam fantastic information about her experience so to arouse his curiosity and get him to try the act out with her. That might have stirred Adam's curiosity in the act.

It seems to me then that Adam did not intend to disobey God's command. He might have acted out of curiosity to find out what the matter was all about. In exercise of the *free will* he was endowed with at Creation, he sinned by making the wrong choice of his own free will.

He was remorseful, though, as shown at the time they covered their nakedness and hid themselves because of their act of disobedience. But it was too late; the sinful act had already been committed. The prescribed punishment for disobedience had to follow.

Last question: since Eve tasted the forbidden fruit (committed the forbidden sex act) before convincing Adam to do the same with her, with whom did she do it—the Serpent? 'No clue' is my humble answer. Your guess?

OBIANYIDO: 'The modern man no longer considers the teaching of Jesus Christ relevant to his needs.'

REPLY: The modern world is fraught with all sorts of social problems and evils. The problems seem to defy solution. Modern human beings have been struggling in their efforts to find the root causes of the problems and the means to the solutions. Obianyido seems to have inadvertently pointed to the very cause of the problems when by asserting, 'The modern man no longer considers the teaching of Jesus Christ relevant to his needs.' I take his point as one of the causes of the evils plaguing modern society. The modern human being, for a better society, needs the teachings of Jesus the Christ.

Disregard for the teaching of Jesus the Christ (or that of other spiritual masters with similar moral substance) is bound to create a moral vacuum. Absence of good moral knowledge and practice of the same in any society is, in turn, bound to make way for cataclysmic social evils. For a long time now, humankind has been witnessing a serious tidal wave of antisocial behaviours all over the world.

Obianyido's observation, though somewhat accidental, is to be taken seriously as the likely root cause of the social problems of the modern world. The question now is, what, precisely, makes up the teachings of Jesus the Christ that can help solve the problems of the world? Here we think of the teachings of Jesus the Christ with compassionate love at the centre. By its nature, compassionate love encompasses humility, civility, honesty, justice, charity, truth, fairness, and other moral virtues, each of which has love for one's neighbour, to the glory of God, as its terminus.

Neglect for the teachings of Jesus the Christ (the Christian principles) was identified as the cause of the ills gnawing at the fabric of British social life and destroying it. Following that, Sir John Major, in his time as the prime minister of Great Britain, made a clarion call: 'Back to basics', where traditional family values, meaning love and respect for the law and people, were to reign in the society. Mr Pattern, the Secretary of Education, realising the antisocial behaviours of children and youths in his time in office, sought to introduce compulsory Christian scriptures into the school curriculum so as to inculcate the Christian teaching (of Jesus the Christ) in the minds of those who make up British society. This was about 1994. Both Sir John Major's effort and Mr Pattern's effort took place in our generation.

The cataclysmic social conditions we are witnessing in many countries today, Nigeria for one, result from the idea that 'the modern man no longer considers the teachings of Jesus Christ relevant to his needs'. This shows there is no better antisocial remedy than the ideas present within the teachings of Jesus the Christ.

In the light of that concern, the deep sense of truth in one of Steve Chalke's statements urges me to invoke his dictum: 'I'm convinced that what Jesus Christ taught makes sense—huge sense—and that it is as relevant and practical today as it ever been.'[26] It makes sense to consider, therefore, that the modern human being no longer considers the teachings of Jesus relevant to his or her needs when modern people are no longer interested in civilisation but in antisocial behaviour.

In this sense, Obianyido bases his saying (i.e. comment) on arrant nonsense!

Disregard for the teachings of Jesus the Christ in any society causes untold social problems. Modern human beings therefore need the teachings of Jesus the Christ for the solution of their social and spiritual problems.

OBIANYIDO: The Holy Book, the Bible, is no longer wanted in developed countries. Once in my college in Britain, a Christian priest handed a load of Bibles to students for free distribution. The rascal students accepted the Bibles for mischief-making. They joked with them, playing a game of throw-and-catch with the Holy Books, until the books were torn to pieces and finally ended up in a metal dustbin.

---

[26] Steve Chalke, *More than Meets the Eye* (2003), vii.

REPLY: That story, no doubt, is a concocted one. It is like an old wives' tale, lacking in reality.

By the way, how can we be sure that Obianyido attended any college when he was in Liverpool? He failed to name his college and the course he was there for. He also failed to tell his readers what he did with his own load of Bibles for free distribution. Those omissions are some of the signs indicating that the story is a made-up one.

I wish to address the story as if it really happened. In such a case, the event is a shameful one. The acts of the students Obianyido describes as 'rascals' and 'mischief-makers' were nothing to write home about. The students committed acts of hooliganism, most unexpected from disciplined students.

Obianyido relies on these acts of hooliganism to say that the Holy Book, the Bible, is no longer wanted in developed countries. His conclusion is senseless. There is a world of difference between the Holy Bible being no longer wanted on the one hand, and the book being no longer useful as a source of moral knowledge on the other. The truth is that even if the book was no longer wanted by the rascals and vandals, it still contains essential moral teachings that are as important and relevant now as they were when first they were given. Any stage of development of a country or society counts for nothing when the teachings of the Bible are disregarded without a substitute substantially the same in terms of content.

To return to Obianyido's story about the rascally and mischievous students and the Bible, why the mischief of the students entertained him and gave him joy beats my scrupulous imagination. He endorsed those ultimately expensive acts of rascality. His irrational and boundless desire to attack Jesus the Christ and Christianity at all costs, as a result of his deep passion and mania for atheism, seems to have, as usual, robbed him of good judgement. Imagine his camping out with hooligans and finding dishonourable pleasure in treating mischief-makers as heroes and heroines. Does he expect applause from his readers for such an ear-itching story?

No primitive or barbaric person, let alone a reasonable person of modern times, would behave like those students, nor would any be thrilled, as Obianyido, by such a repulsive, stupid act, even if one did not believe in Christianity. Yet, Obianyido is thrilled to recount the story of the event in his book *Christ or Devil?* What a slip in rational reasoning! I see his reaction in favour of the students' rascality as dirty.

OBIANYIDO: In my society, Christianity is a lucrative business. Those who claim to be priests and servants of God take advantage of their position in the church to eat what they like and live in the type of building they like. All these things happen in the midst of the poverty of those laity who contribute all their material wealth to the church.

Everywhere, at midnight or in the early hours of the morning, the neighbourhood is disturbed with preaching and shouts of 'Praise the Lord! Halleluiah!' Those church people often pin Christian Union badges on the lapels of their coats or hang them in their offices. Some decorate their cars with the inscription 'When will you come out of sin?' But insensitivity to the feeling of their customers at their places of work does not come under their definition of sin; they treat customers as they like.

REPLY: To begin with, I seek to remind Obianyido of his notion that the Holy Bible is no longer wanted, that the number of church buildings and churchgoers is in decline, and that Jesus the Christ and his followers were the most hated of all religious people in their time. His observations this time, in this present chapter of *Christ or Devil?* are not in accord with his earlier ones. This time he complains that the followers of Christianity are swarming everywhere and disturbing nonmembers.

Some of his observations and complaints against some of the so-called Christians are correct. Fools are sometimes right, though accidentally.

By that I mean that fools sometimes take the correct decisions without making the consciously disciplined effort—whereas the wise consciously follow the path of reason to arrive at the correct decisions.

Yes, some churches' preaching in the early hours and their midnight noisy services disturb the neighbourhoods where they are located. Such behaviours are intolerable, antisocial, and of course, un-Christian.

I have personally observed some such events. Once I witnessed a church pantomime, the actor's intent on behaving like the apostles of old as narrated in Acts 2:1–13 in the New Testament. The church congregation were mesmerised by the so-called charismatic, yet false, pastors and their cohorts who sang, shouted, and faked speaking in tongues and prophesising at the time of my visit. This was not spiritual, in my assessment. As I watched, the congregation fell about like people suffering epileptic fits. The whole congregation indulged in unimaginable hubbub and din, like the biblical Babel. The entire atmosphere of the church was charged with a deafening echo that spilled out into the neighbourhood—the people living close to the church premises. There was a total disregard for the peace and comfort of the nonparticipant neighbours. That, certainly, amounted to a public nuisance. So, Obianyido got his criticism right on this point.

He has another point correct. He is against some ill behaviour of some churches where the so-called Christians show a divide in material wealth. That is, the gap in wealth between the priests/pastors and the ordinary members of the church is too wide to stand as being in alignment with the teaching of Jesus the Christ. The priests enjoy fabulous wealth, while most of the members among the laity who contribute to the financial wealth of the church (from which the priests/pastors derive their wealth) suffer mammoth poverty. That is far from the Christian view that members should contribute to the church's wealth voluntarily to defray the expenses of the church, which, of course, include the maintenance of the priests/pastors who devote their time to the service of the members and to the glory of God: 'A labourer is worth of his wages' (Acts 20:33–35). But the wages should be reasonable and be used wisely.

Paul the apostle, speaking on this subject, suggests that preachers work for their living. They are not to be lazy so as not to be a burden to their followers (1 Thessalonians 3:6–14). Paul said to the elders of the church in Asia, 'I have coveted no one's silver or gold or apparel. Yes, you yourselves know that these hands have provided for my necessities, and for those who were with me. I have shown you in every way, by labouring like this, that you must support the weak. And remember the words of the Lord Jesus, that he said, "It is more blessed to give than to receive"' (Acts 20:33–35). Priests/pastors should take note.

Church priests/pastors who unreasonably enjoy the wealth of the church and impiously exploit their followers are not true Christian leaders.

Where Obianyido's criticism of Christians' behaviour concerns the pinning of badges on clothes (lapels) and inscriptions about Jesus the Christ on cars, I totally disagree with him. No one is hurt by such a practice, although some atheists are likely to develop itching eyes merely by looking at such badges and/or inscriptions.

Finally, I opine that the churches that fail to practise the Christian principles taught by Jesus the Christ and his disciples and apostles are pseudo-Christians, freaks; therefore, they do not represent true Christianity. My book, therefore, does not side with them.

CHRISTIAN RELIGION AND EDUCATION

(CHAPTER 10, *CHRIST OR DEVIL?*)

OBIANYIDO: Is the influence of Christian religion on education in Nigeria positive or negative? Education makers in Nigeria would answer in the positive. But I would disagree with that.

Education in Nigeria originally was directed to producing people who would simply repeat what had been given them. Now, with the overhaul of the curriculum, education has become functional.

In Britain, the Christian religion or religious knowledge has been de-emphasised in the educational system. Only those students whose parents so decide learn religion in school. With this arrangement, British schools no longer pay serious attention to religious knowledge.

Religious education subjected Nigerian children to a ready-made moral code of conduct, thus denying the children the God-given freedom to develop critical thinking and mental growth.

In Nigeria, I once found on a blackboard of a lecture hall of an institution of higher education, 'Follow Jesus Christ our Lord before it is too late.' When next I visited the hall, someone unknown had changed the word *out* in the inscription to *your*, making the sentence read, 'Follow Jesus Christ *your* Lord before it is too late.'

The lecturer warned the students against this mischievous act.

REPLY: In his book, from Chapter 1 to Chapter 10, the latter of which I am at this very time treating, Anene Obianyido has been behaving like a pendulum. Now he uses expressions indicating his belief in the existence of God, and next he uses expressions contradicting that belief. For the matter I am addressing now, he has used the expression 'God-given freedom', showing his belief, once more, in the existence of God.

Whatever the case may be, let me overlook for now his pendulous mind and deal with him in terms of whichever faith I find him professing at any given moment.

Whenever Obianyido found himself in an educational institution, he customarily fell into hallucinations and concocted a story thereafter. About his college (no name) in Liverpool, England, he came up with a story of students playing 'throw and catch' with Holy Bibles. This time, concerning an institution of higher education (again, no name) which he visited twice, according to him, Obianyido spins a story about an inscription on a blackboard involving a lecturer and his students.

I ask, what was his business visiting the institution twice, and with such a short interval in between visits? Was he there as a student, or a lecturer, or an education officer or inspector, or a roam-about who had nothing else to do than to loaf about educational institutions? Imagine! He was there at the right time to witness the lecturer's warning against the students. What was he there for at that moment? His story is starved of the answers to all these questions. How are we sure that his was not the hand that made the alteration in the inscription on the blackboard, assuming his story to be real?

With respect the story, Obianyido wants us, his readers, to take it that the act of the students he described as 'mischievous' were recommendable? He derived some degree of dirty satisfaction in having the incident publicised, and he was euphoric to have witnessed the scene. The fact is that he always finds fulfilment in glamorising and glorifying rascality, vandalism, and similar antisocial behaviours when such are directed against Jesus the Christ, Christianity, or God.

I presume he sees in the antisocial conduct of some students the good products of 'God-given freedom to develop critical thinking and mental growth' which the 'overhaul of the Nigerian educational system', which did away with religious knowledge (an idea he supports), has brought about.

About his suggestion that children be allowed unrestricted freedom, I am not with him on that. Instead, I am of the philosophical view that each human being is born into the world a beast exercising the first law of nature, that of self-preservation, and that if person is left unrestricted, unguided, then he or she will most likely grow very wild and remain detrimental and a big threat to his or her society.

The teaching of good moral religious knowledge can do a lot to cut the wild conduct of humankind down to a civilised size that is acceptable to society. Essentially, the instrument for such a restriction must be the 'ready-made moral code of conduct', which, unfortunately, Obianyido is thoughtlessly against.

My readers, I trust, and Obianyido, I hope, will call to mind the common saying, 'Mr [or Mrs or Miss or Master] so-and-so behaves as one who has not been to school.' In Nigeria, that expression shows disapproval of certain behaviours that are antisocial and unacceptable in a civilised society. This disapproval may be directed against someone even if he or she has been to school and achieved academic qualifications yet lacks in the good moral knowledge and behaviour that good religion teaches. Mathematics, geography, technology, engineering, science, and such do not offer moral teaching; morality is the discipline of religious education.

Obianyido is satisfied that the Nigerian educational system has been overhauled by flushing out or de-emphasising religious education. But I would say that the educational system of Nigeria has been vandalised! The former system was helping to shape the moral conduct of citizens, particularly those who are young, and thus was preparing the younger generation morally for decorous and harmonious social integration in their larger communities when adults.

Obianyido brands the new educational system 'functional'. I dare ask, functional in what sense? I choose to answer that question: functional in churning out graduates with antisocial character. Further, I ask, since the so-called 'overhaul', what has become of the state of Nigeria, politically, scientifically, technologically, economically, socially, and morally? Once more, I volunteer to answer regrettably, the overhaul of the Nigerian educational system, which disregarded religious knowledge and did away with a ready-made moral code of conduct, has opened Pandora's box. Obianyido now sees the result of his vacuous suggestion to do away with the ready-made moral code of conduct that was helping to shape and control the raw nature of humankind. Doing away with the ready-made code of moral conduct creates a dangerous vacuum, which is something that nature abhors. When there is such a vacuum, Nature fills it with her raw, wild state of barbarism. Obianyido must learn that no society can survive as a civilised one without a ready-made code of moral conduct.

Nigeria has, after de-emphasising or doing away with religion, become hell on earth! There are now all sorts of evils there, each type fighting for primacy in the hellish situation. Slowly, the country is sliding towards absolute social chaos. A vivid social crisis reigns in the society as at the time *In Defence of Jesus the Christ* is being written. Prominent among the antisocial problems are armed robbery, fraud (419, its local name), kidnapping, ritual killing of human beings, evil cults in universities and secondary schools, fake churches, and corruption at all levels of public service, politics included.

Today, it takes great courage to live in Nigeria amid these intimidating antisocial problems. Youths roam and loaf about as predators, while the weak and the old (the potential victims) hide away. Where possible, some barricade themselves most of the time in their own accommodations for security's sake. You can be sure every crime and every antisocial mode of conduct known to humankind survives in the country.

Obianyido mentions that in Britain, the Christian religion and Christian religious knowledge have been de-emphasised in the educational system. His shallow thinking was unable to dive deep enough to understand why this is so. Britain has become a multireligious society. Being a Christian country, Britain considered it prudent to apply to its educational system what it reckoned to be Christian principles of tolerance, fairness, and justice. Since British schools are invariably made up of pupils of different faiths, it would be unfair, Britain considered, to emphasise the Christian religion in its schools. Personally, I think this is a case of overtolerance. The country could have gotten around its fear in another way, such as allowing any non-Christian in its schools to opt out of Christian religious education and then to keep Christian religious education going as usual.

Today in Britain, because of the disregard for moral teaching in schools, antisocial behaviour is breeding fast.

Earlier I referred to the views of Sir John Major and Mr Pattern on how to tackle the problem of antisocial conduct among children and youths, by providing them with religious knowledge that emphasises good moral conduct.

The benefits of inculcating good moral knowledge in the minds of citizens at a young age cannot be overemphasised.

The overhauled educational system of Nigeria offers children bookish knowledge without the necessary good moral character to go with it. Today in Nigeria, children no longer respect their elders, their teachers, their parents, the laws of their country, or even God, their Creator! The dictum 'The fear of God [respect for God] is the beginning of wisdom' has lost its credence and credit among Nigerian children (Psalm 111:10).

Finally, we have to accept that religious knowledge, particularly Christian religious knowledge, with its moral teaching in the early years of children's education is the best way of inculcating good behaviour in the minds of children so as to prevent antisocial conduct when they become adults.

OBIANYIDO: Tai Solarin had this to say:

> For twenty years in Mayflower school, there was no religion taught in that secular school. But the much I got to know over the years—that if there were twenty applicants from twenty different schools looking for a job, the ex-May (as the graduates from Mayflower school are known) would get, if not the first place, certainly the second.
>
> On my leaving Mayflower school in 1970, the Mays called a meeting of their own representatives and the new principal, Mrs Odubanjo, and I was also invited. One special request these ex-Mays made was that the new principal keep up the secular atmosphere of the school. There were young men and young women who on leaving school comparing themselves with others feed on the chaff which religiosity is, were convinced that they were miles ahead of their counterparts.

REPLY: Hang on! First of all, let me make a retrospective comment on Obianyido's character. His readers must be confused about his relationship with God. That he supports the Mayflower school only if it is kept secular, and that he believes nothing about religion or God should be mentioned or taught in the school, is indicative of his disbelief in God. On other occasions he seems to believe in God by his use of the expression 'God-given freedom', as I earlier mentioned. The same pendulous mind governs his character on many other matters. As to the question of whether Jesus the Christ ever existed, he believes this time, but the next, he disbelieves. Obianyido has always, throughout his book *Christ or Devil?* shown himself as a very unreliable character by habitually stepping sideways like a crab and moving up and down like a yo-yo. He has no steady mind. His mind is always being rocked by atheism, with which he was fed while he was a student at Mayflower school. His idiosyncratic habit of never, ever making up his mind on any matter before him gives *Christ or Devil?* away as a notorious and unreliable work.

The purpose of religious knowledge is to move one's conduct in one direction, invariably towards civilisation, and to instil respect for God through the path of justice and righteousness. It is, therefore, irrational for Obianyido to describe Christian religious knowledge as 'chaff'.

Obianyido quotes what Tai Solarin has to say in praise of his school, the Mayflower. He basks in the praise because he is an ex-Mayflower student. Being a dimwit, he is unable to see that Tai Solarin is making a cheap advertisement of his school. I see Obianyido as a mercenary using his book as a medium for spreading propaganda in favour of Tai Solarin's faith and his Mayflower school. Solarin wrote his own eulogy, which he garnished with the expression 'founded—without the hand of God', a bit of self-praise, no doubt. What a tantrum that is! What does one expect such a proud person who suffers from egotistical insanity to say about something in which he has a profound vested interest? Should he criticise himself or condemn his own school? It takes the courage of a prudent person to bring oneself to consider one's own work or conduct as bad when such is the case. Tai Solarin lacks that courage.

In the face of that fact, Obianyido is bewitched, unaware that Tai Solarin's utterances are mere vain self-aggrandisement. He believes Tai Solarin's boasting. Why not? Obianyido is an ex-student of Tai Solarin's Mayflower school, and Solarin is his mentor as well as his master in atheism, even though he suffers from delusions of grandeur!

Of all the things I hate, blowing one's own trumpet is first on the list. Had the information in Solarin's claim which Obianyido embraced been presented by a third party in a neutral position, as an observer, then it would have merited consideration. Since the claim proceeded from Tai Solarin with a vested interest in his own school, it is safer to take his utterance *cum grano salis* (with a pinch of salt).

In the old days to which Tai Solarin was referring when claiming that his Mayflower school was among the best, if not the best, of all its contemporary secondary schools in Nigeria, Nigerian secondary schools were classified into two main groups according to the quality of education provided or the students' performance on general or common examinations. There was class A and class B. Class A consisted of government secondary schools and missionary secondary schools. The rest of the secondary schools made up class B. These were private enterprises set up by individuals or a group of individuals who were wealthy enough to do the business. The Mayflower school fell into class B.

In terms of educational facilities, class A schools were far better than class B schools, and produced better results in the Cambridge General Examination, which was being sent overseas, to Britain, to be marked at the end of the students' course, than class B.

The standard score on the general entrance examination (for entry into secondary schools) for class A was very high. Only brilliant or lucky children were able to gain admission into class A. The rest of the children who could not make it into class A were rejects! Those rejects were usually stuffed into class B schools.

In the circumstance I have given, no child would want admission into any class B school if he or she could gain admission to any class A school. The Igbo (a tribe in Nigeria) have a proverb that says, 'Adafusia ebe anaechi ozo jebe ebe analu agwu.' The English translation is, 'One does not voluntarily go for an inferior thing in place of a superior one.' This proverb stirs up two questions, by the way: what circumstance took Obianyido to the Mayflower school's class B (in the western part of Nigeria) from his community (in Eastern Nigeria), and why did he not attend any of the class A secondary schools? The answers to those questions are for my readers to guess.

I am concerned more with the boasting of Tai Solarin than with Obianyido's admission into a private secondary school that was inferior to missionary and government secondary schools.

Tai Solarin's claim represents that his school (Mayflower) turns out graduates far better, academically speaking, than those from other secondary schools, including class A schools. In other words, he claims to be able to turn mediocre students into brilliant graduates, just like an alchemist claims to be able to turn ordinary metal into gold. Well, that is an egocentric, empty claim!

I am prepared to grant Tai Solarin a wish: I grant him his wishful thought that his Mayflower school, where the teaching of good moral conduct, which is what religious education deals in, is proscribed, produces the best academically qualified graduates in Nigeria because God is not recognised at the school. This means that most of the students of the school graduate in their academic discipline as well as in moral bankruptcy.

Besides the use of their academic knowledge in the service of their society, of what other service can such morally bankrupt graduates be to their society than to destroy it as woodworm does wood, or maggot, a carcass?

In any case, one striking fact emerged later about the Mayflower school: it took a new turn, a negative development, towards a terminal crash. The school of atheism capitulated to theism. A Christian church found a place of comfort almost in the heart of the school compound. Christianity, after all, was not kept at bay by the school. The sorry story below about the new development has been culled from *Newswatch* magazine, a Nigerian weekly, of 8 August 1994, page 32. The article is titled 'The Man Died'. The writer of the article is a fine brilliant journalist, Mercy

Ette. I solicited the kind permission of the editor to lift the relevant portion of said article, verbatim, into my writing here: 'He [Tai Solarin] was an atheist. Ironically, some former students of Mayflower, where Solarin pointedly told God to remove "His obstructionist hand", are now big-time preachers. William Florusho Kumuyi, general overseer of the Deeper Life Ministries, is one of them. Religion has even found a berth in the school. The building that attracts a visitor's first attention near the school compound is a chapel. Solarin failed to keep God out of the Mayflower after all.'

The unfriendly and embarrassing interference, by fate, with the school's policy must have been a melancholy event to Obianyido. Since he has a predilection for atheism, as his book bears witness to, he deserves a share in the failure story. The saying 'Except the Lord builds the house, they labour in vain that build it' (Psalm 127) comes true.

Tai Solarin, in addition to witnessing the failure of his school's aim to keep God away from its doors, prematurely passed from our earthly plane. The dramatic failure of Solarin's funfair, with his vain and arrogant boast about his school, 'built without the hand of God', is as strikingly gloomy as his early death is pathetic.

His ambition to be the master of his fate, the captain of his soul, in the ocean of the living came to ruins. His success turned out to be ephemeral—nine days of wandering! 'Pride goes before a fall' (Proverbs 16:18). The events are a sermon for the atheists.

That Tai Solarin passed away prematurely is pitiful. *De mortuis nihil nisi bonum* (May his soul rest in peace). God forgive him, I humbly pray!

OBIANYIDO: Those who claim to be Christians behave in a tremendously horrible way. A growing number of students are now being recruited into these fake organisations and being brainwashed into surrendering a good degree of personal and family responsibility and intellectual growth in exchange for a make-believe spiritual security.

REPLY: Obianyido here considers two types of Christian organisations: a fake one and a genuine one. Which of the two is he criticising and attacking? Answer: both. His is a confused mind!

Earlier he said, 'Jesus Christ and his disciples and their religion were the most hated and despised of all religions.' Also, he had two stories to illustrate his belief that students never like Jesus the Christ, Christianity, or God. One of the stories relates to his time at his college in Liverpool, England, and the other relates to an institution of higher education in Nigeria. Now, in this chapter (Chapter 10 of *Christ or Devil?*), he alleges that students are being recruited into Christianity (whether fake or genuine matters not to our argument). They are not being conscripted, mind you. Does one join, of one's own volition, an organisation that one does not like? If the students show their likeness for Christianity, then Obianyido's later allegation conflicts with and contradicts his earlier stories—the one about the students' game of throw-and-catch with the Holy Bibles at his college in Liverpool, England, and the other about a lecturer, his students, and an inscription on a blackboard in a Nigerian institution of higher education.

Another point: Obianyido writes in Chapter 10 of *Christ or Devil?* 'Those who claim to be Christians behave in tremendously horrible ways.' I like this comment. It means that he recognises that the horrible behaviour falls short of the expected civilised behaviour of genuine Christians. And his use of the words *fakes* and *make-believe* to describe the students he has condemned shows that the horrible behaviours of the students were un-Christian. He sees the Christian standard of behaviour as more civilised and better, socially, and morally, than that of the students. So, he regards the students as not being true Christians. That is a welcome observation by him.

Why then is he thoughtlessly attacking Jesus the Christ and Christianity? That is the question!

CHRISTIAN RELIGION AND MORALITY

(CHAPTER 11, *CHRIST OR DEVIL?*)

OBIANYIDO: According to Rev. N. S. Iwe, 'In view of its human character, Christianity has in the course of human history and in various nations demonstrated itself as the custodian and promoter of human values. Though one may not rightly assert that Christianity has always played this role flawlessly, there is however sufficient historical evidence to justify its claim to it.' I hold that Christianity as practised in my area (Nigeria) has never played the role referred to by the reverend as flawless.

While I was in Liverpool, a white friend of mine visited Nigeria. He came back to narrate how millions of Nigerians profess to be Christians but, in practice, engage in corruption, smuggling, hoarding, robbery, profiteering, bribery, you name it, infesting every fibre of the society. The churches are generally patronised by the corrupt citizens. As a result, it is clear that churches, instead of discouraging crime and immorality, are tempted to promote it.

The situation in Italy is similar: it gives the world a pope and, at the same time, gives it the Godfather, the former leading the world's Christian church and the latter leading the world Mafia.

The United States and other Western countries that are traditionally Christian are laden with corruption and crime.

Russia and its socialist allies, where Christ is hardly mentioned, do not have corrupt or criminal-minded citizens of the type who live in the United States, Italy, and other Western Christian countries of the world.

REPLY: Anene Obianyido agrees with Reverend Iwe but remarks that in his own country, Nigeria, Christians are exceptions to Reverend Iwe's view. In support of the exception, he says that a white friend of his in Liverpool, who visited Nigeria, came back to relate his observations while in Nigeria, to the effect that Nigerian citizens, though professing Christianity, practise corruption. Obianyido goes on to say that Christian churches in Nigeria encourage and support evil. Next, like a racehorse which, after throwing down its jockey, runs all over the racecourse, he runs all over the traditionally Christian countries of the world, describing them as corrupt and criminal. The question is, which Christian countries play the role Reverend Iwe talked about, to which said role Obianyido gives his approval? His readers are left in limbo concerning these conflicting opinions of his.

Again, he jumps, this time to Russia and its socialist allies. His opinion about them: they are places where Christ is hardly mentioned, yet they are not as corrupt as the Western Christian countries. To me, his notion is a total misjudgement of facts. Is he then implying that the teaching of Jesus the Christ (Christianity) breeds corruption? Remember that earlier he supported Reverend Iwe's opinion that 'In view of human character, Christianity has in the course of human history, and in various nations, demonstrated itself as the custodian and promoter of human values.' Does his later view that the citizens of the United States, Italy, and other Western Christian nations are more corrupt and more criminal-minded than those of Russia and its socialist allies tie in with the finding of Rev.

Iwe which he previously accepted? In consideration of his conclusion, which contradicts his earlier one, I feel like saying to him, 'Obianyido, thou art beside yourself. Much atheism doth make thee mad!'

Too, he remarks that Christianity in Nigeria does not play the role of Christians which Rev. Iwe described. I ask, then, whose fault is that. 'You can take a goat to the stream, but you cannot force it to drink' goes a saying. Christianity has a good intention: every country it enters, it seeks to educate the people in good moral principles. If Nigerians fail to accept and practise the Christian teachings for their own social and spiritual benefit, who is to blame? I hold that nonuse or nonpractice of the Christian principles does not invalidate the inherent moral, spiritual, and social values in Christian doctrine. Obianyido seems to write before he thinks; his reasons are many times at war with themselves.

Concerning the communities in Russia and it is social allies, there is no information that Obinayido has ever been to any of those countries. Whatever he says about moral character of the citizens of the countries must be based on hearsay. He has no statistic in support of his points. And he has no measuring rod to show for the comparison he made between moral state of the citizen of Russia (and its Socialist allies) and the moral state of the Christina countries he talks about. In the light of the assertion, he (Obinyido) made that the citizen of Russia (and its socialist allies) have higher moral standard than their counterpart in the said Christian countries is heavily skewed, therefore.

About practical Christianity: All along, in *In Defence of Jesus the Christ*, I have been struggling to separate the genuine Christians from the fake ones. In Chapter 8, I fought to distinguish the correct definition of *Christians* from the botched one given by Obianyido. A genuine Christian is known by his or her acceptance and practise of Christian teachings as laid down by Jesus the Christ. 'By their fruits, ye shall know them' (Luke 6:43–45).

The inadequacy of the character of those who profess Christianity but fail to live up to the standard required of Christians, as in Nigeria, pointed out by Obianyido, need not be passed on to Jesus the Christ and Christianity. The importance of the moral teachings of Christianity cannot be overemphasised.

People without good moral principles are like insects without antennae or with defective ones; they are incapacitated concerning the right means of finding the correct way to build a morally good society.

TRADITIONAL AFRICAN RELIGION—PROSPECT

(CHAPTER 12, CHRIST OR DEVIL?)

OBIANYIDO: Education promotes culture. Our Nigerian education policymakers do no valued the need to teach traditional religion and indigenous culture to our children. The education policymakers therefore portray signs of colonial mentality.

Dr Iwe's view that Africa be freed from foreign culture so that Africans may feel at home with their own is most welcome. African elites talk of revival of culture without realising that religion goes with culture. Richard S. Taylor said it all when he said, 'The culture of a society in whatever stage includes totality of the society's life pattern—language, religion, literature, machines and invention, art and craft.' He adds, 'We cannot free culture from the authority of religion.'

By accepting the Christian religion, we have adopted Western culture, which we practise when we marry, participate in a christening, or celebrate Christmas and Easter. In the same manner, those who practise Islam, Buddhism, Hinduism, or Confucianism have their culture influenced by their religion. If Africa takes up its indigenous religion, then its culture will also fall into oneness with its religion.

Christianity as a religious tradition has had an organic relationship with the social and moral structure of the Western world (populated largely by the white race), moulding its institutions, ruling its education, and influencing its moral and spiritual ideals.

Consider the cultural implications of a black man relating to God only through a white Jewish intermediary, Jesus. It means adopting a foreign cultural tradition of religious rituals.

If Islam does the same in Asia, Hinduism in India, and Confucianism in China, then, given the right education and practice orientation, the black man's indigenous religion will do the same in Africa. It is only a question of time.

There is a gradual switch to indigenous religion, which manifests in festivals such as the Iwaji Yam Festival.

There are, of course, certain practices of the traditional religion that must be abandoned. These include the killing of twins, birthing babies feet first, instead of head first, and extracting the teeth of those who cut their upper teeth first. These practices have long ceased in many places. There are others, including the caste system and witchcraft, especially in connection with trial by ordeal.

REPLY: First of all, let me deal with and put aside Anene Obianyido's suggestion to 'consider the cultural implications of a black man relating to God only through a white Jewish intermediary, Jesus'. His view is that Jesus the Christ, being a white man, would discriminate against a black man (just as he himself discriminates against white people) and would not adequately represent the black man before God. You see! 'A madman thinks every other man is mad' goes a saying.

Obianyido's view is tainted with stark naked racism founded on lack of spiritual knowledge. He is unable to distinguish Jesus from the Christ. Jesus refers to the human being who bears the name but who attained Christhood to become the Christ and hence is called Jesus the Christ (Jesus Christ, for short). The Christ is an aspect of God, the love of God that is made manifest through Jesus and that functions through him as the still small voice which by God's grace is inbuilt in every human being but lies latent or dormant until awakened through absolute righteousness. The Christ, therefore, is Spirit and is universal. It has no colour (black, white, or any other). It is of no nation (not African, not Chinese, not Indian, not a citizen of any nation), and it relates to no race and to no religion. It is for all human beings.

In the Bible, Jesus refers to himself as a human being—the Son of Man. See Matthew 12:32 and Matthew 20:28. In the former, Matthew 12:32, he splits himself into two, sort of, showing his human side, Jesus (the Son of Man), and his spiritual side, the Christ (Son of God), where we read, 'And whosoever speak a word against the son of man, it shall be forgiven him: but whosoever speak against the Holy Ghost, it shall not be forgiven him, neither in this world, nor in the world to come.'

Furthermore, Jesus says, 'I can of mine own self [as Jesus the human being] do nothing. ... If I bear witness of myself, my witness is not true' (John 5:30–31). In this context, Jesus refers to the aspect of God, the Christ in him, as the doer of the divine works that manifest through him, Jesus.

With that knowledge arrived at, the idea Obianyido entertains, that there is a cleavage between the Christ in the black man and the Christ in the white man, is a metaphysical blunder, a bit of scriptural nonsense. The Christ is for all races.

To argue another point: Obianyido welcomes Dr Iwe's suggestion that Africans be freed from foreign culture so that they may feel at home with their own culture. I ask, how? Who, in the first place, has shackled them, or prevents them from feeling at home with their own culture and religion? No one, of course.

The situation is that Africans are easily carried away by the mesmerism of exotic things. They abandon, with ease, whatever is theirs at the sight and knowledge of a foreign model. They had the choice to stick to their culture, their religion, and other things of theirs, provided those things would do no harm to humanity and would not stand in the way of serving God righteously.

About the saying ascribed to Richard S. Taylor by Obianyido, 'We cannot free culture from the authority of religion,' I, to some extent, disagree. Religion, in my humble reasoning, has no authority over culture; what it has is influence, and that influence works persuasively, not by mandate. Even with this, the influence operates more only in areas where the culture is savage or barbaric and therefore unacceptable to righteousness or humanity. In such areas, religion is acceptable as a means of wiping away the evils of the culture. Good examples are given by Obianyido himself when he writes, 'There are, of course, certain practices in traditional religion [and culture, of course] that have to be abandoned. This includes the killing of twins and of babies born feet, instead of head, first.' That means he acknowledges that all is not well, morally and socially, with indigenous African religion and culture. He acknowledges that some changes have been made to address these things, that is to stop the evils. Slyly, he neglects to mention the source of the changes, the thing that gave rise to the stopping of the evils of African religion and culture. Or else he is pretending he does not know, or he has forgotten how the abandonment of those monstrous practises he talks about began.

Let me kindly refresh his memory: the Christian religion he condemns was instrumental in the abandonment of such evil practices. For example, Mary Slessor, a Christian, fought hard to stop the slaughter of twin babies. Even though her grave is still at Calabar, in Nigeria, as memorabilia (a memento, if you like), the fact of her involvement is craftily ignored by Obianyido in his argument. Why? This pertinent question stubbornly remains: why has he bypassed that important fact? Was it *lapses calami* (a slip of his pen)? I think not. Was it a lapse in memory? Of course, it was none of these things. Elementary schoolchildren in Nigeria suddenly could wake up from sleep and, if you were to ask them to, tell you all about Mary Slessor and her great Christian works at Calabar, Nigeria, particularly her success in stopping the killing of twin babies. Obianyido, of course, is aware of the story of the Christian Mary Slessor and her famous religious works. He pretends to be oblivious of that fact and makes a detour to avoid giving credit to the Christian religion. What a crafty character Obianyido is!

Back to Taylor's assertion that we cannot free culture from the authority of religion. As I said earlier, I do not quite agree with that. I hold, rather, that religion is a component of culture, for culture is wider than religion. It contains religion as part of it, but religion does not contain it. In that sense, culture minus religion can still stand. If culture is wiped out (which is impracticable, but I am being hypothetical here), then religion must essentially disappear with it because it is part of culture. The reverse does not seem to be the case.

After all, the word *culture* and the word *religion* denote different things. The two words are readily separated etymologically and terminologically.

This fact notwithstanding, in certain circumstances it all depends on the usage of the words: where they are inseparably fused or are interchangeably used to mean the same thing, a different situation will result. For instance, where the word *culture* and the word *religion* are used in a manner such that each contains the whole of the other so that when we say culture, we mean religion, and vice versa, the two concepts can represent each other. Only in a situation of this nature, the meanings of *culture* and *religion* are the same, and therefore the two are inseparable.

Otherwise, the noun *culture* can be surgically etymologically bisected, and the noun *religion* be carved out from the wider noun *culture*, and then each can live its separate life.

It is therefore only in the circumstance described above that I agree with Taylor that we cannot free culture from the authority of religion—and, I add, vice versa.

In practice, Russia was able to separate religion from culture when it almost abandoned religion while keeping its culture. Even in full Christian countries, one observes a separation of religion from culture: France, Britain, Germany, Italy, and others all have the same religion, that is Christianity, but each has its separate, peculiar culture. The same is true of Nigeria. The many tribes that make up Nigeria share the same Christian religion, but each of the tribes keeps and maintains its separate culture within the tribe. I am speaking of the Yoruba, Ibibio, Ijaw, Igbo, and Ogoni tribes, among other, where all accept Christianity, but each has its own peculiar culture.

Relying on the foregoing information, I conclude that Obianyido is not correct to envisage that 'by accepting Christian religion, Africans automatically accept Western Christian culture'. Christianity originally was Jewish. Later, other countries, particularly European countries, accepted it, but did not accept Jewish culture.

The major activity responsible for transferring and fostering culture from one nation to another is social intercourse—tourism, education, politics, and trade, and, of course, religion to a small degree.

Obianyido's propagation that by accepting the Western world, Christian Africans have accepted the Western world's culture, amounts to scaremongering, therefore. His proposition flops.

It would be prudent for Africans to accept Christian teachings where doing so would refine their indigenous religion and improve their social and spiritual life. They could do so while adhering to their indigenous religion and practising their indigenous culture.

Jesus the Christ and his apostles did not advocate for the changing of religion and culture, but for changes in religious practice and individual conduct so as to refine these things.

Jesus the Christ healed a leper and then let him go so he could show himself to the Jewish priest and give the proper gifts according to Jewish tradition and culture. Then the priest would make it public that the sick had become clean and was no longer to be discriminated against. That attitude of Jesus the Christ illustrates that Christianity is not against traditional religion and culture, provided that neither the culture nor the religion interferes with or hampers service to God. Jesus the Christ reprimanded the elders of the Jewish religion only for putting their tradition and culture before service to God (Mark 7:1–9).

Obianyido pretends to be worried about the influence of the foreign white Christian religion and culture on Nigeria. At the same time, he feigns ignorance of the fact that atheism is a foreign faith which his mentor, Tai Solarin, attempted to smuggle into Africa through his Mayflower school in Nigeria. He even applauds Solarin for that misconceived idea.

Atheism has nothing in common with the indigenous African religion and culture which Obianyido pretends to campaign for. Atheism is diametrically opposed to indigenous African religion, which is based on deity. Obianyido, being in support of atheism, is against deity. Therefore, he is against traditional African religion.

The truth is that Obianyido is a damned racist to the point of xenophobia, particularly when it concerns Jesus the Christ and Christianity. One wonders the reason he suggests teaching traditional African religion, which is deity-based, and indigenous culture to our children and then, in the same book, condemns the teaching of religion in schools in Nigeria, at the same time praising 'Russia and its socialist allies' for de-emphasising religion in schools. Yet again he supports Tai Solarin for setting up a school where religion is not taught. Is he, by implication, saying that indigenous African religion should not be classified as religion? You see!

Already we have noted that Obianyido proposes a hypothesis to teach traditional African religion and indigenous culture to our children in schools, which point was only partially addressed. But there are other sides to the matter. I intend to investigate these next.

Nigeria has various tribes, no fewer than three hundred. Each of the tribes has its peculiar indigenous culture. Schools in Nigeria are not tribally based. Each school is a collection of pupils from the different tribes, and as I said earlier, each tribe has its own indigenous culture and religion, which weaves a web of conundrum: which of the various indigenous cultures and religions is to be taught in school? It is almost impossible to wriggle out of such a web.

Because of this, it is correct to envisage the impossibility of putting Obianyido's proposition into practice, except if all the various indigenous cultures and religions (of no fewer than fifty tribes) are to be taught in schools. There must be an indigenous religion and culture acceptable to all the various tribes for the teaching of indigenous culture and religion to be easily practised. Obianyido's idea is nebulous, therefore.

The proposition becomes more complex when we consider the fact that Obianyido, at the same time of making his proposition, says yes and no to the teaching of any religion at all in schools in Nigeria. He moves sideways (left and right) like a crab, and up and down like a yo-yo, when talking about his proposition. That is because he is being driven about by Christophobia and does not know which direction to follow in order to make his attack against Jesus the Christ and Christianity a success.

Whichever direction he chooses, his attack will be of no consequence to the fact that the teachings of Jesus the Christ offer a panacea for all the ills in the world. I hold that if the teaching of Christianity which entails fairness and justice to all, is inseminated into the culture and the religion of any society, it is expected to give birth to healthy religion and cultural practices for serving humanity and God.

Any religion or culture of any society that opposes beneficial moral changes also opposes healthy social progress. There is the need for mutation where the need arises for better social, moral, and spiritual progress. The Christian teachings are in favour of such beneficial changes, where need be, in societies. The part Christianity has played in many parts of the world (Nigeria comes first to my mind, where the religion intervened in the practices of indigenous religion and culture to stop the killing of twin babies, stop the killing of babies born feet first [instead of head first], stop the killing of babies that cut their upper teeth first, and stop the burying alive of human beings with a dead chief) is striking and unforgettable. With that understanding in mind, Obianyido's campaign against Christianity won't wash. For him to attack Christianity because, according to him, it is 'a foreign white man religion' is unreasonable and unacceptable to civilised minds. It shows him to be an uninformed xenophobe.

Imagine this: Obianyido disapproves of the teaching of Jesus the Christ (Christianity), not on the grounds that the teaching will not benefit Nigerian society, but just because the acceptance of Christianity, according to him, 'means adopting the foreign culture of the white man'. That, to me, is a blind way of reasoning. The Christ, as I have said previously, is Spirit, an aspect within every human being; therefore, the Christ is a universal spiritual being. The Christian religion, which has its roots in the Christ, is therefore not the property of the white man or of any other race; no race or individual is excluded from the Christ concern.

I have reasoned that where the need arises for a better moral society, Christianity should be accepted, or at least its teaching should be adopted for the making of essential moral changes to any religion and any culture. I do not deny that any such adoption of Christianity for the purpose of making changes to an indigenous religion or culture is likely to cause the adopting society a minor case of indigestion, sort of, but I am confident that such likely disturbance will be temporal and, like a toothache, will die off with time, as the benefits of the changes begin to manifest and hold sway.

Obianyido is not in favour that idea; he is for the total rejection of Christianity, and has made no secret his reasons. Evidently, his reasons are precisely four:

The first is that, certainly, he protests against a Jewish white man as an intermediary, Jesus the Christ, between the black man and God, or as a black man's means to God.

The second is that he believes that Christianity was imposed on Africans.

The third is that he thinks Christianity retards progress—scientific, technological, economic, and social—in Africa.

The fourth is that he believes that Christianity damages African religion and culture.

None of those four reasons, in my humble consideration, is viable or convincing. I have previously given my opposing views on these issues. Nevertheless, I wish to expatiate on my views on Obianyido's first reason.

Concerning his first reason, I ask, why is the intermediary between the black man and God causing Obianyido to have a migraine? If one as an intermediary brings to the black man the truth about God and consequent better social and moral life, the prospect of material equality, and the hope for eternal life, why does it matter that the intermediary is black, red, pink, or white, or an Indian, a Jew, or a person of any other race than African? I reckon that for a person who is after the truth and after the best social life, to be mindful of the race, the colour, and the nationality of the intermediary between him or her and his or her quest shows that he or she is a stark naked xenophobe and is deeply enmeshed in racism. The attitude is akin to that of a person, hungry and starving, saying, 'The food offered me may be delicious and good for me, but since it is served in a good white or blue, or foreign, dish, instead of in a black dish or on my native dish, I reject it.' Certainly, such a person either does not know what he or she wants or is not at all hungry. Analogously, Obianyido's rejection of Christianity, which seeks to give Africans, or the black man, good things in life here on earth and the hope for eternal life later, because, according to him, the intermediary between the black man and God is a white Jewish foreigner, is unblinking racism. What blazing stupidity! He in no way understands what Jesus the Christ is or what Christianity stands for, nor does he know what he wants.

According to the Hitopadesha, 'The narrow-minded ask, "Is the one our tribe, or is he a stranger?" But to those who are of noble disposition, the whole world is but one family.'[27] That quote is spot on in terms of Obianyido's attitude towards Jesus the Christ as the link between Africans (the black man) and God.

Civilised minds should see the world as one gigantic room and should see all people, irrespective of their race, colour, or nationality, as one large family. Christianity, indeed any reasonable religion, beckons at the whole world, not minding the people's nationality, race, colour, or geographical boundaries, to embrace the moral knowledge it offers. A good religion like Christianity acts like a pulpit and takes the world as its congregation.

Eagerly, I wish to emphasise that in this particular discussion I am not considering whether or not Africans should go for their indigenous religion and abandon foreign religion. Rather, I am questioning the grounds on which Obianyido stands to suggest that Africans should totally reject Jesus the Christ and Christianity, even though evidently Christianity has many better tangible moral, social, and spiritual benefits to offer. His grounds for proposing the rejection are too swampy and sandy for his quest to rest on.

To enchant Africans and beguile them to accept his proposed idea to reject Christianity, he dubiously offers them indigenous African religion, which he has already found fault with, as a better alternative to Christianity, and calls Christianity 'foreign' and 'the white man's religion' with a white man as the intermediary between the black man and God. Unfortunately for him, he forgets that he has already shown Christianity to be better than indigenous African religion when he pointed out that many evils of indigenous religion should be stopped, and he gave examples of such evils as the killing of twins and of babies born feet first—a wretched admission that the religion is not up to civilised standards (see Chapter 12 of *Christ or Devil?*).

---

[27] G. F. Maine, ed., *Great Thoughts Birthday Book*.

A pertinent question pops up in connection with Obianyido's admission of the faults of indigenous African religion: what initiated the need for flushing out the evils he perceives in indigenous African religion? Answer: the Christian teaching. In turn comes another question, in connection with the first: why has he, like a dumb shadow, glided over the common, yet very important, knowledge that Christianity is responsible for the discontinuation of most of the evils in indigenous African religion and culture? That was very cowardly of him!

I have not forgotten that he alleges that Africans are about to turn away from Christianity and towards indigenous African religion—a case of wishful thinking. He cited the Igbo tribe's Yam Festival as evidence of the turnaround. I disagree with that example. It is a misrepresentation of history. The Iwaji Yam Festival he talks about, among other practices of the Igbo tribe's indigenous culture, survived the sweeping changes in traditional African religion and culture when Christianity fought to refine the original African traditional practices. The Igbo Yam Festival, never having been stopped, later reactivated; it has been enjoying uninterrupted continuity.

Finally, it would be interesting, if it were possible, to see the Igbos, or indeed any African tribe, dig out their long-buried indigenous religious and cultural practices and continue with them, provided nothing in any of the revived practices is repugnant and offensive to humanity and none is irreverent to God.

With that I come almost to the end of Chapter 15 (which is about Chapter 12 of Obianyido's book *Christ or Devil?*—his final chapter).

It follows that he has used all the bullets in his magazine for attacking Jesus the Christ, Christianity, and God, and in the end achieved nothing!

Since his book *Christ or Devil?* ends with Chapter 12, I crave my reader's permission to be allowed a brief comment on his personality.

Personality Traits of Obianyido

From the contents of Anene Obianyido's book *Christ or Devil?* one can gather relevant points for making up Obianyido's personality traits.

Obianyido is Igbo (he hails from the Igbo tribe in Nigeria). No doubt he was born among illiterate peasants in his native land. Fortunately for him, the white Christian missionary school of the Roman Catholic Church came to his rescue and, to some degree, dispelled the mist of ignorance (illiteracy) that shrouded him and made him literate to a fairly small degree.

In his attempt to get into the limelight in his country, he accepted his mentor's (Tai Solarin's) suggestion to write a book, *Christ or Devil?*, which unfortunately criticises and attacks Christianity, and cavils at the teaching of Jesus the Christ, making an all-out assault on his divine personality.

In *Christ or Devil?* Obianyido's main personality traits are exposed, as follows:

(a) Secrecy
    Throughout his book, he is unable to disclose his faith, being cowardly and hypocritical; he simply calls it 'my new faith'. Does that make sense? Yet the signs in his book clinically show him to be a nonbeliever in God, to wit, an atheist.

    He talks about his college in Liverpool, England, without disclosing the name of the college, the discipline he was there to study, or what qualification he obtained from the college.

    He talks about his visits to an institution of higher education in Nigeria but in no way discloses what took him there or mentions the name of the school.

    Several times in his book he uses the expression 'my community' but leaves his readers guessing the name of the community.

What his trade or profession is, he hides from his readers.

This relates to Tai Solarin: Obianyido informs his readers that Solarin visited Europe, but he fails to mention the country or countries in Europe that Solarin visited.

The keeping away of important facts from his readers without any reason provokes the question why.

An Igbo proverb says, 'Oma akwa awu aru malu onweya.' The English translation is 'One who bathes with his or her clothes on has something ugly or nasty about his or her body that he or she wants to hide from others' view.' By that I mean that Obianyido keeps secrets about himself, clearly of things that are not in his favour.

(b) Copycatism

According to Obianyido, Tai Solarin, his mentor, visited Europe and as a result became an atheist. Once he returned to his country, Nigeria, Solarin set up a school where he could sow and spread atheism in Nigeria.

Obianyido followed suit. He went to Europe (Liverpool, England), then went back to his country, Nigeria, thereafter, having become an atheist. Since then, he has been preaching atheism.

(c) Sadism

Obianyido shows himself a sadist. He rejoices at whatever is against or hurts his fellow human beings. Consider these facts: the mischievous acts of the students at his college in Liverpool, England, against their lecturer were a joyful scene to him; the alteration of a lecturer's inscription on a blackboard (against the lecturer) in an institution of higher education in Nigeria he visited thrilled him; and his notion that Jesus the Christ and Peter were crucified upside down pleased him. All these things were a source of joy and pleasure to him.

(d) Chameleonism

Christ or Devil? witnesses that Anene Obianyido is variable—a person of inconsistent character, changing like a chameleon. Originally, he believed in the existence of God. Later he abandoned that belief and accepted the opinion of his atheist friend who went on TV for a debate to say that God does not exist. Later Obianyido believes in the existence of God and uses the expression 'denying the children God-given freedom to develop critical thinking and mental growth'. Another use of an expression indicating his belief in the existence of God: 'God or whatever you chose to call that benevolent force behind Creation'. To all that, add his support for indigenous African religion, which is essentially based on deity.

Let us briefly consider his view on whether Jesus the Christ ever lived in this world. He never doubted that Jesus lived on this earth when he alleged that Jesus 'broke away' from Judaism to form his own religion—Christianity.

When later he learnt that some among the British intelligentsia doubted that Jesus ever existed on earth, he changed his mind and agreed with them. Soon after, he changed again and believed the made-up story in the book *The Holy Blood and the Holy Grail* to the effect that Jesus the Christ escaped his crucifixion and eloped with Mary Magdalene.

Obianyido takes whatever new view before him that suits his desire as his latest belief. He is erratic!

(e) Xenophobia

He is a xenophobic. His deep hatred of Christianity stems from the fact that the religion was brought to Africa by foreign white missionaries. He has unbridled hatred for all foreigners. For that he kicks against the notion that Jesus the Christ is seen as an intermediary between the black man (i.e. Africans) and God.

(f) Uncouthness

He is notoriously churlish, indulging in vulgar, rude, crude, impolite words and expressions that are beyond the pale in describing his enemies and their actions.

(g) Hypocrisy

His mind seems to oscillate between atheism and indigenous African religion, like a pendulum. That is extremely deceitful.

A close and hard study of Obianyido's book *Christ or Devil?* reveals that he is a hardcore atheist.

There is no doubt that his associations with his atheist friends, particularly Tai Solarin, have imbued him with atheism. His claim to indigenous African religion is too fragile and too weak and is limited to the offshoots of the religion, i.e. the ceremonies and festivals that go with the religion, for example Iwaji, masquerade, and weddings—ceremonies that give him some excitement and pleasure. In other words, he is not so much interested in the religion as he is in the exciting earthly pleasures it offers.

It is unimaginable that Obianyido can be in both opposing faiths at the same time, as he attempts to suggest, since indigenous African religion is deity-based, and atheism is completely opposed to deity.

In this case, his attitude is like that of a person attempting to dance to two different strains of music with contrasting rhythms at the same time.

No wonder all along he got the legs of his campaign against Christianity twisted. As a result, he is exposed as a revolting hypocrite—speaking so much in favour of indigenous African religion while, at the same time, slyly being deeply in love with atheism.

Obianyido is an ex-student of the Mayflower school (an atheist school). So are some other people, Mr Kumuyi, for one. Obianyido and his fellow students were fed fat with the concept of atheism at the Mayflower school. Afterwards, all those students, besides him, threw up the evil idea of atheism no sooner than they stepped out of the school gate for good. Kumuyi, an ex-student of the school, abandoned atheism completely and founded, or helped to found, a Christian church, the Deeper Life, almost on the premises of the Mayflower school. Obianyido with his gigantic appetite for atheism swallowed all the principles of atheism he was fed and allowed them to ferment and intoxicate him as is evident in his book.

It is hypocritical of him then to act as one who is mad about indigenous African religion when he is known to be deeply in love with atheism. He is double-faced!

(h) Sycophantism
His sycophantic attitude before his master and mentor, Tai Solarin, who beguiled him into atheism, shows him to be the master's poodle.

(i) Loyalty
Obianyido's loyalty to Tai Solarin made him abandon Christianity upon his return to Nigeria from Liverpool, England, and to become, half-heartedly, it seemed at first, an atheist. Later he became a full-fledged atheist.

No doubt his master Tai Solarin suggested that he write his book *Christ or Devil?* which is against Jesus the Christ, Christianity, and God. Tai Solarin moved aside after having written the preface to the book and stayed by Obianyido's side while he was writing the body of the book. It is no surprise that the book is filled with yeses and nos on the same issue and is very incoherent.

I see the book as a 'poisoned chalice', potentially toxic, as it aims at convincing Africans to disbelieve in God and to accept atheism. So, believe in God and stand firm against the atheists' wiles and cunning, I advise!

'Only fools in their hearts say there is no God' (Psalm 14:1).

God as the Source of himself (and the source of the universe and all therein and without, and all to come into being in the future) of necessity cannot not exist.

With the nine traits highlighted above as building blocks, Obianyido's personality can easily be constructed.

That brings my Chapter 15, which is on Obianyido's Chapter 12, to its tail end.

At this juncture, I intend to recall the subject 'Christianity versus Paganism', which I mentioned cursorily in Chapter 4, then promised to say more about it later, at the tail end of Chapter 15.

Addendum—My Personal Opinion about Christianity versus Paganism

In Chapter 4 of *In Defence of Jesus the Christ*, I reserved my comments on the issue raised by Obianyido that the white Christian missionaries call indigenous African religion pagan. I promised then to proffer to my readers my opinion on that at the tail end of Chapter 15. We have now arrived at that destination. I now intend to make good my promise.

Pagan as a word has a relation, i.e. *heathen*. It makes sense therefore to first explain this relationship. *Heathen* is simply an old-fashioned word for pagan. The two are therefore interchangeable in terms of meaning. Each of the two words is used to describe 'people, belief, practice; religion that does not belong to any of the present main religions', according to one English-language dictionary. To that the *Oxford Dictionary* adds, 'people holding the belief that deity exists in natural forces'.

Since the two words, *pagan* and *heathen*, are substantially the same thing, it will not matter which of the words I employ in my discussion. My choice is *pagan* because it is very extant, and besides, it is the very word used by Obianyido in the context of his complaint.

At this stage I want to make it clear that in the discourse, my description of Christianity refers only to present-day Christianity, the pseudo-, neo-Christianity. By that I mean the Christianity that developed far later than that of the apostles of the New Testament.

To my knowledge, Christianity, for sure, calls indigenous African religion pagan and idol-worshipping. I find nothing wrong with the use of the word *pagan* to refer to indigenous African religion as far as the word goes, when one considers the true meaning of the word as given in English-language dictionaries. The religion does not belong to the present main religions, and also it came into existence long before the main religions of the present day.

As far as Christianity versus Paganism goes, Africans believe that the Almighty God, the Supreme Being, the Creator of the universe and all therein, is Spirit (*invisible* is the nearest description). In order to keep a focus for communicating with that invisible God, African religion chooses an object (or objects as the case may be) as a symbol which they believe has been endowed with supernatural attributes, as a representative of the invisible Almighty God. The symbol is to serve as their object of attention when they worship the Supreme Almighty God. Mind you, in so doing, the adherents to the religion believe they are worshipping the invisible Almighty God, whom the symbol or object represents.

That procedure is followed simply because relying on a mere mental construction of an invisible Almighty God they have never seen and cannot see, without reference to any visible object, seems to the religion incomprehensible, inconceivable, intangible, and meaningless, like a thought about nothing.

Some of the objects for representing God are a river, a mountain, the sun, the moon, lightning, or a tree, all of which seem to be natural forces reflecting the attributes of God. To be precise, indigenous African religion is very much pantheism, which is the belief that God is the force behind natural things.

In some cases, the objects for representing God are carved images which adherents to the religion believe have acquired the attributes of God after certain rituals have been performed on them. The adherents to the religion therefore pay superstitious veneration to those objects.

The representative system is the reason for the classification into small god and big God in the indigenous religion of the Igbo tribe, Nigeria. The small god that represents the big God is called in Igbo language 'Chi', and the big God is represented as 'Chi-ukwu' (Chukwu or Chiukwu). That set-up illustrates the point that indigenous African religion is a form of theology essentially based on a belief in God the Almighty. The philosophy of the theology is the result of the fact of the invisibility of God, who exists but is not seen or physically known.

Paul, one of the apostles of old (in the Bible), observed a similar situation in Athens. While in Athens, he noticed an inscription on the altar of the Athenians: 'To an unknown God'. Having perceived that the people were devout and religious, he told them, 'You have been worshipping Him [God] without knowing who He is' (Acts 17:23–31). By that saying, he meant that they were worshipping God, but wrongly. God is a Sprit one does not see, cannot see, and has never seen. God is to be worshipped directly without anything to represent him.

From the foregoing analysis, one can perceive that Africans, by their indigenous religious procedural way of worshipping God, suffer similar ignorance as that of the people of Athens at the time Paul visited. With this context in mind, I hazard a guess that it is a common misconception to strictly view the pagan religion as idol-worshipping—a notion among the main religions, particularly present-day Christianity, which has, unfortunately, widened the meaning of idol-worshipping to include Satan worshipping.

It is amazing that today the so-called main religions or conventional religions, to a far extent, suffer the same ignorance in their ways of worshipping God as does the pagan religion. The Christianity that emerged from the time of Emperor Constantine of Rome, and its descendants, including present-day Christianity, have portraits, images, and printed pictures of Jesus the Christ, of God himself, of the Virgin Mary, and of saints. The Catholic Church ordains some dead priests as saints, but it lacks the spiritual authority to do that, which amounts to usurpation of God's exclusive prerogative: God, who alone knows the secrets in the hearts of human beings, is the only One who knows who is a saint. All about church buildings—church doors, windows, walls, pulpits, ceilings—one sees images as objects of veneration. Judaism has the Wailing Wall in Jerusalem (the only wall of their holy temple still standing, in defiance of the historical destruction of the temple) before which the Jews pray; Islamism has its square stone building, the Kaaba, in Mecca to boost Muslims' supplication to Allah (God); Buddhists face a statue of Buddha when they meditate; and Hinduism has the River Ganges and the sacred cow as objects of religious veneration.

All the main religions practise, in one form or another, veneration of images, which is against God's commandment (Exodus 20:3–17). Exodus 20:3–5 makes up the second of the Ten Commandments of God that strictly forbids idolatry, i.e. worshipping images of any kind or any form.

In that regard, I hold with the mystics—Jesus the Christ (John 3:24), Paul the apostle (Acts 17:23–31), Moses Maimonides (his writing *The Guide of the Perplexed*), and Joel S. Goldsmith (his book *Beyond Words and Thoughts*, Chapter 10)—and the wisdom which they impart in diverse statements: that God is incorporeal, God is Spirit, and therefore cannot be imaged for worship, but may be worshipped only in spirit. He cannot be represented in any form—tangible or intangible—to which is humanly attached the characteristics or prerogatives of God for veneration or worship.

Most Christian denominations (as well as some other, non-Christian religions), like pagans, superstitiously or ignorantly worship God through such images. That equates with idolatry, which offends the second of the Ten Commandments of God. See my analysis above.

I, therefore, see the pagans, the Christians, and the non-Christian religions that indulge in worshipping, directly or indirectly, images of any form whatsoever as idol-worshippers.

Let's look at Christianity in particular. A book entitled *The Fabulous First Centuries of Christianity*, written by Vance Ferrell, has it that at the time of the Roman Empire, Christianity became impregnated with the principles of paganism. That knowledge kindles the question, what then is the ado about paganism for? For what reason are indigenous African religions singled out as idol-worshipping religions, or why are these religions referred to as pagan to the exclusion of other religions, such as Christianity, of a later time?

Equipped with what we know about present-day Christianity, it is safe for us to distil their attitude towards paganism as a case of the pot calling the kettle black.

Jesus the Christ suggested, 'Judge not, that ye be not judged. ... And why behold thou the mote that is in thy brother's eye, but consider not the beam that is in thy own eye? ... Thou hypocrite, first, caste out the beam out of thy own eye; and, then shall thou see clearly to caste out the mote of thy brother's eye' (Matthew 7:1–5).

Personally, I abhor and condemn icons of any religion that have to do with worshipping God. Therefore, I am of the view that present-day Christianity and other religions that call indigenous African religion idol-worshipping, but at the same time employ icons or images in any form when worshipping God, are wrong. They have no right to their claim of relating better to God than the pagan religion does. They are not entitled to self-justification or to the feeling that their religion is superior to that of the pagan. They are Pharisees: their sanctimonious attitude is hypocritical.

In Chapter 4 I mentioned Vance Ferrell, a religious historian, asserting that pieces of pagan practices were grafted onto Christianity at a later date, making it different from the original Christianity of the Bible. This time let me particularise some of the pagan principles and practices adopted by later Christianity, including the use of candles, bells, incense, and religious images. Christians of today celebrate Christmas on 25 December each year, in remembrance of the birth of Jesus, but 25 December is the date the pagans set aside for the celebration of the birthday of their sun god, Mithra—whereas Jesus, according to the historical record, was most likely born in January. Of the Ten Commandments (from the Holy Bible), Christians refer to the fourth of the commandments when setting aside the seventh day of the week for the Sabbath, Saturday, the day to be kept holy for God, but later Christianity, of its own accord, rejected the day and supplanted it with Sunday, the first day of the week, the day the pagans worship their sun god Mithra. The Easter celebration which present-day Christians observe was adopted from the pagan ceremony for the rising of their god Adonis from the dead. It represents the spring season when dead plants (after winter) spring up once more from their dead selves to live. The list of the things Christianity adopted from the pagan religion goes beyond what I have mentioned. To conclude, Christianity has immersed in paganism for a long time.

It is hard not to observe that since the Christianity of today is heir to the Christianity set up by Emperor Constantine, its practices must, as a consequence, be closely parallel to those of paganism. As for the difference, there is not much difference between the tenets, but there is a difference in the method of practising the tents. It is this difference that creates a loose connection between the two faiths, as a result of which one is deceived to think that the two are not of the same brotherhood. This is my humble observation.

In my assessment, I took a neutral stance and followed the path of dialectics, avoiding theology to the extent that such was possible, to arrive at my observations. It is my humble view that today Christianity and paganism are almost in the same boat—they have intermingled as far as worshipping God goes.

There is no doubt that the promulgation of the National Sunday Law (by Emperor Constantine), which fused Christianity and paganism, played havoc with Christianity, making it worldly. No wonder, since then, Christianity has lost its credentials and its spiritual power. Today, it is spiritually impotent. Unlike the earlier Christianity of Jesus, Peter, Paul, et al., it cannot perform miracles, cannot preach the true gospel, cannot see visions, and cannot prophesy or forgive sins, because the Holy Ghost has deserted it, making it almost an empty shell. It is now in want of spiritual orientation. On many serious occasions, intent on finding the modus operandi or the right orientation, various Christian denominations spring up now and again, here and there in our world. This is one reason for the multiplication of Christian churches. Another reason is a selfish interest in riches and fame!

I will now move forward and introduce my Chapter 16. It is to be my final chapter. I propose to prescribe the subjects of the chapter myself. The format of the chapter is to be designed to follow my free style and fancy. That will allow me to talk more about some issues crucial to the matters raised by Obianyido, which issues I somehow have already shallowly or cursorily discussed, as well as matters relevant for discussion but that were either inadvertently or by prevarication left out by Obianyido.

CONCLUSION

We are at the final stage of *In Defence of Jesus the Christ*. By now you must have observed that the book offers a variety of intriguing scriptural and spiritual subjects, some familiar, some strange, others confusing. Most of them are long-standing questions waiting for answers. What the correct answers to the questions ought to be is a bone of contention between the book *Christ or Devil?* by Anene Obianyido and the book *In Defence of Jesus the Christ* by me.

In my attempt to establish what I conceive to be the correct answers to the questions in Obianyido's book, I locked with him in fiery argument, which contest culminated in the fireworks that characterise my own book, as my readers are to observe.

From the very start to the end of his book *Christ or Devil?*, Obianyido, armed with the most atrocious, abominable, rude, malicious, horrendous, and impolite words and expressions, preposterously abuses Jesus the Christ, Christianity, and God, and attempts to make Jesus the Christ a subject of calumny! In doing so, he relies, for the most part, on the book *The Holy Blood and the Holy Grail*, which made much smoke but produced no fire, and on Tai Solarin, who suffered from delusions of grandeur when nurturing Obianyido in atheism. Both sources lack substance!

My faith is Christianity. I feel unreasonably insulted! I have become much concerned, and in that mood, in my reply, I embarked on paying Obianyido in his own coin, as far as he has indulged in his insulting, toxic attitude against Jesus the Christ and has deliberately distorted his teachings.

In Defence of Jesus the Christ, therefore, fiercely challenges Obianyido's book *Christ or Devil?* I based my aggressive challenge partly on the truism about wisdom in an Igbo (a tribe in Nigeria) proverb that says, 'Akua akugwaghi, na akpata nkukwasa.' The English translation is: 'Assault received without retaliation invites further assaults.' So, I have written aggressively in order to check Obianyido's (and those of others like him) groundless savage attacks against the Christianity of Jesus the Christ, and see if they can turn around to God.

One fact is obvious about *Christ of Devil?*: one does not need to scratch the surface for its aim; it is laid bare on the surface. It is this: Obianyido, with his gossip and propaganda against Jesus the Christ, Christianity, and God, hopes to persuade Africans to abandon Christianity and accept atheism. Take my warning: do not for one moment consider his clamour or cry for his kind of indigenous African religion, because it is a false cry, a sham quest that has been vividly exposed as such in his book, as has been brilliantly shown in some of the proceeding chapters of *In Defence of Jesus the Christ*. So, I see his show of interest in indigenous African religion as a deliberate misdirection.

In all seriousness, I have challenged his hypocritical call for indigenous religion and his diabolical attacks against Christianity. I have lucidly shown that the teaching of Jesus the Christ is socially salutary, morally nourishing, and spiritually beneficial to all societies, and that it powerfully overwhelms the negative propaganda in Obianyido's book and reduces it to impotence.

This last chapter aims at finally dismantling the edifice of propaganda built by the book *Christ or Devil?* so that its mendacious and misleading contents will be exposed as fairy tales.

To do this, I intend to provide a profile of Jesus the Christ and show the ways in which his teachings and demonstrations benefit humanity.

This chapter, for that purpose, is dispensed under three subheadings:

- The Man Jesus the Christ
- His Mission
- His Legacies

The Man Jesus the Christ

Jesus (who became the Christ) was a man of humble birth. His birth took place in Bethlehem, at the time of King Herod's reign (37–4 BC). His parents were Joseph (the father) and the Virgin Mary (the mother).

The Holy Bible has it that Jesus's birth was predicted/prophesised, and that his mother conceived him by 'the power of the Holy Ghost' (Luke 1:30–31).

That he was conceived by the power of the Holy Ghost with Joseph, the mother's husband, out of the picture (not having any biological part to play in the conception) is an issue that has been debated for a long time—even up to date. A chapter of this book has my view on that. I do not intend to repeat it here.

There is another moot point about Jesus. A common opinion holds that he is the Son of God. Many freethinkers refuse to accept this. If the Son of God, in the sense of the word *son* as we commonly understand it and apply it earthly, I join in categorically refusing to accept the assertion. God's spiritual and divine status does not allow biological reproduction of human beings by God. In the spiritual sense? I, of course, say yes: God has children. My reasons for believing thus have been given earlier; there is no need to repeat them here.

At the birth of Jesus, according to the Holy Bible (and *The Aquarian Gospel of Jesus the Christ*), he was traced by Three Wise Men from the

East, who with gifts of gold (a symbol of nobility), myrrh (a symbol of domination), and frankincense (a symbol of sagacious wisdom) paid him homage (Matthew 2:11; *The Aquarian Gospel of Jesus the Christ* 4:3).

Jesus grew up a divine figure, the acme of spiritual master, the apotheosis of morality, the union of all good virtues.

From an early age he displayed matchless boldness, courage, intelligence in scriptures, and unparalleled spiritual wisdom. He was unprecedentedly urbane, among his other virtues. To a maximum degree, he was averse to worldly propensity, and he demonstrated, to an unequalled degree, interest in Holy Writ; he possessed eternal truth and transcendental values.

At the age of twelve or so, he argued brilliantly with spiritual maturity among the doctors of Jewish scriptural law in the temples and synagogues (Luke 2:41–52).

A scriptural book, *The Aquarian Gospel of Jesus the Christ*, which talks about the life of Jesus the Christ in more detail than the popular Bible, informs us that at an early age, while in Jerusalem, Jesus was taken from there by a rich Indian, who became his patron, to India. There Jesus studied Indian scriptures under some Indian spiritual masters. The masters helped to guide him along the spiritual path of Indian scripture (*The Aquarian Gospel of Jesus the Christ* 16–61).

Later, having learnt a lot about the Indian scriptures and showing, at the same time, great intelligence and wisdom in spiritual matters, Jesus learnt about the Brahmin religion in the Shri Jagannath Temple under Lamaas, the priest at the time.

When in Varanasi, a city along the Ganges, Jesus had contact with the Visyas and other masters of Indian scripture. Later, he studied the Hindu religion under Udraka, the Hindu religious leader at the time.

At Lahore, Jesus had contact with Ajanin, a priest, on spiritual matters.

Subsequently, he visited Persia, Assyria, and Greece, one aim being growth in scriptural subjects.

In Alexandra he addressed the seven sages of what was then known as the world.

After having gone through those strenuous, intensive, and extensive experiences in spiritual matters and having faced seven tests/temptations (which, for want of space and time, I do not account for here), Jesus emerged with outstanding success in spiritual affairs. Following his performance, seven spiritual degrees were given him. The highest spiritual title, 'the Christ', was conferred upon him by the sages who were the spiritual masters, the highest authorities in the field of scripture and spirituality during that era.

At around the age of twenty-nine, Jesus returned to his homeland, Galilee, for the second phase of his divine activity (Luke 3:23).

It is right about that age of twenty-nine where the New Testament picks up, once more, the thread of the historical account of Jesus's life from where it had left off.

The above information is the missing historical account of Jesus the Christ's early life. It is from the book *The Aquarian Gospel of Jesus the Christ*, taken from the Akashic records, edited by Levi H. Dowling.

Leaning upon that account, I am prepared to hazard a guess that the gospels of the New Testament omitted the account of the early life of Jesus the Christ (between the ages of twelve and twenty-nine) because the authors of the gospels were not physically in that part of the world— Asia and India—where Jesus the Christ spent his early life, so that part of his life was beyond their direct knowledge.

If that piece of information lifted from *The Aquarian Gospel of Jesus the Christ* is accepted (there is no grounds for its rejection), it fills the gap created by the missing link—the history of the early life of Jesus the Christ (between the ages of twelve and twenty-nine) unaccounted for in the Bible. So that answers the question that has been nagging people for decades as to what happened in the early life of Jesus the Christ, which the Bible fails to say a thing about. What we now know about this, from the information in *The Aquarian Gospel of Jesus the Christ*, is highly persuasive and should be taken as the answer.

As I said earlier, Jesus the Christ returned to his native land at about the age of twenty-nine. At that time, his cousin John the Baptist was announcing the coming of the Messiah, the Christ. Jesus demonstrated that he was the Messiah, the Christ who was to come, by his teaching, his miracles, and his other divine activities. John the Baptist enquired, 'Art thou he that was to come, or do we look for another?' Jesus the Christ made it known to him that he was the One (Matthew 11:1–6).

As part of his preparation for his mission, Jesus was baptised by John the Baptist. In the course of the baptismal procedure, a voice, no doubt God's, came introducing Jesus as his Son in whom he was 'well pleased' and whose teaching should be taken seriously as God's wish (Luke 3:22).

Jesus pleased God with his knowledge of God and his practice of God's commandments, and when he surrendered his humanhood, his worldly propensities, or lusts, and let the Christ (the love, the aspect of God in him) live his life for him. In other words, he gave up earthly pursuits and picked up a wholly spiritual life. That acceptance of the Christ in him to live his life, run his life, and function as his life earned him the sacred honour 'my son in whom I am well pleased', which equates with the title 'the Christ'.

Following hard on the heels of the baptism, Jesus was led by the Spirit into the wilderness. There he was tempted three times by Satan (whatever persuades one to consider disobedience to God, for the sake of serving one's own selfish interests, is of Satan because it opposes God and his commandments). Jesus conquered the temptations and emerged triumphant, demonstrating his Christhood. He became ready for his spiritual mission (Luke 4:1–13).

Next, he started picking and choosing his twelve disciples. These men were to help him in the mission of spreading his gospel.

As his mission took off, some of his people (among the Jews) mistook him for an earthly ruler, a king who had come to deliver them from the coarse hands of their enemies—the Roman authority and some of the Jews' antagonistic neighbours. As Jesus's mission evolved, the Jews' hopes were mercilessly dashed when they discovered that said hopes were outside the frame of the mission: Jesus the Christ demonstrated he was, instead, apolitical, a spiritual leader whose mission was to get sinners to repent and turn to God. He showed he was an itinerant rabbi (teacher) who went about correcting the unrighteous conduct of individuals and the wrong, ungodly teachings of religions, especially Judaism, in order to prepare people for the kingdom of God.

In the frustration that followed the dashing of their hopes, the Pharisees, the high priests, and the elders of the Jewish religion conceived in their minds to find a means of doing away with Jesus. Working in concert with Judas Iscariot, one of Jesus's disciples, the aforementioned Jews made up false charges against Jesus.

Eventually, Jesus was taken before Pilate, being charged, inter alia, of making claim to the kingship of the Jews and saying that he was the Son of God. Pilate and his dear wife shared equally the opinion that he should be discharged and acquitted as they found him innocent of the charges against him.

The accusers blatantly refused to give up. To satisfy the mounting pressure from those Jews, who went on shouting and were adamant that Jesus be put to death, Pilate handed him over to be crucified (John 19:6–7).

Derided, mocked, and tortured, Jesus was subsequently crucified! Two criminals were also crucified alongside him, at a place called Golgotha (Place of the Skull).

The malignant persecution, the acute torture, and the impending death hanging over him at the material time could neither eclipse Jesus's divine nature nor diminish his compassionate character. While at the critical point of death, he prayed, 'Father, forgive them; for they know not what they do' (Luke 23:34).

By that compassionate attitude, he demonstrated a wisdom similar to, but deeper than, that of Diogenes the philosopher, who, when he was told that the people were mocking him, retorted, 'The only people who suffer ridicule are those who allow it to influence them and are put out by it.'[28] That was the very attitude of Jesus the Christ amid the circumstances about him at the time. And the attitude agrees with the truth in the philosophical maxim 'A truly good man can neither be insulted nor disgraced.'

The crucifixion was a regrettable folly brought about by those who carried it out. It was a clear miscarriage of justice!

I invite my readers to imagine the circumstance amid which Jesus uttered the prayer, 'Father, forgive them, for they know not what they do.' That prayer carries the fact that 'to err is human, and to forgive is divine'. The perpetrators of that act of crucifying Jesus, an innocent man, showed their imbecility, and that to err is human, whereas Jesus's response to their action manifested his divinity: 'To forgive is divine.'

In any event, he later gave up the Ghost. What a poignant scene!

After Jesus was certified dead by the Roman authority, Joseph Arimathea was allowed to take his body and bury it. He buried Jesus in his personal tomb (Matthew 27:57–60).

Throughout his life, Jesus demonstrated extraordinary courage, except on three occasions when he could not help but partially display the human side of his being. The occasions are when, during his triumphal entry into Jerusalem, he overthrew the tables of the money changers

---

[28] Plutard, *Makers of Rome* (1978), 65.

and drove the robbers away from the premises of the temple (Matthew 21:12); when he went to Gethsemane to pray, where he said, 'O Father, if this cup may not pass away from me except I drink it, Thy will be done' (Matthew 26:42); and when, while on the cross, he cried, 'My God, my God, why has Thou forsaken me?' (Matthew 27:46).

His reactions on those occasions are understandable from the human viewpoint because they were terrible situations; yet his reactions on each of the occasions were skin-deep.

Besides those occasions, Jesus the Christ, being aware of his innocence and of his good spiritual works, did not fear harm or death. His composure during his arrest and punishment agrees with the saying, 'He that knows himself to be upright does not fear death of a criminal and shrinks from no punishment; his mind is not with remorse for any disgraceful deed, he holds that death in a good cause is not punishment, but an honour, and that death for freedom is glory.'[29]

Jesus did not care and was prepared to give up a human being's most prized possession—his physical life—as a result of his compassionate love for humankind. What a noble sacrifice! Says William Barclay, 'And there are times when the giving of oneself is the greatest gift of all—for that is the gift that Jesus gave to man.'[30]

So Jesus was a mystic, a divine being in human form, an altruist, the epitome of a moralist, a martyr. He practised self-negation, which most so-called Christians of today shy away from.

The biblical history of Jesus the Christ has accounts of his resurrection and his ascension to heaven (Mark 16:6, 14; Acts 1:9 respectively). Those accounts have provoked scepticism and controversies within religious and secular circles. The issues remain unresolved today. *In Defence of Jesus the Christ* does not wish to wade into such somewhat esoteric

---

[29] A. C. Grayling, *The Good Book: A Humanist Bible* (2011).

[30] William Barclay, *Ethics in Persuasive Society* (1971), 71.

matters beyond the boundaries I have earlier traversed in some of the proceeding chapters.

In any case, the divine personality of Jesus the Christ, despite Obianyido's vile attacks against it, remains untarnished, undented. Jesus the Christ remains the most monumental spiritual figure who ever lived on earth. So, he defied the gravity of the opposition and their attacks and won!

NB: I did say in Chapter 4 that Jesus rejected his lower self—his humanhood, the worldliness of his life—and accepted his higher self, the spiritual life, the Christ in him, to manifest through him, i.e. 'the Word [the Christ] was made flesh and dwelt among us' as Jesus the Christ. Approaching the end of *In Defence of Jesus the Christ*, I predict that my readers will, at the end of the book, want to know more about my assertion in Chapter 4 which talks about Jesus's rejection of his lower self and his acceptance of his higher self. What is that about? Unfortunately, this book is not built to accommodate the answer to that question in full. I am, however, prepared to allow a condensed explanation of the issue, just enough to calm the presumed curiosity of my readers.

A human being has a dual nature, consisting of the following two things:

- his higher self (spirit)
- his lower self (flesh).

The higher self is about heavenly spiritual matters, the aspect of God in humankind (that is the Christ). The Christ inclines human beings to show compassionate love in their conduct, which is to translate to righteousness. The lower self is about the quest for the immaterial things of the world—pleasure, fame, power, wealth, etc.—that lead to unrighteousness in character. Call the lower self Satan for an easy description.

Where a person rejects the lower self and accepts the higher self, the higher self rules his or her life and functions as his or her life. In such a situation, the person lives a spiritual life of righteousness. On the other hand, if a person rejects the higher self and accepts the lower self, then he or she allows the lower self to live and rule his or her life. That means Satan takes control over the person's life and inclines him or her towards the unrighteousness of the world, i.e. towards the quest for fame or wealth—in short, serving mammon, not God.

A person cannot surrender to the higher self and to the lower self at the same time. One cannot serve the two masters at the same time. In scriptural expression, 'You cannot serve God and mammon' (Matthew 6:24). Why?

The reason: because the two—God and mammon, or Satan—are diametrically opposed. Each manifests in opposition to the other, God being heavenly, divine, spiritual, and righteous, while Satan is worldly, sinful, and potentially unrighteous.

Jesus demonstrated his rejection of the lower self and his acceptance of the higher self. I refer the three times he was tempted in the wilderness. The temptations were all about choosing between worldly things— wealth, lust, pride, fame, and power, which equates with serving mammon/Satan—on the one hand and choosing heavenly things (humility, simplicity, righteousness, and serving God) on the other. In that situation, Jesus chose the higher self.

By his full acceptance of and surrender to the higher self, and his full rejection of the lower self, Jesus allowed the Christ (the aspect of the God in him) to take over and function as his life. That translates to 'the Word [the Christ] became flesh through Jesus, and Jesus lived among us as the Christ, the Son of God by faith' (John 1:11–14).

Let me highlight this: Jesus was able to make the right choice between the higher self and the lower self when he chose the higher self by listening to the still small voice (of the Christ) within him and obeying it.

Jesus's statement that he had conquered the world derived from the fact that he rejected the lower self (the worldly things of Satan) and accepted the higher self (the heavenly and spiritual things of God) (John 8:23; 16:33). The world is the lower self (Satan, i.e. the ego-man) which he conquered. He conquered the lower self because he listened to and obeyed the still small voice of the Spirit of God in him and followed its instructions.

Do not forget that in humankind there is always the knowledge of good and the knowledge of bad. Jesus had the two during his temptations in the wilderness. He made the righteous choice and rejected the unrighteous. In any situation, the higher self is ever ready to guide a human being to the right choice; in like manner, the lower self is ever ready to guide human beings to the wrong, unrighteous choice. It all depends on individual to make a choice between the two. Whichever choice one makes governs one's conduct.

By Jesus's listening to the still small voice within him (which is best perceived in silent meditation—'Be still and know that I am God' (Psalm 46:10)—he took his decision, accepted the higher self, and became by faith the special Son of God, i.e. conterminous with the Christ.

A question arises: how can one distinguish the higher self from the lower self in order to know which of the two to follow or accept? The answer is that the foregoing distinctive, respective characteristics of the higher self and the lower self are parts of the important knowledge required. In addition is the knowledge that the higher self is invariably presented as in the form of the whispering still small voice within one's inner self. That voice is a relative of conscience and intuition, and to hear it is a calm event that is nonemotional, a state of grace where 'I'-ness (humanhood, the ego) surrenders to God, the great I AM WHAT I AM.

Essentially, the state of the higher self propels one towards righteousness (the best of conduct), which is the opposite of carnal lusts, i.e. the fleeting vanity of worldly things of unrighteousness that are of the lower self. It is most manifest through the medium of silent prayer, or meditation. For that, 'Be still and know that I am God,' says God. This suggests self-surrender to God.

The lower self, on the other hand, displays the direct opposite of each of the characteristics of the higher self. It is emotional and worldly; it seeks after the fleeting vanities of the world and is invariably seduced by it. In the end it anchors in unrighteousness.

This analysis was done to make clearer how Jesus became the Christ, the special Son of God by faith, which I treated only shallowly in Chapter 4.

We have in a nutshell reviewed the personality of Jesus the Christ, shaped during his past incarnations. His life history in this, his last incarnation, reveals that he was born into this world that is full of sin, yet he lived like one dressed in sin-proof overalls and was in no way infected by the vices even though he lived, socialised, and interacted with people in his time who were full of sin.

As we have seen, his lifestyle was patterned to revolve around the kingdom of God, eternal life, with compassionate love as the hub. His teachings, his miracles, and his sympathy and care for the poor and the needy, in short, his care for humankind, which eventually led to his death, made up the focus of his life and showed that he came to this world in this his last incarnation for a special spiritual mission—a mission of redemption.

His special spiritual mission is what we shall consider next.

His Mission

The first glimpse of the mission of Jesus the Christ comes from Isaiah the prophet, who prophesied that John the Baptist would announce the coming of the Messiah and that people should follow the path of righteousness and should turn away from their sins and towards God. From that we came to discover later that the Messiah was Jesus the Christ and that his mission was one of redemption (Matthew 3:1–3).

Later, Jesus the Christ appeared for the teaching of his gospel. While spreading his gospel, he, of his own volition, publicly made known his mission. Time after time, he disclosed that he had been sent by God to persuade the unrighteous (sinners) to turn from their sins and become righteous in order to earn for themselves eternal life in the kingdom of God. In other words, he came for a redemption mission—to deliver people from sin and damnation.

There are numerous Bible references pointing to what the mission was all about. I am quick to mention a few of them at random: 'For God sent not His son [the Christ, through Jesus] into the world to condemn the world; but that the world through him might be saved' (John 3:17); 'I come not to call the righteous, but sinners to repentance' (Luke 5:32); 'For the son of man [who became the Christ] is not come to destroy men's lives, but to save them' (Luke 9:56; 11:23); 'For the son of man [who became the Christ] is come to seek and save that which is lost' (Luke 19:10); 'I [the Christ] have come that they might have life, and that they might have it more abundantly' (John 10:10). With the parable of the prodigal son, Jesus the Christ showed what huge joy would follow the repentance of a sinner (Luke 15:21–32), and with the parable of the Good Samaritan, he illustrated the practical way of caring and showing love to one's fellow beings (Luke 10:30–37). On one occasion he expatiated on the meaning of love for one's fellow being, including caring the sick, those in prison, and those who are hungry, naked, or thirsty, and for a stranger in need of help (Matthew 25:35–45).

Spiritually, a person in a sinful state potentially faces punishment by the law. Therefore, since the mission of Jesus the Christ was to help sinners avoid such punishment by helping them to become righteous, he demonstrated compassionate love for them. Compassionate love therefore is the quintessence of his mission, the summary of his business on earth.

The same compassionate love which Jesus the Christ showed to the world, he struggled to teach the world to show such love in turn, one to the other. Compassionate love is a beacon light that leads the way to salvation, eternal life in the kingdom of God.

At the time Jesus the Christ embarked upon his redemption mission, he found the world laden with social evils. In his redemption business, he focused his attention on tackling, as far as possible, the unrighteousness of the world. In order to convince his audience that he had come from God and therefore should be believed, he performed many divine miracles that were beyond the scope of ordinary humankind: he healed the sick, raised the dead, turned water into wine, walked upon water, cursed the fig tree to whither, and forgave sins (Matthew 9:2).

Jesus the Christ was a repository of spiritual laws, and in course of his mission, he exposed the laws that govern the life of humankind to prepare human beings adequately to earn the kingdom of God. In doing so, he showed indefatigable industry in propagating those laws, because the laws emanate from God.

To make his mission lively, Jesus the Christ displayed nobility and honesty in his character and taught with his life, and expected his audience to follow, his way of life—humble, simple, compassionate love for one's fellow creatures, control over appetite for earthly things, and maximum love for God.

His love for all human beings led him to burst the parochial and racial boundaries set up by Jewish religious practice and reach out to non-Jews—Gentiles and other tribes and races of the world. 'And this gospel of the kingdom shall be preached in all the world for a witness unto all nations' (Matthew 24:14), he said. He socialised and interacted with a Samaritan woman he met at Jacob's well, despite the fact that he was a Jew and the Jews were not socialising with Samaritans (John 4:9–27). By so doing, he demonstrated that all people, of all races and nations, are the children of God, and that his mission concerned the world.

He taught that God knows our needs and made it clear that God is ready to give us all that we need if we first seek his kingdom. Jesus taught that a human being has two deaths: the death of the physical body, which God or humankind can bring about, and the death of the soul, which only God can cause. He taught that there is reward (Paradise) for the righteous, and punishment for the unrighteous (hell).

Unmindful of what the unrighteous Jews' reaction would be, Jesus the Christ reproached them, without mincing words, telling them off for their sinful, ungodly practices and calling them hypocrites (Matthew 15:7-11).

He criticised them for giving attention to their tradition and to man-made rules while disregarding the commandments of God. Here are two examples of such misconduct: (*a*) when the Pharisees and the scribes criticised Jesus's disciples for eating without first washing their hands—conduct against the Jewish tradition (Matthew 15:1-10) and (*b*) when the Pharisees queried Jesus's disciples, who were hungry, for harvesting corn on the Sabbath Day, which went against Jewish tradition (Matthew 12:1-8).

To guide the sinners to righteousness, which leads to eternal life in God's kingdom, Jesus introduced himself (his moral character) as a road map to, a role model for, the kingdom of God: 'I am the Way, the Truth, the Life, no one comes to the Father, except by me' (John 14:6). 'I am the way' means that what the Spirit in Jesus teaches, what he practises, is the way that leads to the Father. Mind that Jesus's practice was being directed by the Christ, which mystically manifested through him and transformed Jesus the man into the Christ. 'To the Father' in the quotation indicates that God is the Father of all; we are all the children of God by creation.

Jesus was not claiming God the Father exclusively for himself; he was not claiming to be the only Son of God. He was, however, claiming to be 'the only special Son' of God, the spiritual Son, by faith. His teaching on how to pray, popularly known as the Lord's Prayer, showed that he recognised that God is for everyone, that we are all the children of God. That is why the prayer begins, 'Our Father' (Luke 11:1). Jesus claimed to be the spiritual Son of God because he knew he had obeyed God to a maximum degree and earned from God the description 'my beloved son in whom I am well pleased' (Matthew 3:17). The 'son' in the quotation stands for the Christ, which Jesus became. He obeyed God by not yielding to earthly appetites of the lower self but by surrendering himself to his higher self to live his life for his Father and function as his life. On that account he was able to say, 'I have conquered, overcome the world' (John 16:33)—he had overcome the lower self!

By his teaching on righteousness, and by rejecting the lower self (the fleeting vain things of the world) and accepting or surrendering to the spiritual heavenly things of God, Jesus demonstrated to sinners how to become righteous. In this way, he was to the sinners what a physician is to the sick (Matthew 9:10–13; 21:31).

That means sinners who accept and practise his teachings are in time cleared of their sins and become righteous enough to earn God's blessings. Given that such is the case, Jesus's teaching is a major part of his show of compassionate love for sinners.

Compassionate love is invariably the mainstay of his teachings. His miracles of healing and his feeding of the multitudes—twice—were both a part of his practical teaching on compassionate love for one's fellow beings.

By teaching and demonstrating compassionate love, he showed people how to be against violence, how to be nondiscriminatory, how to love one's enemy, how to be honest, how to be nonhypocritical, and how to avoid all unrighteous conduct.

From his teachings, one gathers the fact that salvation relates to people's individual conduct. Here are three examples: (a) 'He that loveth father and mother more than me [the teaching of the kingdom of God; the still small voice of God in humankind; the higher self of a human being] is not worthy of the kingdom' (Matthew 10:37–38); (b) 'If any man will come after me [the higher self in humankind, the still small voice of God in a human being], he is not worthy of the kingdom' (Matthew 10:37–38); and (c) 'If any man will come after me [the higher self in humankind, the still small voice of the Christ], let him deny himself [be selfless] and take up his cross [selflessness] and follow me' (Matthew 16:24). These three examples are all about selfless love.

Salvation is therefore not something to be achieved by means of collective venture like a sense of family belonging, like having 'Abraham as the father' (Matthew 3:9), or belonging to a religious organisation that cuts corners, but through the personal conduct of individuals—conduct that is nothing less than a show of compassionate love for one's fellow creatures. On those grounds, Jesus said, 'For behold, the kingdom of God is within you' (Luke 17:20–21). So, look for the Christ in you; listen to the still, small voice of your inner self, along with the higher self, for the kingdom of God. Salvation is linked up with the merit which one's individual moral conduct earns. Jesus said, 'God is spirit; and they that worship Him must worship Him in spirit and in truth' (John 4:24). In that instruction, the word *spirit* appears twice. The first of the two instances refers to God, for certain; the other refers to the mode, the conduct of the individual in worshipping God. It has to be done sincerely, genuinely, and in a heavenly way, not falsely, hypocritically, or perfunctorily as if speaking in relation to the lower self of humankind, which is ever controlled by physical senses. Precisely, Jesus the Christ instructed that for one to worship God righteously, one should turn to one's inner self and listen to the still small voice, the Christ, the aspect of God within ('the kingdom of God is within you'), and follow its spiritual direction. In that situation, salvation is necessarily an individual, rather than a group, concern.

That notwithstanding, group belonging or a religious movement that relates to God is not condemned in matters for seeking salvation. Good religious movements teaching seekers about salvation, about God, could be likened to a kindergarten where one learns the rudiments about God and how to work individually towards salvation. That is what Christianity as a religion is to be about.

Whatever the case may be, the fact remains that Jesus the Christ in his redemption mission revealed that no one can sneak into salvation and the kingdom of God through the back door of religious or family belonging: 'And think not to say within yourselves, we have Abraham to our father' (Matthew 3:9), for that is unproductive as far as gaining salvation is concerned. What counts in favour of one seeking salvation is one's personal/individual conduct. For that, one has to look within oneself, the higher self, for the Christ, who is the kingdom of God within, for spiritual guidance. 'Your heart is the temple of the most living God,' and 'The Kingdom of God is within you,' Jesus the Christ taught during his mission (Luke 17:21). I reiterate.

Looking into one's inner self for spiritual guidance is an individual matter. You carry your own cross and drink of your own bitter cup, where such a thing is spiritually called for; no one does that for another (Galatians 6:4–10).

NB: The often-quoted saying 'Again I say unto you … for where two or three gather in my name there am I in the midst' (Matthew 18:19–20) is not in conflict with the fundamental spiritual principle that anyone's earning of salvation, the kingdom of God, is an individual thing. What is said in the quotation does not displace the fact that salvation must be sought out individually. The two or three (or more) who gather in Jesus's name must each be essentially righteous, and their motive and request must also be righteous. That is a sine qua non for the Christ (the love of God, the Prince of Peace, the righteous Son of God) to be in their midst and for God the Father to answer their prayer. The mere fact of togetherness is nonproductive as a means of attracting or earning answers to one's prayers.

For that, the mission of Jesus the Christ was not about setting up a new religion, but about refining and cleaning up the existing ones so they could join in teaching individuals the right way of serving God. No wonder that when he healed the sick, he asked them to go and sin no more, but also to give the priests of whatever religion to which they belonged their thanks (Mark 1:40–44). Jesus did not ask the healed to join his religion, for he had none and had no intention of forming one. The purpose of his redemption mission was not to set up a religion, but to correct the wrongs of the then existing religions and the immoral conduct of individuals.

He, however, had 'a church', and the few people he asked to follow him were those he needed in his church, who were to help in spreading his gospel to the people of the religions then in existence and to individuals in numerous societies.

Jesus's mission then was to turn sinners from their sins and towards God by giving them the correct interpretations of the scriptures as regards God's commandments. Plus, he enjoined his church to spread those teachings. Those teachings—the correct interpretations of the commandments of God—were later gathered and came to form a body of doctrine, a compendium of scriptural and spiritual principles later known as the Christian teachings. And the members of his church and other followers of his were nicknamed 'Christians' in Antioch (Acts 11:26).

In Chapter 2 of his book *Christ or Devil?*, Anene Obianyido alleges that Jesus the Christ broke away from Judaism and set up his own religion—Christianity. That is trash! This notion of his stems from his poverty of scriptural and spiritual knowledge. Jesus the Christ was born into Judaism and remained in it, but not to the exclusion of other religions, as his redemption mission had a universal outlook and was not attached to any religion up to the end of his life on earth. During his mission, he was simply criticising the leaders of religions, particularly that of his people, the Jews, for misinterpreting the scriptures and misapplying the laws, thereby leading followers astray.

He went on to correct their religious teachings and had to teach the truth about the kingdom of God.

Jesus asked Peter to lead the church, once Jesus had left the earth, in spreading the correct teaching. The symbolic handing over of the key to Peter was all about the spreading of the correct teaching so as to lead the seeker to heaven. Jesus the Christ was not against any religion that taught the correct commandments of God; he was against those among the people who did not accept him and his correct teachings of the commandments of God: 'He who is not with Me is against Me, and he who does not gather with Me scatters abroad' (Matthew 12:30).

Obianyido's view that Jesus the Christ intentionally founded a religion of his own—Christianity—simply because he said to Peter, 'And I say unto thee, that thou art Peter, and upon this rock I will build my church; and the gates of hell shall not prevail against it' (Matthew 16:18), is a total misunderstanding of the original meaning of the word *church*. Jesus the Christ said, 'Build my church,' not 'Build my religion.'

Church in classical times meant no more than a body of people who went about spreading their master's or leader's teachings to society. In this incident, Jesus the Christ was the Master and Peter and others were his followers. Church did not equate with religion. There has been a shift in meaning of the term church. Today the term *religion* is almost interchangeable in meaning with the term *church*, meaning a building where worshippers gather and where rites and ceremonies are performed. Church does not stand for religion.

The evolution of the word church is a subject for philology, which is outside the ambit of *In Defence of Jesus the Christ*.

That is that.

Not being after a new religion, Jesus the Christ continued, during his lifetime, to attend the synagogues and temples of Judaism until his departure from our earth. If he were after a new religion, he was in a better stead to found it himself than to delegate the job to Peter or someone else. Even his disciples, including Peter himself, despite what Jesus the Christ had said to him, continued to attend the Jewish synagogues and temples. As the church of Jesus the Christ, for spreading of their Master's gospel, the synagogues and the temples gathered seekers of the kingdom and offered them the opportunity to spread the Master's gospel to many at a time. Evidently Obianyido is operating under a misapprehension when he alleges that Jesus the Christ broke away from Judaism to form his own religion, i.e. Christianity.

So, forming a new religion was not part of the spiritual mission of redemption, which was the reason Jesus the Christ came to the world. His mission centred on teaching the truth about the kingdom of God to redeem sinners, i.e. turn them from their sins and towards God.

For his teaching the truth about God's kingdom, among other reasons, some of the Jews, previously mentioned, became confrontational with Jesus. Yet with uncompromising spirit, founded upon God's fiat, Jesus defied them, going on in the face of the hostility to stick to the course of his mission.

When he got to the end of his mission, he heaved a sigh of pleasure and satisfaction, thanking God for having sent him on the mission and making it possible for him to accomplish it. The whole of John's gospel, particularly chapter 17, verse 4, is about Jesus's joy for having accomplished his mission: 'I have finished the work which Thou giveth me to do' (John 17:4).

Today we know that evils exist in our society only where the teachings of Jesus the Christ are not accepted, or are accepted but not put into practice. 'Christian ideal has not been tried and found wanting. It has been found difficult and left untried,' writes G. K. Chesterton (1876–1936).

This man whom I write about is Jesus the Christ, who pleased God (Luke 3:22). He was, on earth, the archetype Son of God, a perfect model of what God expects of all human beings. In fact, his redemption mission represents an oasis in the vast human desert of unrighteousness.

The world, from Jesus's era to the present day, has drawn upon his rich store of wisdom in the oasis in its effort to tackle its social and spiritual problems.

The oasis of wisdom formed by Jesus's mission is what I regard as containing his legacies to the world. At the heart of that wisdom lies his teaching on compassionate love.

His Legacies

In Chapter 6 of *In Defence of Jesus the Christ*, I mentioned that Anene Obianyido, in Chapter 3 of his book *Christ or Devil?*, referring to Jesus the Christ, asks, 'And how far did his teachings agree with real-life experience and modern reason?' Then I gave a very terse reply in passing, hoping to elaborate later. That elaboration now comes under the subheading 'His Legacies'.

Those who, like Obianyido, doubt the benefits derivable from the mission of Jesus the Christ should read, for a start, Joel S. Goldsmith, here quoted:

> It has been said many times, and claimed by many persons [Obianyido among them], that the teaching of Jesus Christ is so impracticable that it could not possibly be adopted to our modern life. This seems strange when we remember that according to biblical accounts, this so-called impracticable way of life healed the sick, raised the dead, and provided supply for those who needed it, stilled the storm, and brought peace where there had been discord. This way of life has been called impractical, and yet nothing in the religious history of the world has ever been quite as practical as was Jesus' teaching. It was difficult, but it was practical. And so, in these modern days, we, too will find that living as the master [Jesus the Christ] taught is difficult, but also that it is practical.
>
> The fact that a religious teaching can bring about the healing of physical and mental ills, that it can lead to an increased sense of supply and provide safety and security, that it can bring an inner peace and a release from the world's major problems, warrants calling that teaching practical.[31]

---

[31] Joel S. Goldsmith, *The Contemplative Life* (1994).

The preceding quotation is talking about the teaching, with its benefits, which Jesus the Christ bequeathed to the world. The benefits relate to compassionate love for the recipients. Compassionate love, therefore, is the epicentre of the legacies of Jesus the Christ to humankind. The world is still enjoying these legacies; the world needed them at the time of Jesus on earth and needs them in this modern time. They are ageless.

The philosophical thought of Richard Chenevix Trench points to the life of Jesus the Christ in terms of the high moral quality he demonstrated to the world by his teachings and his lifestyle: 'Every noble life leaves the fibre of itself interwoven forever in the work of the world.' The tree of compassionate love planted by Jesus the Christ during his time on earth still bears fruits of social benefit in our present generation. It recycles itself timelessly. It was that tree that he instructed his disciples and apostles to continue watering by his symbolic handing over of the key to Peter, as mentioned earlier.

Jesus's followers, headed by Peter and Paul, propagated his teachings, and his later followers are still doing so for the benefit of humankind. Paul once said, 'In all things I have shown you that so toiling one must help the weak, remembering the words of the Lord Jesus Christ, how he said, "It is more blessed to give than to receive"' (Acts 20:33–35). That was a teaching on philanthropism, on charity, as a model of selflessness in serving God through serving one's fellow human beings. Speedily, we are here reminded of the parable of the Good Samaritan given by Jesus the Christ, and the feeding of the multitude (on two occasions). Those teachings are about compassionate love with its moral virtues, which Jesus the Christ asked that we practise.

On another occasion Paul said, 'Remember this, if you sow little you won't get much grain. But if you sow generously, you will get much grain' (2 Corinthians 9:6). This saying also is about doing good, being righteous, so that good may follow the doer on a pro rota basis.

All these teachings by Paul (and those by other apostles of Jesus the Christ herein not mentioned) were offshoots of the teachings of their

Master, Jesus the Christ. Note, too, that following the teachings, Paul underscored compassionate love as the essence of all good action and conduct. He declared, 'The greatest of all virtues is love' (1 Corinthians 13:1–13). To the Ephesians, Paul conveyed the same teaching on compassionate love. In all, the teachings of the disciples and the apostles of Jesus the Christ were the legacies they received from their Master, Jesus the Christ.

The apostles of Jesus the Christ faced some problems sometimes. Some of the problems were internal, and others were external to their circle. Among the internal was the matter of racial and tribal discrimination. The Jews among the members were against the non-Jews. This related to the question of admission of non-Jews into their fold for the service of God. Boldly and tenaciously, that evil was fought against with the spirit of the example given by Jesus the Christ. Consequently, the evil was uprooted.

Remember, Jesus the Christ taught that there should be love one to another, and gave examples, one of which was the parable of the Good Samaritan who did show love to a total stranger in need. It was with such a teaching as a legacy that the apostles stamped out discrimination from their midst. When the Christian church at Antioch wrestled with discrimination, they were told by the apostles who were there that no discrimination would be tolerated in their circle. The result was positive and firm.

Following those decisions, the Greeks, the Africans, and others formerly discriminated against were taken into the Christian fold (Acts 11:1–20; 13:1–3): Simon called the Black (Niger), a dark-skinned African; Lucius, who came from Cyrene; and Manaen, with a court background, were all received without further ado. The ungodly conduct of Peter and Barnabas, who had stopped eating with the Gentiles of Antioch because of their discriminating attitude, kindled Paul's outburst. Paul at once reprimanded the discriminating members who were Jews, instructing that there should be no discrimination (see the book of Galatians, particularly 3:28).

In Acts of the Apostles in the New Testament, we are informed that 'to demonstrate the end of discrimination, the Jews shared the gospel with the Gentiles'—for example Peter with Cornelius, Paul with the Philippians, and Philip with the Ethiopian eunuch.

Also in Acts, we learn that Timotheus, the son of a Gentile father, worked with Paul among the Jews (Acts 16:1–4).[32]

The apostles' external problems related to the persecutions they suffered at the hands of some outsiders, some of whom were disgruntled, miserable Jews. These were some of the legacies of Jesus the Christ enjoyed by the generation of the earlier apostles.

Now we turn to the question posed by Obianyido: 'And how far do his [Jesus the Christ's] teachings agree with real-life experience and modern reason?'

In order to answer this question adequately, I pose my own question: what is the real-life experience, socially, morally, in the modern world? We are in no doubt that the modern world is riddled with serious social problems: racism, which Obianyido in this twenty-first century practises against the Christian missionaries just because of their colour and foreignness; suppression of the weak by the strong; suppression of the poor by the rich; corruption; unfairness; and so on. Everywhere, between nations, between races, within nations, within tribes, and within families, there is quarrelling, squabbling, fighting, wars, and all sorts of social evils. No one can deny that. Nigeria, the country Obianyido hails from, currently has more than its share of such social evils.

In a situation such as this, modern reason necessarily needs to direct and focus attention on searching for the best means of solving the problem of social chaos. In my humble view, the teaching of Jesus the Christ on compassionate love passed down to our modern world as a legacy holds the key to the solution.

---

[32] Bruce Kaye, *Obeying Christ in a Changing World* (1997), 124–25.

Those trees, I repeat, of compassionate love planted by Jesus the Christ in a small area in Bethlehem, Judea, during his time on earth are being slowly passed on to our modern world by some of the dedicated Christians of today. In many places the trees are growing; in others, some are bearing the fruit of good conduct in individuals and within organisations for a better society. The modern world is witnessing the social and spiritual nourishment from the legacies bequeathed to the world by Jesus the Christ being timely drawn upon for tackling the grave social problems of many modern societies and calming things down. That is no wild claim, for without the legacies, the world's problems would have, by now, snowballed to create a social cataclysm and bring hellfire to earth.

Brian Kaye briefly relates the salutary effects of Christianity on the world when he says that Christianity gave to the human race a sense of the worth of an individual, be that individual a slave, a free person, a male, a female, a Gentile, or a Jew, or from some other nation or class. Without the teachings of Christ, there would have been no St Francis kissing the beggars, no Mother Teresa of Calcutta tending to the poor. Because of the teachings of Christ, there is Elizabeth Fry to campaign for prisoners; Christian Aid; Caritas of the Roman Catholic Church; the Salvation Army, founded by William and Catherine Booth; the Young Men's Christian Association; and the Young Women's Christian Association. There was Frederick Douglass (the abolitionist and reformer); Mary Slessor (the Queen of Calabar, Nigeria), who helped to stop the killing of twin babies in Nigeria—her grave in Duke Town, Calabar, Nigeria, is still there as a monument reminding us of her great Christian work; and Florence Nightingale, a nurse, nicknamed 'the Lady with the Lamp', who during the great Crimean War spent her time sympathising with and compassionately comforting sick and wounded soldiers (she was inspired by the spirit of Christian teaching bequeathed by Jesus the Christ to the world).

The book *Obeying Christ in a Changing World* talks of the work of Father Damien in the midst of lepers and mentions that his good progress there is a part of the legacies Jesus Christ left for the world, even though wars, crusades, and inquisitions (against innocent freethinkers) were once wrongly carried out in the name of Jesus the Christ.[33]

As I write, the late Nelson Mandela of South Africa, a devout Christian, quickly joins the list. Before he left our world, the spirit of forgiveness, which Jesus the Christ demonstrated by teaching and by action, led him to forgive the callous white colonial power of South Africa which unjustly persecuted him and imprisoned him for about twenty-seven years for no other reason than his having asked that his fellow black South Africans be accorded justice and freedom in their own country.

All charity organisations and individual philanthropists of the past and the present were aroused, and the emerging ones are all being aroused, to act according to the moral legacies of Jesus the Christ.

The legacies, which remain invaluable to any society, gather strength from generation to generation. All I am saying is that the catalogue of personalities and organisations pursuing treatment favourable to human beings all have their roots in the legacy of compassionate love given to the world by Jesus the Christ and fostered by his followers.

Yes, it is true that some time ago, in the Middle Ages, certain organisations, notably, the Roman Catholic Church (professing Christianity), embarked upon a Crusade that entailed violence and evils against some human beings, mainly the freethinkers. Their conduct was evidence of a very serious derailment from the track of the teaching of Jesus the Christ. Be that as it may, *abusus non tollit usum* (misuse does not nullify proper use). Changes for the better have been made, and improvements in the conduct of some Christian churches are slowly creeping in.

The view of the proficient writer and literary critic A. N. Wilson, in respect to the matter of the legacies from Jesus the Christ, is worth mention, lest it be forgotten. According to him, 'the biblical statement *Talitha cumi* (Damsel, arise) (Mark 5:4), said by Jesus the Christ to Jairus's daughter, became the rallying cry among nineteenth-century

---

[33] Bruce Kaye, *Obeying Christ in a Changing World*, 249–55.

feminists.'[34] He also refers to Doctor Zhivago's remark to the effect that history began with Jesus the Christ as contained in the gospels and that Jesus the Christ's teaching on compassionate love for one's neighbours (fellow human beings) is to be seen as the supreme form of living energy.

Other scriptural authorities and mature thinkers air their opinions of the usefulness or benefit of the teachings of Jesus the Christ throughout time, up to the present day. Keir Hardie, who led the Labour Party in England for thirty-three years, recognised sin as the basic problem in life. At the end of his career, Hardie said that if he had to live his life over, he would give all his strength to preaching the gospel of Jesus the Christ. Dr G. C. Weiss opined that 'that which actually makes Christian men and women become genuine missionaries is their arrival at certain convictions from the Bible regarding God's world plan and their Christian responsibility towards the world according to that plan. Those convictions drive them to the mission field year, after year, in faithful selfless service.' Continuing, he said, 'The mere spirit of adventure or philosophy is not sufficient to do this. But an understanding of scripture and sound conviction of its demands on believers will not allow the missionary to do otherwise.'

Andrew Sirrett, a Canadian pharmacist, wrote, 'There came up before me most vividly my great sin of omission, any failure to tell those who know not the gospel.'

Professor Mackenzie, mentioning Buddha, Socrates, and Jesus the Christ as reformers, went on to say,

> Similarly, Jesus was no ascetic or recluse. He came eating, drinking and was familiar with the ideas and habits of his people, even of those that were regarded as outcasts and degraded. But he had also his time of retirement, temptations in the wilderness, withdrawal to mountains.

> This combination of active participations and reflections, withdrawal enabled him to sum up the morality of his

---

[34] A. N. Wilson, *Jesus*, 151–52.

notion, and by summing it up to set it upon a deeper basis, which fitted it to become the morality of modern civilized world.[35]

Philosophising in *Resistance*, William Penn Patrick wisely reasoned, 'History records countless events which prove the point. For example, the greatest of all men overcame the most severe form of resistance and in so doing gave birth to Christianity. Had Jesus run from his opposition, we would not know his name today, nor would we have available for use those great and wonderful truths he brought forth for men so that man could find his individual greatness.'[36]

'The teaching of Jesus the Christ lays stress upon the compassionate love for men and contains sayings of infinite wisdom and universal application.'[37] Some of the sayings, including parables, of universal application deserve to be mentioned: 'You cannot serve two masters at the same time and serve both well' (Matthew 6:24); 'Do not cast your pearls to the swine which will trample upon them' (Matthew 7:6); 'Do to others as you want them to do to you' (Matthew 7:12); 'If the blind leads the blind, both shall fall into the ditch' (Matthew 15:14); and 'Every city or house divided against itself shall not stand' (Matthew 12:25)—among others.

A few of Jesus's wise parables include the parable of the prodigal son (Luke 15:11–32); the parable of the tenants (Mark 12:1–9); the parable the wedding banquet (Matthew 22:1–14); and the parable of the workers in the vineyard (Matthew 20:1–6)—among others.

The wisdom in these sayings and parables of Jesus Christ is a part of the legacy which modern world is making use of.

The great Indian sage Mohandas Ghandi once told the British viceroy of India, 'When your country and mine shall get together in the teaching

---

[35] John S. Mackenzie, *A Manual of Ethics* (6th edn).

[36] William Penn Patrick, *Resistance*.

[37] *New Standard Encyclopaedia*.

laid down by Christ in his Sermon on the Mount, we shall have solved the problems not only of our countries, but of the whole world.'[38]

In a simple expression: 'The legacy of Jesus Christ is gentleness, compassion, and humility.'[39]

Bruce Kaye opined, 'The scripture does not present a detailed Christian social order, but it does give a basic truth about God and man; the realm of justice and humility and brotherhood, and what God detests.'[40]

Further, I once more draw attention to the wisdom of G. K. Chesterton. This wise man knows where to lay the blame for the ills of the modern world and knows where lies the panacea to these problems. He observes, 'The Christian ideal has not been tried and found wanting. It has been found difficult and left untried,' as quoted earlier.

E. G. White, mentioned previously, adds, 'In the heart renewed by divine grace, love [compassionate love—I prefer this expression because it has a strongly distinctive meaning from sensual, erotic love] is the principle of action. It modifies the character, governs the impulse, controls the passions, subdues enmity, and ennobles the affections. Thus, love cherished in the soul sweetens the life, and sheds a refining influence, on all around.'[41]

Although so far the list of the benefits from the legacies Jesus the Christ bequeathed to the world—past and present—is sufficient to convince any doubting Thomases of the beneficial use we have made and are still making of such legacies, three more special aspects of the legacies, indirectly albeit loudly, ask to be included. These are events from his life history. One is about his date of birth, another is about his date of death, and the third is about his Last Supper with his disciples (popularly known and celebrated as Holy Communion today).

---

[38] *Watch Tower* (1986), 6.
[39] Turif Khalidi, *The Muslim Jesus*, 15.
[40] Bruce Kaye, *Obeying Christ in a Changing World* (1977).
[41] E. G. White, *Steps to Christ*, 59.

Christmas is the Christian festival when the birth of Jesus is celebrated on the twenty-fifth of every December. I would be at fault if I were to disregard the celebration and not treat it as part and parcel of the legacies of Jesus the Christ.

Throughout the Christmas season, the social climate is such that people wear extraordinary cheerful moral garb. Presents (gifts) are exchanged among people; enmities seem to disappear; faces shine with spiritual smiles; care is taken of the weak and the poor by the strong and the rich. These events electrify humanity and bring people in line with high moral character. Almost all faiths are swept into the excitement by the strength of the celebration.

To be precise, the teaching of Jesus the Christ on compassionate love (loving one's neighbour) universally comes true during Christmastime.

The Last Supper is an important part of the legacies, though it particularly concerns Christians. I intentionally left it to be treated last, my reason being simply that it has been misunderstood and needs some explaining. This is my scriptural opinion about it: Christians of today call it the 'Holy Communion', which is something that Christians regularly celebrate. During the celebration, churches are in the habit of repeating the ritual in the same demonstrative manner shown by Jesus the Christ without following it up practically with the necessary teachings or lessons it was to convey. That, to my scriptural understanding, makes the celebration as unproductive as the barren fig tree cursed by Jesus the Christ (Matthew 21:18–19). In this sense, the Last Supper, or Holy Communion, has become a mere bit of excellent acting (a drama), but spiritually impotent and fruitless.

The Last Supper was meant to be a demonstrative teaching used by Jesus the Christ to symbolically impart lessons on compassionate love, to be practised in our daily life.

According to the Holy Bible, 'Jesus the Christ took bread and blessed it, broke it and gave it to his disciples and said, "Take eat, this is my body." Then he took a cup of wine gave thanks to God and gave the wine to them saying, "Drink ye all of it; for this is my blood of the New Testament, which

279

is shed for many for remission of sins'" (Matthew 26–28). The gospel of Luke adds, 'This do in remembrance of me' (Luke 22:19). That is to say, 'I am Love, so when you love others you remember me, and when you remember me you love others.' The whole scenario was a demonstrative teaching on compassionate love through the sharing of what one receives or has. The personality (Jesus the Christ) stands for an embodiment of love, peace, and humility. The bread represents his body; the wine, his blood. By analogy, Jesus the Christ demonstrated that love (which he represents) should be possessed and shared with fellow human beings. People should share what they have among themselves by helping the needy, and love always must be shown, when necessary, in daily practical life. It is not a thing to be done on occasion only, or at intervals, say, once every Sunday, but a thing that is to be part of living that is continuous. Also, no one who needs love is to be excluded from the sharing of the love.

Another lesson is on the giving of thanks to God, the Source of what the disciples were to share with Jesus—the bread and the wine. That showed the need for one to be appreciative and thankful to the Source of whatever good or benefit one receives.

The washing of the feet of the disciples is part and parcel of the Holy Communion; therefore, it is part of the practical teaching of the Last Supper. It showed humility, simplicity, selflessness, and compassionate love. It was to teach the disciples the need for readiness to serve anyone, whenever and wherever the need may arise; the social status of the one who serves and that of the receiver of the service should not be taken into consideration—should not matter—so long as the receiver of the service needed help and the one who rendered that help could capably give the help. Here the parable of the Good Samaritan raises its magnanimous head once more as a vivid practical example.

I have pointed to the inherent lessons of the Last Supper. Following the name or the description Last Supper, I ask, why was the Last Supper made the Last Supper by Jesus the Christ?

The Last Supper was made the last on purpose: Jesus the Christ waited until he had come to the final stage of his mission to use the Last Supper as a practical way of summarising his teachings. The lessons of the Last Supper told all that Jesus the Christ expected everyone to learn and practise as a result of his mission. It seems to me that present-day Christianity does not quite comprehend the lessons of the Last Supper. I do hope that Christians will learn these lessons inherent in the Last Supper, and will teach them and practise them, or risk incurring the fate of the biblical fig tree that was full of leaves but bore no fruit.

Having said all that, I do not categorically assert that Christians are totally wrong in their manner of observing the Last Supper (the Holy Communion). The commemoration of the event is essential and is in order if done as a memory refresher and is further put into practical use in daily life—i.e. in the sharing of compassionate love. Otherwise, it is no more than just mimicking Jesus the Christ, and no social or spiritual benefit will be gained.

The bread and the wine Jesus the Christ shared with his disciples was ordinary (common) but turned holy after he had prayed over it.

Regardless of all that is universally known about the divine personality of Jesus the Christ, especially respecting his strong campaign for the practice of compassionate love in daily life as a moral and spiritual means for promotion of human dignity and service to God, the pessimist Obianyido sees nothing good about him, and he uses the most foul language against him in an attempts to make him a target of calumny! Imagine his thoughtless opinion that 'modern man no longer considers the teaching of Jesus Christ relevant to his needs' (see Chapter 12 of *In Defence of Jesus the Christ*, which is about Chapter 9 of Obianyido's book *Christ or Devil?*).

Though I have already challenged his nefarious views about Jesus the Christ, I intend here to fortify my challenge with the opinion of Vance Ferrell.

Vance Ferrell, a writer, describes, in a nutshell, the personality of this man Jesus the Christ, whom I have almost to the limit of my scriptural and spiritual knowledge talked about, by saying,

> Ancient writers, modern writers, atheists and religionists—all have declared Jesus Christ to be the most amazing man in all history! His outstanding unselfish teachings, presenting a level of morality above that of all others; His influence on the lives of people down through the centuries that followed; the marvellous transformation of human lives for the better in those who have surrendered their lives obediently to him; the forgiveness of sin and enabling grace to obey the Ten Commandments which he grants to those who submit to his control; the wonderful hope of a world to come, which he imparts to his followers; all this and much more, place him on a level above all others. He who became a man in our God, whom we reverently worship.[42]

Any intelligent person who cares to study the life history of Jesus the Christ, especially pertaining to his legacies, and mull over them will find that there are enormous social and spiritual benefits to the legacies of Jesus the Christ to humankind, and will be compelled to hold that Obianyido's thoughtless opinion that modern humankind no longer considers the teaching of Jesus the Christ as relevant to their needs is the most arrant piece of folly, ill-conceived and self-consuming. There should be no doubt at all about the huge relevance of the teachings of Jesus the Christ to our present generation, particularly when we think of the chaotic social state of our modern world.

Vance Ferrell is not alone in asserting that Jesus the Christ, of all teachers of the scriptures of various religions and all spiritual personalities who ever lived in this world and those still living, is the greatest in the field of scripture and spirituality.

---

[42] Vance Ferrell, *The Fabulous First Centuries of Christianity* (2006), 637.

In this book, mention is made of several opinions of numerous reliable authorities in scriptural affairs, all saying substantially the same thing as Vance Ferrell, but in diverse ways.

Anene Obianyido has failed to observe, as others have, the glaring fact that the legacies Jesus the Christ left to the world are beneficial to humankind.

The likely reason for this is that, as we can see in *Christ or Devil?*, Obianyido can only speak through his master's voice, and his master is a staunch atheist. He is too attached to his master, Tai Solarin, and is too loyal to him. He became a follow-the-master man, the master's poodle, with no direction of his own—acting like a zombie! In the wise saying of A. C. Grayling, 'Loyalty is a virtue, but only when it is principled. Unquestioning allegiance to a cause, a faith or an individual is bad because, by its nature it is too easily made an instrument of wrongdoing, for when instructions are blindly followed they are thereby potentiated. Even as an instrument of good its value is unequivocal, a loyal servant is the vehicle of another's intentions, therefore little praise is due to him beyond the mere fact that he yields himself to his master.'[43]

Obianyido, being morally malnourished and lacking in religious knowledge, senselessly attacks and defames Jesus the Christ in his book *Christ or Devil?* In the course of his cycles of life (reincarnations), during which times he morally sacrificed pleasures and other vain trappings of the world at the altar of righteousness and divinity, Jesus earned himself divine status—'the Christ', an aspect of God—during this his last incarnation. It is in vain that Obianyido and his master, Tai Solarin, begrudge Jesus his hard-earned divine status.

Despite all the rantings and calumnies of Obianyido against Jesus the Christ, he remains the most admired and the most successful scriptural and spiritual teacher and leader who ever lived on earth.

His life gave the world the most precious spiritual gem. The modern world is always in dire need of peace but seems not to know the best way

---

[43] A. C. Grayling, *The Meaning of Things* (5th edn, 2002).

to go about getting it. I am of the strong conviction that the teachings of Jesus the Christ offer the world the sure *highway* to this peace. What does Obianyido want? His attempts to denigrate Jesus the Christ fail. His book *Christ or Devil?* attacking Jesus the Christ is blind, deaf, and lame. *In Defence of Jesus the Christ* seeks to make it look dumb too.

It is hard for any rational, sober person to deny that Jesus the Christ's sacrificial service—his teachings, and his selfless love for humankind and concern for their suffering—if conscientiously studied and practically followed, offers humanity a better life than does any other teaching in this life—or in the life to come, I surmise.

Paul's warning: 'Beware lest any man spoil you through philosophy and vain deceit, after the tradition of men, after the rudiments of the world, and not after Christ' (Colossians 2:8).

The history of Jesus the Christ and his undeniable beneficial legacies to the world—both ancient and modern—are welcome facts. *Res ipsa loquitor* (The facts speak for themselves).

The legacies have the potential to give the world—groups and individuals—peace and progress—in short, a better life in this world and in the world to come after death, if tried.

My treatise is now tapering off, as it is about to end. At this juncture, I am suffused with happiness because I resolutely and fiercely tackled the thoughtless views of the atheists—Anene Obianyido and Tai Solarin— against God, Jesus the Christ, and Christianity. Though that be the case, in so doing, strictly speaking, I meant no offence (i.e. *absit invidia*, to borrow from the Romans).

If the aforementioned atheists ever become sober enough to reflect on my attack and thoughtfully consider the positive side of it, they are likely to realise that in the end it is all for their good: for their spiritual edification, their better knowledge, a better life in the present, and the good of their future.

When one is walking towards a destructive destination, it takes only gentle persuasion to turn the person around. But where one has already arrived at the destructive destination, as, indeed, have Obianyido and Tai Solarin, it necessarily requires far more than a mere gentle approach to rescue the person from destruction. At that point, it requires fierce, sturdy effort to extricate the person from his or her already attained wrong destination, before this person can be directed to the right destination. Jesus the Christ applied vehement pressure to Saul of Tarsus (later, Paul, the apostle of Christ) in order to turn him round from his deadly pursuit, which was made possible by his religious ignorance, and orient him towards positive spiritual knowledge of his heavenly destination (Acts 9:1–20).

So, intent on bringing Anene Obianyido and his atheist friend Tai Solarin out of their senseless atheism so as to direct them to a spiritual destination—God (among other reasons previously given)—I treated them the way I have in my writing.

In this way, I believe that the gate to spiritual wisdom, which leads to a better life, has now swung open, waiting to welcome them with immense joy, if they care to think again and turn to God.

Once more, the 'Christian ideal has not been tried and found wanting. It has been found difficult and left untried' (G. K. Chesterton). Here is my terminus ad quem.

Modestly, I rest my case.

Readers, give your verdict.

Gratias tibi ago (Thank you).

Dominus vobiscum (God be with you).

Adieu!

Printed in the United States
by Baker & Taylor Publisher Services